EXCITEMENT!

. . . is the only word that describes paddling through the Lehigh Gorge, whether it be in a raft, kayak, canoe, or any other type of boat – even on an inner tube or inflatable pool furniture.

Paddling down the Lehigh River is not only a thrilling whitewater adventure, it is also a scenic tour through backwoods territory on a watercourse whose tree-lined banks have hardly changed since the time of Columbus. Visible signs of civilization are sparse above the metropolitan areas near the confluence with the Delaware River.

You don't even have to be on the river to feel the exhilaration in the air. During whitewater releases, you only have to visit the access points, or hike or bike along the Lehigh Gorge Trail, and you're sure to hear the screams and laughter of paddlers on the water: an incomparable vicarious experience that might encourage you to contact a raft outfitter and sign up for a trip that you'll never forget.

The present volume is laid out like a spinal column: sections of the Lehigh River are stitched together to form the supporting structure, while the tributaries extend to either side like ribs. Each stretch of river is described in detail so that paddlers and anglers will know what to expect. Each runnable tributary is treated in similar fashion. This way there won't be any untoward surprises that might bring a boater to grief.

Some streams are covered primarily because of their fishing potential.

The focal point of the Lehigh River watershed is the Lehigh Gorge: a canyon that stretches approximately 25 miles as it carves a twisting path between mountains that tower nearly a thousand feet on either side. The vista alone is worth the effort to see it. But to paddle along the bottom of the canyon, and stare upward at the thickly forested slopes and sheer cliff faces, adds a fillip that enhances the experience a quantum leap above the extraordinary.

In addition to the Gorge there exists a number of paddling and fishing opportunities that are often overlooked. Narrow upstream sections meander idly through wilderness tracts that few paddlers or anglers ever think about, much less appreciate. The lazy current in downstream sections, where the river is broad, provides easy-going paddling for families with small children who will enjoy a layback day on the water, and a quick swim in the shallows to escape the summer heat.

The Great Falls of the Lehigh is a spectacular 20-foot drop in the riverbed.

Then there are the major tributaries: Aquashicola Creek, Bear Creek, Black Creek (2), Buckwha Creek, Coplay Creek, Hazle Creek, Hokendauqua Creek, Indian Creek, Jordan Creek, Little Lehigh Creek, Lizard Creek, Mahoning Creek, Monocacy Creek, Mauch Chunk Creek, Mud Run, Nesquehoning Creek, Pohopoco Creek, Quakake Creek, Sandy Run, Saucon Creek, Sawmill Run, Shades Creek, Stony Creek, Tenmile Run, Tobyhanna Creek, Trout Creek (2), Tunkhannock Creek, and Upper Tunkhannock Creek. The Great Falls of the Mud is a combination of two waterfalls followed by a boulder-filled cataract that stretches for a hundred yards.

These shallow streams become runnable after large rainfalls. Some of them are slow-moving and placid: perfect for a quiet day's outing. Others consist of wild rapids and steep gradients that rival the mighty Lehigh.

And let's not forget the canals that were constructed in antebellum days. Some of these are flooded and are easily accessible to anglers, and to paddlers who want to cruise still waters that don't run deep. The Lehigh Valley watershed has it all.

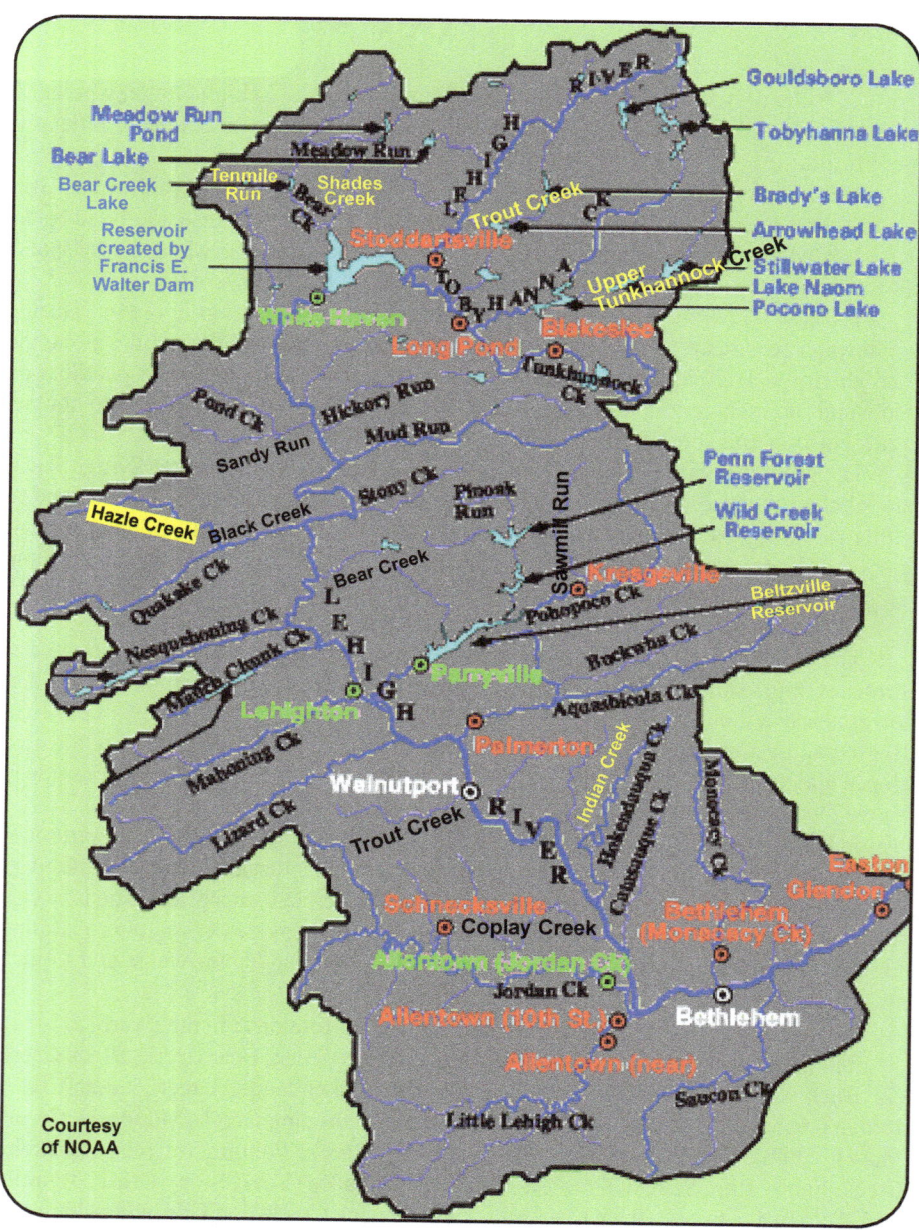

Map of the Lehigh River and its major tributaries (not all of which are runnable). The colored circles with a black dot denote streamflow gauge sites, not the center of the nearest named town. According to USGS WaterWatch, Little Lehigh Creek has only one gauge, not two as shown. Note that only Long Pond is natural. The other pond and lakes are artificial impoundments (reservoirs).

LEHIGH RIVER PADDLING GUIDE

PLUS TRIBUTARIES LESS PADDLED

BY GARY GENTILE

Bellerophon Bookworks

Copyright 2016 by Gary Gentile

All rights reserved. Except for the use of brief quotations embodied in critical articles and reviews, this book may not be reproduced in part or in whole, in any manner (including mechanical, electronic, photographic, and photocopy means), transmitted in any form, or recorded by any data storage and/or retrieval device, without express written permission from the author. Address all queries to:

Bellerophon Bookworks
3 Lehigh Gorge Drive
Jim Thorpe, PA 18229

Additional copies of this book may be purchased from the same address by sending a check or money order in the amount of $20 U.S. for each copy (plus $4 postage per order, not per book, in the U.S. Inquire for shipping cost to foreign countries). Alternatively, copies may be ordered from the author's website and paid by credit card:

http://www.ggentile.com

This book is dedicated to Cheryl Novak, who ran shuttles for me so that I could paddle waterways whose put-ins and take-outs were located far apart.

Picture Credits

All uncredited photographs were taken by the author. Front cover photo shows a rout of rafts plowing through the lower Rock Garden on the Lehigh River. Back cover watercraft from top to bottom: inflatable rafts, canoe with flotation bags, hard-hulled sit-in kayak and inflatable sit-on kayak, tire inner tubes, stand-up paddleboard, and inflatable catamaran.

International Standard Book Numbers (ISBN)
1-883056-50-0
978-1-883056-50-6

First Edition

Printed in U.S.A.

CONTENTS

INTRODUCTION — 7
- Historical Sketches: Canals, Railroads, Lawsuit — 10
- Personal Pre-Park Reflections — 19

LEHIGH RIVER (in Sections)
- 0 - Headwaters to Lehigh Road — 28
- 1 - Lehigh Road to Phillips Road — 31
- 2 - Phillips Road to Game Land Road (North Bridge) — 33
- 3 - Game Land Road (North Bridge) to Game Land Road (South Bridge) — 35
- 4 - Game Land Road (South Bridge) to Lackawanna State Forest access — 36
- 5 - Lackawanna State Forest access to Route 115 — 37
- 6 - Route 115 to the Francis E. Walter Dam — 38
- 6.5 - The Lost Mile — 44
- 7 - Francis E. Walter Dam to White Haven — 45
- 8 - White Haven to Rockport — 48
- 9 - Rockport to Jim Thorpe (and Glen Onoko) — 53
- 10 - Jim Thorpe to the Lehigh Gap — 66
- 11 - Lehigh Gap to Canal Park in Allentown — 72
- 12 - Canal Park in Allentown to the Delaware River at Easton — 76

LEHIGH CANALS
- 1 - Jim Thorpe through Weissport to Parryville — 81
- 2 - Bowmanstown through Palmerton to Lehigh Gap — 83
- 3 - Walnutport to Lockport — 84
- 4 - Treichlers — 86
- 5 - Laurys Station to Northampton — 87
- 6 - Catasauqua to Allentown — 88
- 7 - Allentown through Bethlehem and Freemansburg to Hopesville — 89
- 8 - Glendon to Easton — 91

MAJOR TRIBUTARIES
(FROM UPSTREAM TO DOWNSTREAM)

Explanatory Remarks	92
Trout Creek (and Brady Lake)	94
Tobyhanna Creek	98
Upper Tunkhannock Creek	116
Tunkhannock Creek (and Long Pond)	118
Bear Creek	125
Tenmile Run	129
Shades Creek	131
Sandy Run	135
Mud Run	137
Stony Creek	148
Black Creek	150
Quakake Creek	155
Hazle Creek	157
Bear Creek (and Little Bear Creek)	159
Nesquehoning Creek	162
Mauch Chunk Creek (and Mauch Chunk Lake Park)	170
Mahoning Creek	175
Pohopoco Creek (and Beltzville State Park)	177
.....Sawmill Run	185
Lizard Creek	188
Aquashicola Creek	193
Buckwha Creek	195
Trout Creek	197
Hokendauqua Creek	199
Indian Creek	203
Coplay Creek	205
Little Lehigh Creek	207
Jordan Creek	211
Monocacy Creek	217
Saucon Creek	223

APPENDICES

Watershed Clearwater Revival	226
Linear Measurement	233
Streamflow	235
Adversity	237
Books by the Author	238

INTRODUCTION

Paddling Guide to the Lehigh River Watershed

The Lehigh River watershed hosts backwater and wilderness areas that are supreme in their beauty, remoteness, and diversity. This book focuses on the water routes. Its companion volume – *Lehigh Gorge Trail Guide* – focuses on hiking, biking, and off-road jogging.

I first fell in love with the area when I started paddling the Lehigh River with the Mohawk Canoe Club. Throughout the years I have canoed the river dozens, perhaps scores of time. I have also kayaked the river, but I am at heart an open-boater. I always said to myself that someday I would like to live near the river. Now I do.

Most paddlers visit the Lehigh River solely to challenge the whitewater rapids for which it is famous, particularly in the Gorge. Summer weekends find hundreds, perhaps thousands, of people paddling downstream in rafts, kayaks, canoes, inner tubes, even inflatable sleeping pads and lawn furniture. After moving, I looked into the possibility of paddling the streams, creeks, and runs that feed the centerpiece river.

I was disappointed to learn that most of the time these tributaries were nearly waterless. For example, when I scouted the Mahoning Creek, I saw that I could walk on the streambed without getting my shoelaces wet. But several weeks later there was a two-inch rainfall in the space of 24 hours. Suddenly the stream was gushing. Together with Cheryl Novak, my constant companion, we decided to give the creek a try. Without knowing what to expect, we put my 17-foot Old Town Tripper in the narrow waterway west of Lehighton, in Normal Square, where Mill Road crosses the creek.

The current was fast, surging downstream with respectable speed through backwoods that could be reached only by bushwhacking. No trails marred this hinterland. The thin watery ribbon was a highway through untrammeled forest that lay close to civilization yet was partitioned from it by a fringe of forest.

Suddenly we burst into a vast open glade. It was the golf course of the Mahoning Valley Country Club. The winding creek carried us to a foot bridge whose steel supporting girders were slung too low to permit the canoe to pass underneath. Under the astonished eyes of a pair of golfers, we beached the boat on the left bank and carried it over the grooved path to the downstream side of the bridge.

One of the golfers must have been an octogenarian. He put his hands on his hips, and said in amazement, "I've been golfing here for 60 years. Never seen a canoe before." That was the moment when I realized that people rarely paddle the feeder streams in the Lehigh River watershed.

The Lehigh River was the main attraction. The Lehigh Gorge was the cornerstone. By and large, boaters ignored the other water courses; most outsiders probably didn't even know they existed. Locals knew the names of the streams. They even fished in them. But on only two occasions have I found anyone paddling down them: a pair of kayakers on the lower Lizard Creek, and another pair on a short middle section of the Jordan Creek. Later I met two hardcore extreme kayakers, but not on the water.

Granted that the smaller streams were somewhat seasonal – they could be run only during spring snow melt or after a large downpour – but they held qualities that the big river lacked: charm and solitude.

I was hooked!

Before the floodtide receded, I ran my canoe down the Nesquehoning Creek. I paddled solo because Cheryl was not a whitewater canoeist. I didn't run the creek blind, however. The previous winter I had scouted the worst part of it by bushwhacking through dense stands of rhododendron along the rocky banks, from Industrial Road to the confluence with the Lehigh River: a distance of four miles. There was only one cascade that required portaging.

Let me explain about scouting and portaging. These are common techniques that are employed in wilderness canoeing, and I wrote the book on wilderness canoeing – quite literally: *Wilderness Canoeing: the Adventure and the Art*. The book was based on years of experience in organizing and paddling multi-week canoe trips through the Canadian northlands, from Labrador to the Northwest Territories. My longest trip was on the George River: 380 miles that took a month to paddle.

When you are uncertain of the severity of the water that lies downstream, you beach your boat and walk ahead in order to examine the rapids so as to determine if they are runnable in light of your load and level of expertise. If not, you either use the painters to line the canoe between boulders along the bank, or carry the boat over short drop-offs, or portage around dangerous cascades and waterfalls.

I was able to scout the Nesquehoning Creek easily. I also scouted the Quakake Creek and Black Creek by riding my mountain bike along the adjacent railroad service road. Other creeks in the Lehigh River watershed can be scouted by hiking them in low water – but that's a lot of work. Creek beds tend to be difficult for hiking: loose rocks have been rounded by erosion and are covered with moss and slippery vegetation. Hiking poles are strongly recommended.

Cheryl and I once hiked a mile up the Little Schuylkill River, from Route 54 to the impoundment, in thrice the time it takes to walk that distance along a well-worn dirt path. I hiked alongside some of the streams, but mostly I studied the streambeds from bridge crossings, and made interpolations of probable difficulty based on the approximated gradient. Without knowing the obstacles that lay between viewing points, I had to run them blind, and trust my experience to get me through unscathed: by lining, carrying, or portaging.

The purpose of the present volume is manifold: to inform my readers what they can expect to find on the Lehigh River, to introduce them to the subtleties and enjoyment of transient streams in the watershed, and to save them the trouble of scouting by describing the impediments that block straightforward passage, so they can decide if a particular stream is one that they want to paddle.

There's more to the Lehigh River watershed than the Gorge. Much more.

Fish Tails, or the Angling Angle

I do not consider myself an angler. Until last year, I had not fished in Pennsylvania waters since I was too young to require a license. Even then, all I ever did was pluck a few sunfish out of Pennypack Creek, in Philadelphia.

In Salisbury, Maryland – my mother's hometown – I used to catch bluegills, catfish, and silversides (that's what we called them) in the Wicomoco River. I never kept them. I measured them, wrote down the species and length, and put them back in the water. I made it easy to get the fish off the hook: I either crimped the barb flat or filed it off. When I returned to my grandparents' house after a day's fishing, my grandfather would ask, "Where are all your fish." I showed him the page in my notebook.

INTRODUCTION 9

All my adult fishing has been done on wilderness canoe trips in Canada, where I caught pike, walleye, trout, and arctic char. I cleaned, cooked, and ate every one. Once I got two for one: a walleye in the stomach of a pike. Those were the days. I told these fish tales in *Wilderness Canoeing: the Adventure and the Art*.

This background might not qualify me to write about angling in the Lehigh River watershed, but I'm going to do it anyway. I won't write about tackle and technique because my angling readers likely know more about those subjects than I do. But I am going to mention some personal observations, and comment about small secluded streams that out-of-towners might not know about.

Although I have caught plenty of trout in big rivers in Canada, I had no idea that they could live in such tiny brooks as those that exist in the Lehigh River watershed. After moving to Jim Thorpe, my first experience with the tenacity of native trout occurred when Cheryl returned from a walk with the dog, and told me that she saw a 6-inch fish in Robertson Run: a Lehigh River tributary that measures less than a yard across and that nowhere has a depth that is greater than a foot. I know, because I have hiked its entire length. I was surprised. Perhaps shocked

Later, I met an angler on Broad Mountain where the Eastern Loop crosses Jeans Run: a rivulet that is only a wee bit larger than Robertson Run. He told me that he had just caught three native trout (which he released). He said that he had to sneak up on the pools in which they lived; if they saw him approaching, they hid among the rocks and would not emerge as long as he was in sight – or for a long time after he left. They were uncommonly shy.

The first time I actually spotted one myself was when I was hiking up an unnamed stream on the east face of Broad Mountain. The stream measures slightly more than a mile in length. In places it is as wide as six feet across, but where it is wide it is only a few inches deep: barely more than my scree collar. This stream is one of my favorite places to visit because it boasts a two-tiered waterfall that stands 30 feet in height. My first time there, I was skipping from one shallow puddle to another when a native trout rose out of a puddle, skittered along the ground through half an inch of water for a distance of 3 feet, and disappeared into another puddle. Now I was more than surprised or shocked. I was astounded.

Since then I have come to accept that native trout can exist in the tiniest of runnels. I suppose that the reason for this is that they don't rely on baitfish or worms for sustenance, but can eat flies and other insects that land or fall on the surface. How they manage to survive the winter when the streams are frozen and covered with snow, I don't have a clue.

With all of the above being said, I doubt that there is any natural or artificial waterway in which native trout don't thrive. For that reason, in the present volume I have mentioned certain streams that deviate from the primary focus of the book (which is paddling): those that are too difficult for boaters to reach, or too small to paddle, or too wild and woolly to run without incurring disaster.

I should also like to mention that hundreds of minor tributaries to these unfavorable streams harbor populations of native trout just waiting to be caught. But most of you know that already.

Major fishing tributaries that are excluded from individual chapters are (from north to south): Hickory Run, Leslie Run, Drakes Creek, Glen Onoko Run, Jeans Run, Catasauqua Creek, and numerous others both named and unnamed.

HISTORICAL SKETCHES

Canals

In order to put usage of the Lehigh River into perspective, I will briefly describe the commercial origins and recreational evolution that led to its present designation as a free and open river for everyone to enjoy.

The impetus for commercial exploitation of the Lehigh River was the discovery of anthracite coal in the late 1700's. The commencement of navigation harkens to the beginning of the 1800's. The inspiration for marketing coal as a viable commodity came from the minds of Josiah White and Erskine Hazard. It may be that these partners were the first visionaries of the Lehigh River watershed.

The actual discovery of coal in Pennsylvania is shared by a number of individuals at different times and places. At first its use was limited by two factors: the difficulty in getting the black stone to burn, and the logistics of transportation to places where it was needed the most.

It is generally conceded that White and Hazard were jointly responsible for the accidental discovery of the way to get anthracite coal to burn. The usual practice for obtaining heat from bituminous coal was to ignite it in the open air, the way logs are burned in a fire pit. Under these conditions, anthracite coal merely smoldered and then was extinguished. After numerous trials to get anthracite coal to burn in an open furnace, the furnace door was slammed shut in disgust. Within minutes the coal burst into flame: a white smokeless flame instead of a black smoky flame, and a flame that generated more heat than that obtainable from bituminous coal.

Eureka!

At that moment, White and Hazard joined the scientific brotherhood of Archimedes.

Mountains adjacent to the Lehigh River were packed with coal. Extracting it was fairly simple and economical because most of the seams lay on or near the surface. The costly and labor intensive part of the undertaking was conveying the product to metropolitan areas where it could heat homes, make fires for blacksmiths, and generate steam for industrial processes. At first, lumps of coal in baskets were carried on the backs of mules. Later, wooden arks or barges were floated down the river when the water level was sufficient for the purpose.

But the Lehigh River was capricious. Most of the time it was dry enough to walk. Only during snowmelt season and after a fierce rainstorm did it hold enough water to float a boat. All too often, watercraft were destroyed by freshets that flowed wildly out of control. So White and Hazard envisioned a grandiose plan whose contemplation today would cause people to shake their heads in disbelief, and to brand the pair as lunatics. The two businessmen proposed to tame some 3 dozen miles of river by means of an extensive series of dams, canals, locks, dead waters, and towpaths.

Work commenced in 1818. For three years, hundreds of workers plied picks and shovels on the enormous task of digging some 35 miles of canals alongside the Lehigh River. Workers also chipped enough stone blocks to construct 9 dams and 49 locks. Upon completion, the canal system stretched from 2 miles above Jim Thorpe to the confluence with the Delaware River, at Easton. I fear to contemplate how much such a project would cost today, even with modern earthmoving equipment.

Historical Sketches

I apologize for condensing such a prodigious a task into a paragraph, without elaborating on the tremendous obstacles that must have been overcome in the process. For information about existing remnants of this system of canals, see the chapters in the present volume under Lehigh Canal.

The construction of the canal prompted the building of the Gravity Railroad, from Summit Hill to Mauch Chunk. Upon completion, coal that was mined from the rich mountains in Panther Valley was transported by rail to the river, then by canal boat down the Lehigh River to Easton, thence down the Delaware River to Philadelphia – all under the corporate banner of the Lehigh Coal and Navigation Company.

Next in the taming of the Lehigh River came an extension of the canal, from White Haven to Mauch Chunk, This 26-mile stretch required 20 dams and 29 locks. It opened for business in 1839.

The acceptance of hard coal as a source of fuel required a fair amount of promotion. People who were used to burning soft coal (bituminous) in open fireplaces were reluctant to change. Once anthracite coal caught on – and caught fire – people quickly learned how efficient it was. Anthracite generated more heat per weight of product than bituminous. Plus, anthracite burned not only hotter but cleaner.

Eventually, anthracite became the coal of choice for steamships, and remained the fuel of choice for the next hundred and fifty years, until the advent of motor vessels that were propelled by diesel engines. When the *Monitor* charged into the Battle of Hampton Roads on March 9, 1862, the steam for her newfangled engine was provided by boilers whose furnaces burned anthracite coal. She left no telltale smudge of black smoke in the air to announce her fast approach.

Following the success of the Lehigh River canal system, other canal systems were

This woodcut from *Harper's Weekly* shows coal chutes loading canal boats on the Lehigh River at the bottom of Pisgah Mountain.

constructed. The canal along the Delaware River stretched from Easton to Bristol (outside Philadelphia). A connecting lock at the confluence of the Lehigh River with the Delaware River enabled continuous service along the length of both canals.

Canals then transported more than coal. They handled freight of all kinds. In due course, they carried passengers both upstream and down.

This woodcut from *Harper's Weekly* shows Mauch Chunk as a thriving coal port, transporting black carbon on canal barges and railroad cars.

Railroads

Starting in 1836, track was laid piecemeal along the Lehigh River, but railroading did not get into full swing until the 1850's. That was when Asa Packer, soon the guiding light of the Lehigh Valley Railroad, assumed a controlling interest in the company. Growth became exponential under his expert direction. He extended tracks not only along the Lehigh River, but throughout eastern Pennsylvania so as to connect with track laid by other railroad companies.

Packer continued in this monumental task until his death in 1879.

I do not mean to give railroad expansion short shrift, but there is little more to be said other than that railroads kept expanding, and expanding, and expanding – and taking over more and more of the freight business: similar to the manner in which the canal system took over more and more of the wagon business that preceded it.

The real boost for railroading in the Lehigh River watershed came in the 1860's. Unfortunately, the boost was the result of a catastrophe in which hundreds of people were killed: a flood on so grand a scale that it caused irreparable damage that shifted the balance of freight competition from canal boats to railroad cars.

The Great Flood of 1861

According to the records of the Lehigh Coal and Navigation Company, "About the time the flood attained its maximum, the booms erected by the lumbermen in the pools near White Haven gave way, releasing from 200,000 to 300,000 saw logs, which, swept down by the current with resistless force, occasioned great damage to the works

Historical Sketches

along the whole extent of the line . . .

"The effect of the logs upon the canal and guard banks, both on the Upper and Lower Sections, was also very damaging, in many places battering down the protection walls, and plowing up the embankments, thus affording to the impetuous current an unobstructed way for the completion of the ruin, by washing away the now unprotected and loosened earthwork."

Literally overnight, nearly every dam was destroyed. Hundreds of canal boats were smashed to splinters; most were never recovered. The damage was so severe that the Upper Section (from White Haven to Jim Thorpe) was abandoned. Railroad beds and trestles in the Lehigh Gorge were damaged, but train companies were able to make a quick comeback. Now the only way to transport goods through the Lehigh Gorge was by freight train: the harbinger of things to come.

The great flood also washed away homes and businesses that lined the banks of the mighty river. W.H. Gausler was a mule driver when the great flood of 1841 disrupted river service for three years. By 1861 he was a prosperous businessman. He recorded, "On June 6, 1862, I lost by a freshet, my house, lumber yard, coal yard and boats. My family got out of the house at one o'clock in the morning with only their night clothing. All went down the Lehigh River. There was not enough left to build a fire."

Lehigh River debris continued its course of destruction when it entered the Delaware River. According to B.F. Fackenthal, "The surface of the water in the Delaware at Riegelsville was covered with lumber, logs, houses, barns, pit sties, hay stacks, bridges, canal and other boats."

Demise of the Canal System

Flooding was a perpetual problem along the Lehigh and Delaware Rivers. Railroads continued to grow as large-scale floods kept disrupting service on the canal. Tracks and beds were not immune to flood damage, but they could be repaired much faster than damaged dams and locks. Thriving railroad communities sprang up like weeds. Long before the turn of the century, railroads constituted the primary motive force along the Lehigh River.

Then railroads reigned supreme . . . until the advent of paved roads and automobiles.

The canal system did not die a sudden death. Instead, it slowly wasted away as railroads grew healthier. The long lingering dissolution did not terminate until 1942, by which time the cost of maintenance and repairs exceeded the meager profit that a dying coal business generated. The canals were abandoned to nature.

Flood Control

The Great Flood of 1862 was only one of many that plagued the inhabitants of the Lehigh River watershed. It was preceded by the great flood of 1841, and succeeded by so many, much larger floods that cresting records were constantly being broken. In some cases, flood waters rose more than 20 feet above the streambed – so high, in fact, that towpaths between the Lower Section canals and the river were sometimes submerged, making the river appear twice as wide as it was under normal circumstances.

Over the years, raging torrents again and again swept away buildings that bordered the banks of the Lehigh River. Hundreds of people were killed.

In 1955, hurricanes Connie and Diane devastated the eastern United States with widespread flooding. Eastern Pennsylvania was particularly impacted. Nearly half the area's streamflow gauges recorded discharge rates that were more than double their previous records. The Lehigh River crested at over 23 feet, which surpassed all previous records. The Delaware River crested at more than 40 feet, which also set a new record. More than 100 people died in Pennsylvania alone. Pennsylvania property damage was estimated at over $70 million.

Nature's one-two punch in less than a week fostered a new era of flood awareness that resulted in Congressional legislation that was aimed at the prevention of future disasters by erecting dams where they were needed the most. The one that is pertinent to the present volume is the Bear Creek Dam. The U.S. Army Corps of Engineers completed construction of this mammoth earth-and-rock structure in 1961. The amount of water that it was designed to impound was 108,000 acre-feet, equal to nearly 5 billion cubic feet, or some 35 billion gallons.

No sooner was the dam completed than, in 1962, the COE expanded the dam's purpose to include water supply and recreation. "Water supply" meant that extra water was stored and could be used to compensate for droughts in the Delaware River basin. "Recreation" meant that limited releases could provide whitewater conditions for rafting and canoeing activity. Five whitewater releases were scheduled each year. It must be kept in mind that these additional uses were secondary and subservient to the first priority of flood control.

In 1963, after the death of Pennsylvania's Congressional Representative Francis E. Walter, the name of the dam was changed in his honor.

Lehigh Gorge State Park

In 1972, with the idea of creating a new State Park, the Commonwealth of Pennsylvania purchased the abandoned railroad bed on the right bank of the Lehigh River, from White Haven to Glen Onoko (2 miles north of Jim Thorpe). The State then continued the process of land acquisition by purchasing property adjacent to the Lehigh Gorge. After 8 years of preparation, which included surfacing the railroad bed with crushed limestone, the accumulated property was turned over to the Pennsylvania Bureau of Parks, which led to the creation of Lehigh Gorge State Park.

The Lehigh River had long been a playground for whitewater enthusiasts. Now the park actively promoted other outdoor activities such as hiking and biking.

In 1988, Congressional legislation authorized the use of the water in the reservoir for recreational purposes. This set the stage for increasing the number of whitewater releases from 7 per year to more than 20, as well as establishing low-water releases for angling. Equally as significant, all these releases were *scheduled*. That meant that users could *plan* events.

Without a dam, the Lehigh River was runnable only during snow melt season and after a rainstorm, whenever one might happen to flood the river. With a dam, not only were whitewater releases guaranteed to occur, but they were guaranteed to occur on *weekends*. In a society whose occupational prerogative was based on working from Monday through Friday, scheduled weekend release dates that were guaranteed to occur meant that most boaters were assured of paddling opportunities on days when they were free from their jobs.

Weekend scheduling had a spin-off benefit: it encouraged the establishment of businesses that catered to rafting. These outfitters attracted unskilled paddlers who

Historical Sketches

Looking upstream at the Francis E. Walter Dam and reservoir.

could now float down the river in multi-person inflatable rafts, accompanied by experienced guides to steer them through the rapids. These thrilling whitewater tours increased the number of river users exponentially. Activity has been escalating ever since.

When I paddled the river in pre-park days, I rarely saw more than half a dozen boats, and all of those belonged to the group I was paddling with (the Mohawk Canoe Club, which issued a printed schedule of all its trips throughout the year). Occasionally we had a kayak or two. I never saw a raft. I never saw another group, either at the put-in, on the river, or at the take-out. The Lehigh River was largely shunned because whitewater canoeists numbered in the minority, and the small kayaking contingent within the club sought more challenging streams.

I don't mean to imply that Mohawk Canoe Club members were the only ones to paddle the Lehigh River. Other boaters could have been on the riverine conveyor belt but out of phase with us, or using different access sites. And other boaters may have paddled the river on days that were not on the Mohawk schedule. My point is that there was very little boating on the river in those days.

By comparison, on whitewater release days last year, I saw not hundreds, but literally *thousands* of paddlers on the river. Granted that the vast majority of these were rafters, but the high number of kayakers was not to be discounted. The only canoes I saw (other than mine) were high-performance whitewater canoes that were completely filled with flotation bags except for the cockpit area. My Old Town Tripper was definitely out of place; it attracted strange looks and not a few comments. Even my Dagger Reflection drew undue attention. Yet my ABS canoes from yesteryear were a big step forward from my original aluminum Grumman.

At the Rockport access, I strolled among hundreds of enthusiastic rafters who were standing in line to board rafts that outfitters had inflated and carried down to the water. The exhilaration in the air was so thick that it was tangible. The chatter was constant, the grins were enormous, the pacing in place was nonstop. Girls and young women

A fleet of rafts weaving a zigzag route through rapids between boulders. The people's excitement is palpable. The very atmosphere radiates anticipation and exhilaration. To witness such an event is to share the experience vicariously. To have the experience is incomparable.

started screaming as soon as they stepped into their raft.

On the water, people of both sexes and all persuasions hooted and howled like banshees. Bailer battles were constant. Squirt guns added to the amusement. Most rafters whooped and held their paddles overhead when they saw me taking pictures from the bank. I didn't see a soul who wasn't having a grand time – perhaps the time of their lives.

Outfitters launched groups of rafts in assembly-line fashion, then kept the groups together and separated from other groups once they were underway. Each group might contain 20 rafts or more; each raft could hold as many as seven people. Thus the average flotilla carried more than a hundred happy passengers. Rafts were launched from half a dozen access sites. Groups played hopscotch as they paused for lunch or breaks.

Kayakers spaced themselves between groups of rafts, or stationed themselves at rapids in which they wanted to play, then floated out of bounds whenever rafts drifted through the standing waves.

Due to hydrodynamics and differences in hull configuration, slender canoes can move faster over water than fat rafts can move. Whenever I padded my canoe through the Lehigh Gorge, I passed one raft flotilla after another, and never had any difficulty in worming my way through the masses – although I did have to duck past a few water fights. It was all in fun. Great fun.

In pre-park days, the annual number of Lehigh River paddlers counted in the hundreds. Nowadays the number counts in the tens of thousands. Plus, the Lehigh Gorge Trail has enabled non-boating anglers to reach fishing holes that were previously inaccessible to them.

The only fly in this river ointment – other than fishing flies – is water availability.

Historical Sketches

And perhaps a tendency toward fickleness on the part of the COE. In years of drought, scheduled releases may be reduced in volume in order to conserve drinking water that is being held in reserve for communities in the Delaware River basin.

For example, 26 whitewater and 12 angling releases were scheduled for 2014. Water was released as scheduled throughout spring and summer, with volumes for paddlers ranging between 750 and 810 cubic feet per second: perfect for canoeists, although rafters and kayakers might have preferred more. No one complained.

Four of the releases were scheduled for October: two whitewater releases of 4,000 cfs over the weekend of October 11 and 12, and two angling releases of 300 to 400 cfs on Friday, October 10 and Monday, October 13. First, as a result of the summer drought, the COE reduced the whitewater releases to 1,700 cfs for Saturday and 1,000 cfs for Sunday. Still respectable.

As the weekend approached, the COE cancelled all four releases. The volume of water that was released on those days was 145 cfs: not enough to be useful for any purpose. Yet three days later, on Thursday and Friday, the dam released 1,750 cfs in order to reduce the reservoir to its optimum winter level. Go figure!

Lehigh River Lawsuit

Pennsylvania recognizes two categories of waterways: navigable and non-navigable.

Navigable waterways are those that have been used for commercial navigation any time in the past. They are owned by the Commonwealth and are held in trust for the benefit of the public. To quote the Pennsylvania Fish and Boat Commission, the agency which manages and regulates State waterways, "The rights of the public in public waters are quite broad and extend to fishing, boating, wading, floating, swimming, and otherwise recreating."

Non-navigable waterways – that is, waterways that do not have a history of being used for commercial navigation – are treated slightly differently. Again, to quote the Pennsylvania Fish and Boat Commission, "Title to the beds is held by the adjacent riparian landowner. If the adjacent riparian landowner owns property on only one side of a non-navigable waterway, he or she owns to the middle. When a non-navigable waterway flows through someone's property, he or she owns the entire bed of the waterway."

Although riparian landowners can prevent fishing or wading in non-navigable water, they cannot "prevent the public from boating or floating in non-navigable water . . . because there's a 'navigation servitude' that gives the public the right to use the water for purposes of navigation only. This servitude does not extend to fishing."

The way it was explained to me by a Regional Supervisor of the PFBC's Bureau of Law Enforcement, riparian landowners own the streambed of non-navigable waterways, but the Commonwealth owns the water that flows over the streambed. The water is public property. Think of paddling on a non-navigable stream as akin to walking along the edge of private property, say, on a street or sidewalk; or hiking along the border of a State Forest without stepping over the boundary line onto adjacent private property. Being close to private property is not the same as being *on* private property.

This is good news for boaters because it means that they can paddle on any waterway in the State as long as they access the waterway from public property (a park or bridge, for example). But they cannot access a waterway by crossing private property unless they have permission from the landowner. Nor can they wade on the streambed in the course of navigating the stream.

Enter John Andrejewski. That is, in 1995, Andrejewski entered the Lehigh River from riparian land that he co-owned with his father. Once on the river, Andrejewski fished and waded upstream and down until he stood on part of the riverbed that lay adjacent to property that was leased by the Lehigh Falls Fishing Club. Members of the fishing club told him to leave. Andrejewski refused because he, according to court documents, "believed that the river was within the public domain."

After repeated "transgressions," the fishing club filed a suit against Andrejewski, "seeking a declaration that the two-mile portion of the Lehigh River located through its land is not navigable and thus, not owned by the Commonwealth and instead, is its own private property."

Andrejewski prevailed by presenting "substantial evidence regarding the navigability of the portion of the Lehigh River located between its land."

The fishing club appealed. Andrejewski received more help than he possibly could have imagined. "On appeal, the Department of Conservation and Natural Resources of the Commonwealth of Pennsylvania, the Department of Environmental Protection of the Commonwealth of Pennsylvania, the Pennsylvania Fish and Boat Commission, and the Pennsylvania Federation of Sportsmen's Clubs have all filed *amicus curiae* briefs. . . . All four *amicus curiae* support the trial court's conclusion that the Lehigh River is a navigable waterway."

The Superior Court found no reason to reverse the opinion of the lower court. Attorneys for the fishing club argued that, although much of the river had been navigable in the past, the stretch under consideration (between the Great Falls of the Lehigh and the Francis E. Walter Dam) was no longer navigable.

In reviewing relevant case law, which went back to colonial times, the Superior Court found, "Appellant attempts to overcome these cases by pointing out that different sections of the Lehigh River were being examined. We find this fact to be irrelevant. Rivers are not determined to be navigable on a piecemeal basis. It is clear that once a river is held to be navigable, its entire length is encompassed. Appellant owns land along the Lehigh River, which has been declared navigable by our Supreme Court . . .

"We cannot piecemeal by piecemeal re-examine the navigability of an acknowledged public waterway. The relevant case law necessarily is old since the issue of what rivers are public rivers became important early in the history of our Commonwealth. The Lehigh River unquestionably historically has been considered by our Supreme Court as a navigable, public waterway. Since Appellant's land is on the Lehigh River, the public has the right to fish on the portion of the river located through its land. Order affirmed."

The affirmation concurred with the lower court's ruling that "the Defendant has the right to fish the bed of the Lehigh River for its length."

The right to fish included the right to wade or otherwise walk through the water on the riverbed, because Pennsylvania owns the riverbed and holds it in trust for public commerce and recreation. These rights were granted not only to John Andrejewski, but to everyone.

John Andrejewski has my heartfelt thanks for sticking to his guns and protecting a cherished public resource from privatization.

Reflections

Personal Pre-Park Reflections

My very first paddling experience occurred underground. I was spelunking in Virginia when I encountered a sink hole at whose bottom flowed an unexplored river. I bought a 4-person inflatable life raft, lowered it 70 feet into the sink hole to a ledge above the water, climbed down after it, inflated it with a hand pump, lowered it 20 feet to the slowly moving surface, and climbed down a rope to board the raft. My companions on this trip were Tom Gmitter and Al Dubeck.

We paddled half a mile upstream before the ceiling sloped down and met the water. We explored some side tunnels along the way back to the exit.

Later, I used the raft to paddle down Bushkill Creek. My fellow paddlers were Ken Nonemaker, Pete Regan, and Joe Thompson. The stream was flooded with March snow melt so we all wore wetsuits. Partway down the stream, the raft struck a sharp rock that ripped an enormous gash in the starboard pontoon; it deflated instantly. For the next several miles, we shivered in the frigid water while clinging to the port pontoon until we reached the take-out.

By that time I had joined the Mohawk Canoe Club. I didn't own a canoe, so for the first couple of years I paddled tandem with other members who taught me the fine art of canoeing. My two primary instructors were Jim Seyler and Charlie Schrey. On my first trip down the Lehigh River, I paddled bow in Charlie Schrey's 17-foot aluminum Grumman. We didn't have airbags in those days. We relied on skill and experience to make it through the rapids. Charlie gave me tips on whitewater paddling strokes as we splashed through the waves.

We ate our midday meal at Lunch Rock. My repast consisted of a can of Sloppy Joes. Once back on the water, I started to feel unwell. I barely had time to recognize the symptoms of food poisoning when we entered the first stretch of standing waves. About halfway through the rapids I vomited so violently that undigested food particles were forced through my nostrils. Charlie did all the paddling while I kept vomiting.

After Charlie steered the canoe into an eddy, he calmly spoke only a single word: "Seasick?"

I was unable to speak until I cleared my nasal passages by inhaling water through my nose. Although I liked Sloppy Joes, ten years passed before I was able to eat it again.

On another occasion, our group was approaching Bear Creek when I heard gunshots ahead and to the left. Then I saw the splashes of bullets in the water a hundred feet ahead. I backpaddled hard and shouted a loud warning. The shooting stopped, and someone called out from the woods near the stream, "Sorry! Didn't know anyone was there." We passed Bear Creek safely, never saw the shooter, and did not hear a resumption of firing.

Then there was the time I led the group through a rapids, and pulled into an eddy to wait for the rest of the boats. Lo and behold, a string of grapevines overhung the water – and the wild purple grapes were perfectly ripe. I ate as many as I could before catching up with my companions downstream.

By this time I had bought and sold an aluminum Grumman, and invested in one of the first Royalex boats to hit the market. Royalex was the brand name for a high-impact

Mohawk on the Lehigh. In those days I strapped a waterproof Nikonos II camera around my neck.

thermoplastic resin whose acronym was ABS, for acrylonitrile butadiene styrene. Ironically, or coincidentally, the canoe was manufactured by a company called Mohawk.

My Mohawk got its first real test on the Riviere du Chef in Quebec, Canada. The other three boats on the three-week trip were standard aluminum Grummans. Everyone laughed at my plastic boat. They called it the Rubber Ducky, after a popular song based on a bathtub toy in a children's television series. They didn't laugh for long. In the narrow upstream shallows, the aluminum hulls came to a screeching halt every time they struck a barely submerged rock, as if the hulls and the rocks were two components of Velcro. The Rubber Ducky slid gracefully over rocks like skates on ice.

It didn't take long before Kendra Schieber (my partner) and I were elected as scouts. We led the way through every rapids and rock field, so we could direct the high-friction boats to the clearest passage.

Back on the Lehigh, I kept noticing that water often flowed over the gunwales amidships as I passed through tall standing waves, despite my powerful backpaddle strokes. This was annoying because my technique was correct and I hit the waves at the perfect angle. It was more annoying when the Grummans followed the same path and remained dry. I soon determined that the problem lay in the low freeboard. This started me on a quest to find a different boat.

The one I settled on was an Old Town Tripper. It had 13 inches of freeboard instead of the Mohawk's 11 inches. It also had a soft V-shaped bottom instead of the Mohawk's flat bottom; this difference in hull configuration enabled the Tripper to track better on flat water and in the wind. Now I could plow through standing waves without having to pull into a downstream eddy afterward, and bail.

About this time I took kayak lessons from Mohawk Canoe Club member Walt Daub. I practiced the Eskimo roll in a pool until I could roll back up every time. After I bought a kayak, I made a few short flat-water trips until I thought I was ready for the Lehigh. The trip proved to be the end of my kayaking career.

As we often did in those days, we (the Mohawkers) did a double trip: from White Haven to Jim Thorpe instead of from White Haven to Rockport or from Rockport to Jim Thorpe. I enjoyed crashing full speed through standing waves without having to backpaddle. One time I got a little too rambunctious and got flipped by a rogue wave. I rolled upright in the middle of the rapids and kept right on going as if nothing had happened. My first whitewater Eskimo roll! And my last.

Reflections

The problem was not my kayaking skill, meager though it was, but pinched nerves from a previously broken leg. The sitting position aggravated the chronic pain so much that I was forced to take my left foot off the pedal between rapids, and stretch out my leg in order to obtain partial relief. The trip was so agonizing that by the time we reached the train station, I could hardly stand when I disembarked onto the stony shore.

I sold the kayak and went back to open-boating, where the kneeling position was tolerable. But my kayaking experience was not all wasted. I learned about the efficiency of paddling solo with a double-bladed paddle, instead of using the inefficient J-stroke to counteract the boat's deviation.

By then I had long since forsworn wooden paddles. I had two Iliad paddles (for me and a partner) which in my opinion were the best ones on the market. If longevity means anything, I still have them and still paddle with them. The T-handle shaft was made of plastic-coated aluminum; the oversized blade was made of durable fiberglass. I called the manufacturer and asked if they could make a special, double-bladed paddle for me. Kayak paddles averaged 7 feet in length. For canoeing I needed one that was 10 feet in length. I specified that the blades should not be curved and offset like a kayak paddle, but flat and on the same plane.

Iliad took my specifications and went one better: they designed a detachable paddle in which the shaft of one 5-foot section fitted into a socket in the shaft of the other 5-foot section. There was no loss in strength because the shaft-and-socket overlap was doubled in thickness. Thus each section was the approximate length of a single-bladed paddle. This made the paddle easy to carry and store.

I added one modification: I fabricated drip catches that I made out of neoprene. I cut circular swatches of neoprene from wetsuit material, then cut doughnut holes in the middle of them. These neoprene drip catches could be slid up the half-shafts when the paddle was separated. This way, when water dripped off the blade and down the upheld shaft, it dripped off the neoprene catch and fell into the river outboard of the hull. This kept my hands dry as well as the inside of the boat: a godsend when the water was cold. Nowadays, my home-made invention is manufactured commercially.

I also modified my canoe. I added epoxy resin skid plates to the bow and stern. I glued neoprene kneeling pads to the floor. I installed thigh braces to add support for reaching and bracing in rapids. I placed the kneeling pads and thigh braces in three positions: in front of the two seats for tandem paddling, and behind the front seat for solo paddling. When I paddled solo, I leaned against the back of the front seat and faced the stern of the canoe.

After I was equipped to perfect my technique of solo canoeing with a double-bladed paddle, the Lehigh River became my special playground. I did some trips on the Youghiogheny, and I paddled down the Tohickon on annual release dates. But mostly I ran the Lehigh Gorge – over and over again.

On one wildcat trip that comes to mind, we decided to start from the dam, camp downstream of Rockport, and finish at the train station the following afternoon. The Saturday whitewater release not exceptionally high, but it was fun for all concerned. Little did we know that this was only a one-day release. When we crawled out of our tents on Sunday morning, we learned that the COE had shut off the water. The Lehigh River was a nearly dry gravel bar. We had to walk most of the way to Jim Thorpe, dragging our boats by the painters.

Now for my most memorable Lehigh River odyssey. . . .

The Mohawk Canoe Club has a long tradition of awarding medals to anyone who paddled 500 miles in a calendar year. Although I did a fair amount of paddling, I spent most of my extracurricular time in scuba diving. Then there were hiking and backpacking (both locally and out west), rock and mountain climbing, plus skiing and snowshoeing in the winter. With all these activities, it was nearly impossible for me to paddle 500 miles in any twelve-month period.

My opportunity arose one year when I went on a long wilderness canoe trip on the Riviere du Chef in the province of Quebec. Three straight weeks of paddling added some 300 miles to my tally. By the end of November I was only 50 miles short of earning the medal. No club trips were scheduled for December, so it was left for me to paddle the required mileage on my own. Knowing how important it was to me, two club members agreed to help: Walt Hauser and Jim Howie.

For my last hurrah of the year, I planned three consecutive days of paddling for mid-December. As the target weekend approached, a great storm swept through the eastern States, deluging the area with rain and bringing plummeting temperatures.

Walt met me at the Jim Thorpe train station on Saturday morning. The river was in flood. I had previously paddled the Lehigh at discharge rates ranging from bare minimum all the way to 3,000 cubic feet per second. This day the discharge rate an imposing 4,000 cfs. I had never seen it so high. To make conditions more challenging, the temperature stood in the mid 20 degrees Fahrenheit.

We packed our gear, transferred a boat, left one vehicle behind, and headed for White Haven. There we had to stand in the freezing air to change from street clothes to paddling wear. Walt struggled into a full wetsuit. I donned the drysuit that I habitually wore for cold-water diving, plus a neoprene hood and neoprene three-fingered mitts. No sooner did we start on the river – Walt in a kayak, I in my Tripper – than the wind picked up and snow started to fall – sideways! We found ourselves paddling in a full-scale blizzard. This was going to be an endurance trip.

Difficult as it may be to believe, the river was less challenging at 4,000 cfs than it was at lower discharge rates. This was because the boulders that ordinarily created standing waves and hydraulics were buried so deep that the water leveled out as it passed over them. Likewise with drop-offs and ledges: the extreme depth filled them in and smoothed them over. There was very little whitewater. The raging torrent created monstrous swells that became a roller coaster ride moving with phenomenal speed.

I don't mean to imply that there weren't any rocks or standing waves, but they were few and far between. Mostly we were propelled at a breakneck pace over immense rollers with high crests and deep troughs. This was not particularly threatening as long as I kept the boat aligned with the current.

My biggest problem was wind spray. Water that slapped against the side of the hull splashed higher than the gunwale. Most of it was blown straight over the canoe without falling inside, but some of the drops struck the inside of the opposite gunwale, and dripped down to the floor. Soon the interior was filmed with half an inch of icy water which I didn't dare to bail out because I was afraid of missing a crucial stroke and turning broadside to waves. I constantly had to fight the wind that twisted the boat with a will of its own.

Visibility was reduced to a hundred feet by large snowflakes that filled the air like white confetti at a victory parade. From the middle of the river we could barely see the banks. We concentrated on watching the water ahead.

Reflections

Then a loud whistle sounded from the left side of the river. A down-bound freight train was slowly overtaking us – and I do mean slowly. We were moving with exceptional velocity. The engineer stepped out of the cabin of a black locomotive, and stood on a section of catwalk. He stared at us in evident disbelief. He shook his head and raised his arms with a shrug, as if to say, "What the hell are you guys doing?"

Canoeing through a raging snowstorm in subfreezing temperatures was not one of my druthers, but now that I had started, I was committed – or would have been committed had the engineer been a psychiatrist.

Two other events occurred in short order. Over the blast of the wind I heard Walt shouting. I took my eyes off the rapids ahead to spare a glance to my left. He did not appear to be in trouble. He steered close to me so I could distinguish the words he was mouthing before the wind whipped them away. He said that he was having vision problems; he was seeing some kind of shadowy shapes in front of his eyes, and blinking would not make the shapes go away or clear his vision.

I saw the trouble immediately. His crash helmet was coated with ice from windswept spray that froze on the smooth outer surface. Water had dripped down the center of the helmet's forehead and formed a 3-inch icicle that hung down like the nose guard on the iron helmet of a medieval knight wearing plate armor for a jousting match. When I explained the situation, he reached past his brows, snapped off the icicle, looked at it in his hand, and tossed it overboard.

Meanwhile, I was uncomfortable and needed to change positions by sliding either up or down the seat I was leaning against. That's when I discovered that I couldn't move. The slush in the bottom of the canoe had frozen solid around the legs of my drysuit. I couldn't break free. I was panic-stricken by the realization that if the canoe was dumped by a tremendous rolling wave, I would trapped under the boat, and would not be able to break free until the ice melted – if I could hold my breath that long.

I chopped the ice with my paddle blade until I was able to move my legs. For the rest of the trip, I constantly swished my legs back and forth and from side to side, in order to prevent them from getting beset in the ice.

We couldn't have taken-out at Rockport even if we had wanted to. There was no way to land as the raging current swept us past the steep-walled access.

Lunch Rock was a blur that I hardly noticed as we sped past the eponymous geological feature.

We raced along for the next 10 miles as if we were in a slalom, except that there weren't any obstacles. Most of the rocks were totally submerged, and the few large boulders that protruded above the surface were easily avoidable. There was plenty of maneuvering room because the swollen riverbed overflowed the banks, and low-water boulder fields were hidden under tons of rushing water.

We rounded the Oxbow in a flash, then entered the upper part of the Rock Garden. By this time the snowstorm had reduced itself to flurries. Visibility increased to a hundred yards or more. The wind moderated – but an errant gust caught me just as I crested a tall roller. Before I had time to correct the angle, the canoe plunged into the trough at a very slight angle. The starboard bow dipped beneath the oncoming wave . . . and the boat flipped over in the blink of an eye.

After I surfaced I struck out for the canoe, which rolled back upright and floated barely awash. I hung onto a gunwale, tucked my paddle under the thwart, and tried to steer the boat to shore as I rounded the bend into the lower Rock Garden. No go.

A cold day in the Rock Garden.

I swam for a quarter mile without making much sideways progress against the ferocious torrent. Finally I saw an exposed boulder ahead in midstream. I angled toward the only haven in view. I managed to reach a position directly upstream of the boulder, then let the speeding current carry me down to it. I couldn't grab the boulder because the rounded surface was smooth. Instead, I intentionally slammed into it, then scrambled and crawled on top, swinging the canoe into the trailing eddy in the process.

Walt was nearly out of sight downstream. He was facing me and paddling hard to stay in place. The only thing he could have done to help was to stay in position and catch me as I drifted past him. Then I could grab onto his kayak while he paddled toward shore. I waved to let him know that I was okay.

I rolled the canoe upside down, dragged it onto the boulder, and flipped it over. I eased the dewatered boat back into the eddy, then crept into it. The current quickly carried me past Walt. He peeled off and followed me. After that we – or I – had no more complications. We reached the train station five hours after our departure.

We sat in the car and wolfed down the lunch that we had not stopped to eat on the river. The heater helped to take off the chill. After we completed the shuttle, Walt drove home while I drove to Jim Howie's house in New Jersey.

Jim and Joan were writing Christmas cards when I arrived at their door. Their daughter Carol was visiting for the weekend. Outside, the ongoing storm continued to pummel the area: first with snow, then with sleet, then with freezing rain. I was glad to spend the night with friends inside a well-heated home.

The morning brought little relief from the weather. There was no more precipitation, but after the freezing rain stopped, the fluctuating temperature had dropped into the teens. The Howies' house was set back in the woods at the end of a long uphill driveway. Every limb on every tree on the property dazzled pure white with frost: a fairyland scene out of a Disney movie.

My Chevy Blazer was coated with a thick layer of ice that froze the doors shut and filled the keyholes. From the gunwales of the canoe, upside down on the roof, hung fat icicles nearly a foot in length.

Jim helped to chop the canoe free from the rack and set it on the ground. It looked

Reflections

weird with long icicles protruding upward, like stalagmites growing on the floor of a cave. We hefted to canoe onto the roof of his car. I used lighted matches to melt the ice in keyhole of the driver's door. It took a while to chip the thick veneer of frozen water off the windshields of both vehicles. Finally we got underway to the Musconetcong River: a frequent trip for Mohawkers and one that I was familiar with.

    We left my Blazer at the take-out. Jim dropped me off at the put-in. I did not expect to get wet on this trip – the Musconetcong was a smoothly flowing river with hardly a riffle to mar safe passage, and with only one short dam to portage on the right – so I did not wear my drysuit. I wore long-johns, woolen trousers, and so many layers over my chest and vital organs that I lost count. A woolen ski cap kept my head and ears from freezing, ski mittens and woolen liners kept my hands warm, and my feet were nice and toasty in black Army-surplus Mickey Mouse boots that were designed for soldiers who fought in the Korean War in winter.

    I was faced with the same frosty wonderland that surrounded Jim's house. The ground and the trees were covered with snow which was laminated with invisible coats of ice from the previous night's storm. I have never seen a sight so awesome; so inspiring. Gawking at the untrammeled countryside was almost a spiritual experience. And I had 15 miles of this dream world to pass through. My one regret is that I did not take a camera to record the ineffable beauty.

    There was hardly a breath of wind, yet the forest crackled constantly from the weight of snow and ice that bore down on branches which then rubbed against nearby neighbors. Time after time I heard tree limbs snap and break away, then crash to the forest floor. This constant threat led to two close calls with death.

    In the first incident, a massive ice-laden branch snapped off a tree on the right bank. It must have weighed a couple of hundred pounds. It splashed into the water not 10 feet forward of my bow, and sank. A second or two later I drifted right over top of the still-swirling water. If the heavy branch had landed on me, or if it had struck the canoe and sunk it, I would have been seriously injured, or killed, or drowned.

    In the second incident, the trunk of a 50-foot-tall tree broke off at the base and fell right across the river some 30 feet ahead of me. At that point the Musconetcong was 50 feet wide. The tree was set back from the left bank nearly 10 feet. I happened to be paddling close to the right bank. A few seconds after the fully mature tree and all its branches struck the water, I drifted through the 8-foot channel between the top of the tree and the right bank. I couldn't have planned it any better.

    Unable to withstand the excessive weight of snow and ice, there was a continuous onslaught of falling trees and branches in the bordering forest. I did not witness any more of them hitting the water.

    The most spectacular event was yet to come. Before I describe it, I need to preface the incident with some personal background. My father was an electrical contractor. During summer vacations, I had worked with him on residential jobs and housing projects since the age of 10 (when society was more rational and open-minded, and children were allowed on construction sites). Later I served a 4-year apprenticeship and spent 10 years employed as a commercial and industrial electrician. I worked on everything from tall office buildings (where I walked high steel before the floors were poured) to hospitals, chemical plants, refineries, and a plutonium waste treatment plant. I installed high-voltage electrical panels; did control work on complex low-voltage installations; performed maintenance on the presses at the *Philadelphia Inquirer*; hooked up service

A freezing day on the Musconetcong (taken after the trip).

cables; worked on warehouses, homes, and apartment complexes, both construction and renovation; and so on. I also took chemistry courses in high school and college. My point is that I am extremely knowledgeable about the science of electricity.

Between my put-in and take-out there was one place on the Musconetcong where the river and a road came close together. As I approached the convergence, I heard a strange crackling sound that reminded me of radio static, or the crinkling of paper bags. What I saw was a phenomenon that few people have ever seen, even electricians: a perpetual short circuit.

The weight of snow and ice on the distribution lines was so enormous that the catenary of the upper cable sagged until it came into contact with that of the lower cable. By design, the insulation on transmission wires that were strung in the open between utility poles was comparatively thin, because heat that was generated by normally flowing current could be dissipated by the air. When these two cables touched, the heat of flowing electrons and concomitant magnetic flux burned through the insulation of both cables. Normally, a short circuit would have tripped the protective circuit breaker. In this instance the circuit breaker didn't trip. Here's why.

A short circuit creates an overload in the load-bearing conductor. Nowadays, magnetic circuit breakers trip only milliseconds after detecting a preset overload in the milliampere range. Ground fault interrupters actuate even faster. But in those days, electrical circuits (both distribution lines and household conductors) were protected by *thermal* circuit breakers. I've been out of the business for a while, but I don't think that thermal breakers are in use any more.

A thermal circuit breaker operates (or operated) on the principal of heat: it trips (or tripped) when it detects a preset rise in temperature (such as that which would be generated by a short circuit). On transmission lines, breakers are installed in transformers (those cylinders at the top of utility poles). Transformers are not placed on every pole, but are spaced over a distance in order to compensate for voltage drop (line loss).

Reflections

On this particular day, the outdoor temperature was so low that the heat generated by the short circuit was dissipated in the air before it traveled along the wire and reached the circuit breaker. The result was a short circuit that kept on shorting.

I suspect that everyone has seen a "short" at some time during his life. It's a tiny ball of light about half the size of a BB shot, and lasts barely a split second before the breaker trips and stops the flow of electricity.

The ball of light that I observed was larger than a basketball: a giant coruscation of interacting electrons that simulated ball lightning (if such a phenomenon exists), and that did not terminate during the time I drifted past it: perhaps a minute or two.

I apologize if my readers aren't as fascinated by this electrifying sensation as I was, but I still am. For me, with my knowledgeable appreciation of its rarity, if not uniqueness, it was a mind-boggling once-in-a-lifetime occurrence.

It was nighttime by the time I returned to the Howies'. The house was blacked out. I was stunned because Jim had invited me to come for dinner and spend the night again. Now it looked as though he and the family had gone out and left me in the lurch. I felt my way through the garage to the door that they commonly used to enter the house. It was unlocked, so I pushed it open and poked my head inside. They were sitting in the dark around the dining room table. The only illumination came from a gasoline lantern on the kitchen counter and a handful of candles that were spread strategically throughout the house.

It was a power failure. The whole neighborhood and much of central New Jersey was suffering from downed transmission lines. Who would have thought!?!

Joan cooked dinner on a gasoline camp stove. Jim had a fire going in the living room fireplace. Carol tended the fire. I helped to tote in some wood. We spent the evening huddled in front of the fireplace, like pioneers in a log cabin in colonial times. When the others retired to their bedrooms, I slept on the floor as close to the fire as I could get. My job was to stoke the fire throughout the night; my payment was the warmest place in the house. The best word I can use to describe the way I felt that night is "romantic."

I said goodbye in the morning and left to make my final mileage on the Delaware River. I put-in about 15 miles above New Hope. The temperature rose over the freezing mark, and made it to the low 40's by afternoon. The river was in flood as a result of all the precipitation and now-melting snow. I didn't have to worry much about whitewater on the Delaware, whose gradient is nearly flat. I cruised along swiftly, knowing that there was only one obstacle between me and my destination: the weir dam at Lumberville. I knew from previous experience that I had to shoot through the opening in the center, so I paddled idly in the middle of the river.

I got confused when I passed under bridges that I thought were located farther downstream. I must have been daydreaming, for suddenly I recognized New Hope ahead. I passed under the bridge that connected the quaint artist community with Lambertville, beached the canoe on the downstream side, and scrambled up the slope to the downtown area. Yes, this was definitely New Hope.

What happened to the Lumberville Dam? The water level was so high that the dam was completely submerged. I had passed over the dam without even knowing it.

I hitchhiked up Route 32 on the Pennsy side, drove my Blazer to New Hope, put the canoe on the roof, and headed for home in Philly. In due course I proudly received my 500 mile medal. I had certainly earned it.

LEHIGH RIVER

Section 0: Headwaters to Lehigh Road
Distance: 4.0 miles
Travel time: 3 hours
Adversity level 3: Very challenging
Walkable but not runnable
Gradient overall: 34 feet per mile
Gradient breakdown: Bog to Lake Drive = 13 feet per mile
Gradient breakdown: Lake Drive to end of Lower Klondike Pond = 54 feet per mile
Gradient breakdown: End of Lower Klondike Pond to Lehigh Road = 30 feet per mile

The Lehigh River has three primary sources. The "official" origination – that is, the source that is given on the U.S. Geological Survey topographic map – is a bog south of Pocono Peak Lake: not a natural lake but an artificial impoundment that was created to serve a housing development. Water under this reservoir seeps through forested ground for half a mile before accumulating a sufficient amount to become noticeable as a stream that fills a bog.

At first the bog is little more than a soak: a soggy wetland filled with tall marsh grass and inhabited by frogs, water striders, and flying insects. Water pools around hummocks. Farther "downstream," the bog spreads in width to the length of a football field. A quarter mile later the bog assumes the appearance of a pond in which the marsh grass is submerged and only occasional hummocks mar the smooth glistening surface.

The "pond" is not geological in nature, but biological. The reason soon becomes apparent: the hip-deep water is impounded by a beaver dam that spans a restriction in the muddy streambed. Two more beaver dams follow in quick succession. Downstream of each dam, the water is little more than a trickle which is often unseen because of the thick marsh grass that grows in great profusion, much like hair on a chia pet.

The bog where the Lehigh River officially begins.

Lehigh River Section O

Lehigh Pond

This bryozoan was living in Lehigh Pond. It is a colony animal: a group of individual zooids similar to coral. This specimen was the size of a football.

The "river" makes its first public appearance when it passes through four culverts under a bridge on Lake Drive, one quarter mile north of Route 507. At that point the streambed measures some eight feet in width, although at some places downstream it shrinks to only a couple of feet across. Now the seep turned trickle exhibits true flow.

The streambed consists of a rocky substrate, most of which is exposed above barely moving water: perhaps only slightly more than can be sprayed through a garden hose. Now the surrounding dry land is a forest of hardwoods and hemlocks, and the ever-present rhododendron.

Nearly half a mile past Lake Drive, the "river" meets the drainage from Lehigh Pond. This aptly named body of water originates in a bog that is located in State Game Lands Number 312. A hardly perceptible measure of water seeps southward into this pond, which has the appearance of a giant spermatozoon. The oval-shaped "head" of the pond is slightly longer than a football field, and three times as wide. The "tail" extends south for 300 yards. At the end of the pond, a narrow dribble may (or may not) flow for a couple of hundred yards to the main watercourse.

At this point a circular pond some ten feet across and several inches deep is inhabited by crayfish, snails, and inch-long fish with the diameter of a pencil lead. Once

I saw a fish that measured three to four inches in length: species unknown to me.

Lacking any perceptible infusion of water, the rivulet continues the same as it did before. Suddenly the stream broadens and deepens: ten feet wide and hip deep. Fantasies of a navigable waterway soon dissolve with the appearance of another beaver dam: the first of seven along this narrow stretch. Most of these dams are well maintained: the spaces between limbs chinked with mud. Fresh beaver chews and a waterside lodge attest to current occupancy.

The water is only a few inches deep on the downstream side of each dam. Then the depth increases until the site of the next dam, after which the process starts over again.

The next two landmarks are a decrepit wooden walking bridge and a power line right-of-way. The power line service road fords the river through water whose depth wouldn't cover a 12-inch ruler.

The next landmark is the West Fork: the third in the sequence of bogs that merge to form a river that is still no wider than a backyard creek. The West Fork comprises the biggest bog of all: one that extends more than two miles northward. Yet the confluence is all but invisible: lost among the thick vegetation that lines the right bank of the primary watercourse. A minimal amount of water, if any, is added to the main flow.

Finally, the meager stream flows into an impoundment known as the Lower Klondike Pond. This reservoir measures half a mile in length, and is shaped somewhat like a kidney bean. The dam is located at the opposite, or southwestern end. It is from the outflow of the dam that the first section of the Lehigh River – *still* the size of a small run – may on occasion become runnable.

It is from this point that the Lehigh River commences its serpentine course through wild forests and between tall mountains as it grows into a great waterway that offers limitless recreational opportunities to rafters, kayakers, canoeists, tubers, and anglers – when sufficient water is available, or is made available.

Looking toward the dam from the end of Lower Klondike Pond. By the size and extent of weeds on the bottom, the reservoir appears to have been empty for quite some time.

Lehigh River Section 1

Section 1: Lehigh Road to Phillips Road
Distance: 2.8 miles
Travel time: 1 to 2 hours
Gradient for flat water: 10 feet per mile
Adversity level 2: Challenging
Needs 400 % on the Lehigh (Stoddartsville) gauge
Gradient: 25 feet per mile (total)
Gradient for running water: 38 feet per mile

Note the split gradients. The total gradient is misleading because the first 1.3 miles consists of impounded water in which nearly all the drop occurs at the two dams. The gradient of the water that runs for 1.5 miles gives a better understanding of the streambed for the rest of the way to the end of the section.

Park on the grass-covered road on the east side of Lehigh Road, then portage your boat to the river upstream of the bridge. The first quarter mile is an absolute mess of floating logs and fallen trees, in water too deep or with a bottom too muddy to stand in (or on). Basically it's a swamp. You have to climb onto the deadfall, balance yourself, and drag your boat over wood to the next watery space, then do it again a few feet farther on: and again, and again . . .

I lost count of the number of times I did this, but my best guess is six to eight. It was challenging but it sure wasn't fun.

After you gain clear water, duck under the railroad bridge – and I do mean duck. The clearance was so low that I had to remove my knapsack *and* life vest, then bend forward with my head touching the deck, and press my belly against the center thwart. What a hassle.

The reservoir known as Larsen Lake was a welcome relief. The dam builder was thoughtful enough to pour cement staircases on either side of the dam. I dragged my canoe up one set of steps and down the other.

A channel connects Larsen Lake with another reservoir that is called Lake Natalie on USGS topo maps. The channel passes under 4th Street. The next dam is located at the northwest end of Lake Natalie. Once again the dam builder was considerate enough to construct a gradual slope on either side of the dam, making for an easy drag.

Running water commences at the outflow of the dam. Now the real trouble begins – not with the gradient as you might expect, but with deadfall. The gradient is fairly constant with no ledges or drop-offs. A few small boulders litter a streambed that measures 15 to 20 feet from bank to bank: more than adequate for the purpose of avoidance. I paddled smoothly through a dark forest that was punctuated by so many houses that there was no sense of wilderness or isolation. The water was so shallow that I could never get my blade fully submerged. I grated over rock bars with little effort – until I encountered the first logjam of many.

From that point onward I constantly had to disembark into shin deep water in order to lift or drag my canoe over barriers which never seemed to end. I spent more time climbing over tree trunks than I spent in paddling.

Take-out on the left bank downstream of the Phillips Road bridge. A small pull-over is located some fifty feet away.

After completing this section, I decided that it was not worth the effort. The adversity level in the statistical sidebar is based on the amount of deadfall, not on the effort of paddling.

For a short trip on open water, launch a boat at the 4th Street bridge and explore the reservoirs at opposite ends of the channel. I saw one angler fishing from the left bank downstream of the bridge. Two others paddled kayaks along the channel and fished in both reservoirs.

When all is said and down, the fishing opportunities are more attractive than the boating prospects.

looking downstream into Lake Natalie from the 4th Street bridge. Note the kayaks in the distance.

The cascade in Section 2.

Lehigh River Section 2

Section 2: Phillips Road to the north bridge on Game Land Road
Adversity level 3: Most challenging
Distance: 3.5 miles   Needs 400 % on the Lehigh (Stoddartsville) gauge
Travel time: 1-1/2 to 2 hours   Gradient: 39 feet per mile

This section is a dream trip in comparison with the previous section. There is absolutely no deadfall so you can paddle straight through without interference. Well, almost . . .

Except for a one block stretch, the adversity level is more like 2 than 3. Let me explain.

Put-in at Phillips Road, on the left bank downstream of the bridge, and downstream of the rock dam that you can see from the bridge. I ran Sections 2 and 3 in one continuous sweep, so I ran the dam on the right with no problem: the canoe simply slid over the rocks and dipped into the river without taking on any water. A hundred yards downstream lies the only fallen tree that spans the banks. But there was enough headroom for me to duck under the root end alongside the left bank.

After that it's clear sailing for the next mile and a half. Pure fun is the way I remember it. The trees on either side provide a modicum of insularity. The streambed is rocky but not scratchy, although I tagged a few submerged boulders here and there. The 20-foot space between banks was adequate for avoiding the occasional exposed rock. And best of all, the gradient is consistent and the rapids are constant, with no standing waves higher than a foot or so.

Then comes Route 435. If you're paddling an open boat, hug the left bank as you parallel the road. Slide over the foot-and-a- half ledge. Avoid the sharp right turn under the bridge. Land on the left bank at the angle of the turn in the river. Disembark. You have to walk for the next block with your boat in tow.

The cascade under the bridge drops 10 to 15 feet, and after a short gap encounters another cascade . . . then another. None of these cascades can be run in an open boat with any hope of success. For expert kayakers it may be a different story.

Lest I misrepresent myself, I am not an expert kayaker and never was. When I used to kayak whitewater I was at best an intermediate. Keep this in mind when I say that I think these cascades can be run by an expert kayaker. And don't take my word for it. Scout it first, and make up your own mind.

Canoes have to be lined, dragged, or portaged. There is a shallow ledge on the left bank under the bridge. I walked along this ledge while holding onto the left gunwale with my right hand, and while keeping a firm grip on the stern painter with my left (in case I slipped and the canoe got away from me). On the other side of the bridge I dragged the boat up the dirt embankment and through the woods to a point below the first cascade.

Then I pushed the boat into the water and waded through the marsh grass to the next cascade. There I took hold of both painters and lined the boat down the rocks. I continued lining through the short pool and past the third cascade. Mission accomplished. The whole operation didn't take more than 10 to 15 minutes.

The process was less challenging than a first glance at the cascades might imply. They look scary at first, and that's a good thing. The feeling of impending doom will keep you from being overconfident.

After the next bridge – a block and a half past Route 435 – there is only one more obstacle. You'll see it before the twin bridges of Interstate-380: a rock dam that stands some 3 feet high. I beached the boat on the left bank, dragged it through the tall marsh grass – collecting a large number of burrs and stickers in the process – and relaunched immediately below the dam. It didn't take more than a minute.

Now the fun recommences. From here to the take-out the water flows fast over a fairly consistent gradient. The whitewater was almost constant, with standing waves between one and two feet in height, but none higher. With deep strokes I could nearly always touch bottom. I sashayed from bank to bank in order to avoid exposed boulders. There was no deadfall.

The forest on both sides added a touch of seclusion that was broken only briefly by the appearance of widespread houses and a single bridge.

The take-out at the bridge must be anticipated. The final cascade looks impassable upon approach, but you'll quickly learn that you can thread your boat through the boulder field without getting stranded. Keep toward the left side of the river, then hug the bank as you near the bridge. Just as the bow is about to pass under the bridge, turn sharply to the left and poke your nose into the eddy. Paddle hard. The current will grip the stern, turn the boat 180 degrees, and shove you gently against the abutment. Paddle one more stroke so that the bow touches the embankment. Climb ashore and drag the boat uphill through the weeds to the parking lot.

I strongly urge whitewater paddlers to run this section. Despite the cascades between the two bridges, it's as close to pure fun as it can possibly get.

Lining a canoe is a standard wilderness technique that is employed when rapids are too risky to run with a firm likelihood of success: when swamping or dumping means losing gear and possibly the boat as well. Notice the painters leading from the ends of the canoe to the rock. By holding both painters, and either drawing in slack or letting out line, I can guide the canoe safely through whitewater. The process is not difficult but it takes some practice to perfect.

Most of Section 2 is fast-flowing whitewater which is punctuated by boulders that force boaters to navigate a zigzag course that has no let-up.

Lehigh River Section 3

Section 3: North bridge on Game Lands Road to south bridge on Game Lands Road (or Plank Road)
Distance: 1.5 miles
Travel time: 1/2 hour
Adversity level 2: Challenging
Needs 800 % on the Lehigh (Stoddartsville) gauge
Gradient: 41 feet per mile

Although I paddled this section and the next one as a continuous run, I have divided my trip into separate sections because of the great disparity between the characteristics of the streambed. The two defining differences are gradient and obstacles. Read both sections and you'll see what I mean.

Section 3 starts at the Section 2 take-out, on the left bank immediately upstream of the north bridge on Game Lands Road (or Plank Road). Park in the clearing but don't block the gate. I ran this section and the next one when the streamflow gauge at Stoddartsville registered 750%. Even then I scraped a few rocks during my downhill slalom. These scrapings would be hang-ups at lower levels. Experienced paddlers could run this section at higher levels: kayakers certainly, canoeists cautiously.

The gradient is fairly consistent with no ledges or drop-offs: just stretches of steep incline over rock gardens that don't seriously present any problems. For that reason I encourage whitewater enthusiasts to run this segment despite the obstacles, which come in three varieties: whitewater, boulders, and logjams.

Whitewater is expected with this kind of gradient, so you won't be disappointed. Boulders are a nuisance, especially when there isn't much maneuvering room. Yet I was able to avoid the midstream boulders by simply going with the greatest amount of flow, which fortuitously passed around or between them.

Two downed trees lay across the stream where the width is 15 to 20 feet; neither one posed an imminent threat. The first one lay high enough that I was able to pass beneath it by putting my paddle inside the canoe, leaning flat on the center thwart, and ducking my head all the way down. The trunk didn't touch my life vest.

The second one cleared the water by only a couple of inches. Despite the high flow rate, I had no difficulty standing in the water as I lifted my boat over the trunk, clambering over it myself, and climbing back inside. The water rose to just above my knees.

The total gradient of Sections 3 and 4 is 24 feet per mile: an average that is greatly misleading because it makes Section 3 appear less challenging than it is, while it makes Section 4 appear more challenging. These erroneous adversity levels would be a disservice to my readers. If Section 3 seems too short to make the effort worthwhile, skilled or adventurous paddlers should consider adding it to Section 2. Less skilled paddlers, or those who prefer to avoid obstacles, should avoid this section altogether.

The take-out at the bridge is easier said than done. A rock garden diverts nearly all the water to the left bank, where it tends to sweep a boat against a phalanx of rhododendron bushes that grow so large and dense that they reach over the water and block access to shore. I didn't take-out here because I ran Sections 3 and 4 together, but it seemed to me that the current would press a boat under the thicket and either tip over the boat or knock the paddler out of it.

To avoid this potential catastrophe, I ran straight ahead and beached my canoe on the rounded rocks where the water took its nasty turn to the left. I then dragged the boat 20 feet or so and put-in again immediately upstream of the single-lane bridge, which has plenty of headroom. I could have taken-out on the right, or at a number of places on the left but upstream of the bridge.

Lehigh River Section 4

Section 4: South bridge on Game Lands Road (or Plank Road) to Lackawanna State Forest access
Distance: 4.0 miles
Travel time: 1 hour
Adversity level 1: Not challenging
Needs 800 % on the Lehigh (Stoddartsville) gauge
Gradient: 17 feet per mile

This section has no obstacles and a gradient of only 17 feet per mile. Now you can see why I didn't lump both sections together. As noted in the previous section, a combined gradient of 24 feet per mile would present misleading information about the true conditions of either section. This 4-mile stretch consists of nothing but fast flowing water with occasional exposed rocks that are readily avoidable because of the greater width of the stream: say, 30 to 40 feet on average.

I would go as far as to call this section a family trip that paddlers of all ages and experience levels can paddle without fear of coming to grief. Besides, the water was never deeper than the length of my blade. If you somehow manage to tip over your boat, stand up and walk to shore. The most challenging part of this section is shoving your boat through the vegetation that separates the water from Game Lands Road. The south bridge is a good put-in because parking is available there. There are also other clearings farther downstream where you can park several vehicles and have easy access to the water.

Take-out at the Lackawanna State Forest access by cruising over the sluice and turning sharply into the eddy on the right bank. This is the put-in for Section 5. The wide grassy trail to the parking area measures a hundred yards in length. By the way, the current gave me such an assist that I paddled both Sections 3 and 4 in an hour and ten minutes: 20 minutes for Section 3, and 50 minutes for Section 4. And I wasn't even racing.

Below: Cheryl Novak photographed me downstream of the Section 3 put-in.

Right: Access between Sections 4 and 5, showing the wider breadth of the river.

Bottom right: The broad reaches and rugged banks of Section 6.

Lehigh River Section 5

Section 5: Lackawanna access to Route 115
Distance: 6.5 miles
Travel time: 1-1/2 to 2 hours
Adversity level 1: Not challenging
Needs 400 % on the Lehigh (Stoddartsville) gauge
Gradient: 12 feet per mile

Paddling this section is not necessarily a novice trip but it's pretty close. There is no deadfall to worry about, and no ledges or drop-offs. With 30 feet of maneuvering room, the few exposed boulders are avoidable. And there is just enough whitewater to keep it interesting: low whitewater, that is, consisting mostly of riffles with standing waves no higher than a foot. If you've never paddled any kind of whitewater, this is the place to begin and learn what all the fuss is about.

I don't mean to give this section short shrift, but there's not much more that I can say about it – except do it.

The gradient is low and consistent. It's nearly impossible to get into trouble. By not paying attention, the worst you can do is get stranded on a rock. If somehow you manage to upset your boat, stand up: the water is seldom more than knee deep, and often less. Walk to shore.

Dwellings are not intrusive because they are few and far between. This means that the river is bounded by forest. A couple of wild turkeys flew across the water in front of my boat. There were lots of ducks and a few Canada geese. One beaver leaped from the bank into the water at my approach.

There's one bridge to pass under: Locust Ridge Road, a mile and a half from the put-in. When you see the pipeline clearing, you're only half a mile from the take-out. Otherwise, the river is bordered by trees and is comfortably distant from traffic noise.

When you come around the final bend you'll see the Route 115 bridge in front of you. Take-out at the USGS gauging station on the left bank. A set of cement steps leads up to the intersection of the highway and Caughbaugh Road. Sadly, your pleasant trip has ended.

NOT TO WORRY!

Great Falls of the Lehigh is located in Section 6, not Section 5. Turn the page and read all about it.

Lehigh River Section 6

Section 6: Route 115 to the Francis E. Walter Dam

Distance: 8.5 miles
Travel time: 2 to 3 hours

Adversity level 4: Extremely challenging
Needs 200 % on the Lehigh (Stoddartsville) gauge
Gradient: 26 feet per mile (overall); 24 fpm true

Many paddlers might opt to avoid this section because of the Great Falls of the Lehigh: an imposing 20-foot waterfall that is breathtaking to behold. In actuality, two other hazards are arguably more insidious impediments. Both of these hazards relate to river access, and smack of conspiracy.

As noted in the previous section, the best access is next to the U.S. Geological Service stream gauging station, located on the left bank upstream of the Route 115 bridge. Although a perfect out-of-the-way parking area is located directly across the street from this most suitable access point, the township has erected a no-parking sign there. I stopped long enough to unload my canoe, but that is no guarantee that this short-term lull in forward motion would prevent the receipt of a citation. The convenient parking area and sign-posting might be a money-making scam, like a reduced-speed trap, to lure people into violating a local ordinance.

No other parking areas are to be found in the vicinity, so you have to find a distant place to park, then walk along the shoulder to the bridge.

As soon as you float under the bridge you'll hear the sound of crashing water. The Great Falls lies just around a slight curve to the left. Steer toward the right bank. The flow does not accelerate as the water approaches the drop-off, so don't be afraid that the loud noise portends immediate danger. About 20 feet from the top of the falls there is a deep notch in the bedrock. Drive your boat into this notch. Step out of the boat into knee-deep dead-water.

Adjacent property owners guard the waterfall with fanatical persistence, aggressive shouting, and vociferous threats, but as long as you don't climb up onto the high embankment 10 feet overhead, they cannot legally obstruct your passage: the streambed belongs to the Commonwealth of Pennsylvania, and therefore is public property. Abusive sentinels are eager to harass paddlers from the safety of their yards – like junkyard dogs that bark at passers-by. Thus they callously imperil boaters by insisting that they have no right to walk ahead in order to scout the safest route.

The thunderous roar of the river as it rushes over the drop-off can be deafening. The flow along the edges is slow and relatively calm. The first time I canoed this section (with Cheryl paddling bow in a 17-foot Oldtown Tripper), the water never rose above my knees as I walked downstream along the solid rock wall. I lined the canoe by holding onto the painters and letting the slight current at the edge of the river propel it downstream.

Lining can be effected easier with two people – one holding the bow painter and one holding the stern painter, each letting out line or pulling it in as necessary – but I had no trouble in guiding the canoe alone as I waded across flat underwater bedrock. I kept wearing my life vest in case I slipped, but found the footing firm.

At low water, a dry ledge extends beyond the edge of cascading water. The canoe ran up on this ledge, almost of its own accord. I stepped onto the rock and dragged the canoe across a broad flat area to another dry ledge well past the waterfall – this because the waterfall is shaped somewhat like a horseshoe. This 15-foot drop might seem insurmountable, but it isn't. I pushed the canoe over the lip beyond the balance point, let the weight of the bow tip it downward, and held onto the gunwale until the bow touched the rock below. Then I let the canoe slide along the ledge below by letting the stern painter slip slowly through my fingers. The climb down was effortless because a narrow slot contains steps that are cut naturally across bedding planes.

I dragged the boat another thirty feet to still water beneath the rapids. My description might make the carry seem scary and arduous, but it's less challenging than it sounds. Except . . .

On another occasion I ran this section solo at high water: 478 % on the Stoddartsville gauge. This was a totally different situation, and one that needs to be disclosed with emphasis.

The sound of crashing water was appalling as I slid my canoe into the notch. After I stepped out of the boat, a thin jet of water that was forced upstream through a separation between an exposed boulder and the sheer rock wall created an eddy current that kept pushing the boat out of the notch and into the downstream current. There was nothing to tie the painter to while I forged ahead on foot to examine the waterfall. I had to take the boat with me.

I held onto the stern painter, but I controlled the canoe by gripping the right gunwale. I walked the boat to the top of the falls. The ledge that had been dry on my previous passage was now gushing with overflow. It did not threaten to wash me over the lintel, but if I had let go of the boat it would have been propelled over the ledge into the maw of rushing water.

I think I would have been terrified if I had not previously carried over the waterfall when the water was low, and knew in advance how to effect the carry. As it was, I was strongly apprehensive about the predicament I had gotten myself into – and how I was going to get myself out of it. Carefully I swung the boat around my legs into a foot of water that was speeding over the ledge. Instead of simply balancing the canoe on the lip, I had to hold it back: an act that took all my strength.

I let the gunwale slip through my hand. The boat reached the balance point in a flash, tipped over, and was nearly ripped out of my hand. The bow struck the rock below harder than I wanted, but no damage was done. This time I was paddling my 15-foot Dagger. Due to the shorter length, I couldn't get the canoe to slide but had to leave it wedged the way it was. The climb down was easy because the set of stepped ledges, which led down through a narrow notch like a handmade staircase, was dry.

Ironically, this largest drop was the easiest part of the carry. The broad flat bedrock that had been high and dry on the previous occasion was now part of the river. The lower five-foot drop led into a seething cauldron instead of onto the next lower ledge. I couldn't line the boat because the raging torrent was frothing away from shore into the worst of the current. The gunwales would have been overwhelmed instantly.

I shinnied along a shoe-wide ledge by holding onto bulges in the rock. There were no firm grips. What had been a simple carry before was now a precarious undertaking. My feet were barely on dry rock and the boat was in the current and tugging hard to pull me off my perch. I crouched so as to let the boat slide across my lap, or at least my left knee. The force of the current against the stern swung the boat partway around. I wanted to slide my hand along the gunwale but I couldn't do it. The best I could do was to direct the way the boat was going to fall. It lunged abruptly, slid off my knee, and plunged 5 feet into a slow-moving pool below, yanking me off the ledge in the process.

The canoe struck the water. I fell face-first into the boat with the grace of a flying elephant. I landed so hard that my hat's chinstrap stop was driven loose. The hat flew off my head into the water, where it was drawn away and sucked under the hull. I managed to push myself off the seat or thwart (I don't remember which), got my body back on the rock, and miraculously retrieved my hat before it was washed away. I lost my grip on the canoe, but caught the stern just as it was about to drift out of reach. I had made it to the bottom of the waterfall not by touching down but by crash landing. I was unhurt.

In retrospect, two people would have had an easier time of negotiating the lower ledge because one could have swung around the rock face and taken the bow of the boat in hand while the other held onto the stern.

I have described these maneuvers in exacting detail because I want my readers to know that the waterfall can be bypassed. I strongly suggest, however, that before you try this maneuver with a boat, you scout it without one. Wade from the bridge along the right bank during low water: 100 % or thereabouts. Thus unencumbered, you won't have any trouble in climbing down the waterfall and getting the lay of the land – and the feel of the ledges. Have no fear: you can climb back up the ledges and the embedded staircase, then wade back to the bridge.

I should also mention the possibility of carrying down the left bank. The tricky part is making sure that you don't get sucked over the falls. I didn't do it but from the right bank I saw how it could be done. Hug the shore as you drift in the slow water above the drop-off. The bank is guarded by trees. It curves outward (to the left, away from the center of the river), leaving only ten feet of still water in which to turn sharply into the pool along the bank before touching the fast water that pours over the drop-off. There is not enough distance to back-ferry into the pool. Instead, you have to angle the boat toward shore and paddle hard so as not to get caught in the fast flow. A broad series of ledges is spaced casually like steps with extended treads all the way to the bottom of the rapids, a distance of about 50 feet. This part of the carry is easier than the carry along the right bank, and you can do it while keeping your shoes dry.

The fallacy of this maneuver is getting onto the ledge before getting washed over the waterfall. I think it can be done in low water, but after observing conditions during high water, I would not want to try it. Instead, I now think it can be done by hugging the left bank to the turn, exiting the boat, walking it through the shallows to the upstream ledge, then dragging it onto the ledge far upstream of the waterfall.

Whichever way you carry, after the excitement is over, take a moment to look up at the large stone structure atop the embankment at the base of the falls (on the right bank). You'll see the ruins of a nineteenth-century gristmill. On the map this area is called Stoddartsville, but you won't see anything that looks like a town, and the U.S. Postal Service doesn't recognize the name. Do not approach the gristmill for a closer look or you might get involved in some contretemps when local zealots call the cops.

During times of low water, the rest of the trip may not be exciting by comparison but it is well worth the ride for its scenic beauty and isolation. The breadth of the river is 40 to 50 feet. Slight gradient and gentle curves along stony beaches and tree-lined banks provide a laid-back cruise unless you run aground in shallows. Parts of the river can be scratchy.

The broad peninsular clearing that appears on the left bank about 2 miles below the Great Falls is part of Cape Acahela, a 242-acre reservation that is owned by the

Lehigh River Section 6

Great Falls in the background, ruins of a mill on the left.

Boy Scouts of America. The camp has been in continuous operation since 1916. It focuses on Boy Scout and Cub Scout activities in both summer and winter.

When I paddled past this spot, a black rope was stretched across the river at the waterline. The first time, the ends were tied to trees only a foot or so above the water: too low to afford passage underneath. Half the length of the rope dipped into the water in the center of the river. I paddled over the lowest point of the catenary, and was able to glide over the rope without getting tangled.

The last time, the rope was tied higher up the trunks so that the bottom of the catenary rested right on the surface. That time, I hugged the left bank and ducked under the rope; I had trouble in scraping over the rocks in the shallows. The right bank looked passable in similar fashion.

No matter how it's tied, this rope is a hazard to boaters who may not notice its presence, especially in high water when the current runs fast.

A quarter mile past this point the Tobyhanna Creek pours in from left.

A description of my high-water trip should whet the appetite of boaters of all persuasions. I paddled in fast-moving water from the moment I left the waterfall. Even the occasional pools flowed with ripples. After the Tobyhanna, the additional water increased both the depth and the speed of the current. I blasted along without effort.

There was nothing but wilderness on either side of the river. Luxuriant forest stretched away from the banks as far as I could see. A bald eagle flew overhead and landed on a tree limb ahead of me.

The streambed was perfectly consistent. There were no ledges, no drop-offs, no boulders, and no hydraulics: just accelerating water that alternated between riffles and standing waves. It was as if the river had been groomed. Most of the standing waves stood a foot or so in height. Every once in a while I plowed through a stretch of 2-footers that were spaced conveniently far apart.

The trip was mile after mile of raw fun, and it would have continued that way had it not been for the wind. Whereas the head wind above Stoddartsville pushed my boat backward faster than the mild current propelled it forward (I paddled both sections together this time without taking-out or putting-in at Stoddartsville), now the head wind acted merely as a brake that relieved me of having to backpaddle through the worst of the whitewater. I merely steered and let the wind reduce my speed enough to prevent the bow from cutting through the waves and letting water splash over the gunwales.

The geography changed some 5 miles below the Great Falls. For one thing, the land above the banks receded so that opposite tree lines stood half a mile apart, across a vast flood plain. For another, I noticed high-water marks on the vertical embankments: horizontal grooves that indicated previous impoundment levels. I did not realize at the time that I was now paddling through rapids that were usually submerged when the reservoir was maintained at a higher level. But more on that later.

The lower water level presented less flat water and more running water. And the water was accelerating due to a local increase in the gradient. Now the surface dipped more steeply and 2-foot standing waves were commonplace. The largest waves were avoidable: they tended to bunch together on one side of the river or the other, but they never extended all the way across.

The real problems were the increase in wind speed and the change in direction: 25 to 30 knots broadside. I had to fight so hard to prevent the boat from being swept ashore that I was literally paddling perpendicular to the flow, toward the right bank, and rolling over 1-foot waves. Whenever I encountered taller waves, I turned the canoe into them so as not to get swamped – but every time I did so I was blown closer to the left bank.

I fought with all my strength for 5 to 10 minutes, losing ground over river width with each passing second. Finally I was slammed against the rock wall where the river made a sharp turn to the right. In other words, I was pinned on the outside of the curve where the current was the fastest and where the standing waves were the highest. Strong current continued to drag me downstream, with the port hull scraping past rock toward a protrusion that pointed toward the opposite bank. I was powerless to stop my downstream progress.

Understand that if it had not been for the wind, I could easily have passed along the inside of the curve where the current was slower and standing waves were shorter. Now I had no choice but to play the hand I was dealt.

As the boat was dragged past the point of the protrusion I tried desperately to paddle into the wind and across the river. I didn't make an inch of progress. I was swept downstream sideways into 2-foot standing waves which, if I hadn't straightened the boat, would have swamped me. I barely turned in time to slip between the waves and the rock wall, which I struck again. Then the boat was spit around another but slighter protrusion into a long series of mammoth waves that stood so tall that I found myself looking *up* at the top of the tallest one: it was 4 feet high!

I had no choice but to try to hit the rapids head on. Fighting the wind, I swung the boat around only a split second after I plowed into the first 2-footer. In fact, the boat was still pivoting as I drove into that first wave. I was then driven across a series of waves, each one taller than the one preceding it. Within a second or so I crashed into the 4-footer. This wasn't a simple standing wave but a writhing mass of whitewater that was half the size of a Volkswagen. The water must have been deflected upward from a huge submerged boulder.

The boat flew over the top and slid down the other side. An errant wave slapped the starboard hull. Water that was splashed upward was blown into the boat by the fierce wind. I took on about a gallon of water. Then I passed over a couple of 2-footers into a long series of 1-footers. After that came fast-moving rollers.

All that happened in the previous four paragraphs took less than ten seconds.

Lehigh River Section 6

The reservoir is a popular area for ice fishing. Because the water level is reduced in winter, vehicles can drive across the lower road and onto snow-covered land. The upstream wall of the dam can be seen to the right. The lower road is submerged in summer.

I cruised around the bend into flat water, where two anglers were fishing from a motor boat. I beached the canoe on a sandy bank within hailing distance. I rested for ten minutes before flipping the canoe to dump the water.

Now for some reflection and introspection. I repeat: had there been no wind I would have skirted the standing waves by taking the inside of the curve. I did not tackle the whitewater on purpose. My druthers would have been to bypass it entirely. The reason I didn't get swamped or dumped was a combination of fortuitous circumstances.

First: leading to the final 4-footer was a series of shorter waves whose heights were graduated from low to high. The bow of the canoe was light because I was paddling solo. These two factors joined to lift the boat from the lower waves to the higher ones, as if I were being pushed up the rungs of a low-angled ladder.

Second: I had the great good fortune to pass over the final 4-footer precisely in the middle. If the boat had been only a few inches off center, either the bow would have been deflected or the boat would have slid down the slope into the swirling hole on either side, or both.

This reminds me of one of my open-boat trips down the lower Youghiogheny. Paddling solo in my Oldtown Tripper, I passed over a gigantic pillow and slid sideways into a hydraulic below the adjacent boulder. I swam and dragged my boat to shore. After reconstructing the moment of destruction, I apprehended that if the canoe had passed over the pillow only a few inches to the left, I would not have slid down the slope. So I portaged the canoe upstream and ran the rapids again. I carefully gauged my alignment, kept the boat a bit farther to the left, and stayed afloat without taking on a drop of water.

This time, on the Lehigh, I was lucky enough to hit the perfect spot. My guess is that if I were to repeat that run a hundred more times, and try to take an open boat over the pillow, I would get dumped every time. Of course, as I noted above, I would never have gone that way voluntarily.

Back on the river, I fought strong headwinds for the next mile and a half. When I rounded the final bend and headed for the planned take-out, my first thought was that it had been stolen. The spot where I told Cheryl to meet me now stood 50 feet up a rocky bluff. The last time we were here, the reservoir was full and the road on the upstream side of the dam was underwater. The take-out was supposed to be on the right bank near the parking lot, with the submerged macadam serving as an apron.

Now the reservoir was nearly empty, the road was passable, and vehicles were parked on a sandy beach on the left side of the dam. I realized that this was the best take-out, and so did Cheryl. So ended an exciting trip: not with a bang but a whimper.

The gradient in the statistical sidebar is not necessarily meaningless, but it *is* subject to interpretation. Two factors that throw off the calculations are the sudden drop at Great Falls and the flexible level of impoundment by the dam. The drop at Great Falls is permanently set at 20 feet, but the impoundment level fluctuates in accordance with an equation that balances the amount of recent precipitation with the current status of containment: that is, the quantity of water impounded depends upon long-time variations between drought and flood.

Sometimes the gravel roadway upstream of the dam is fully exposed and drivable. At other times the middle is submerged under many feet of water.

The water level at the dam also affects travel time. The higher the level, the more the reservoir backs up the riverbed with water that doesn't flow. The lower the water, the more flow is available to propel downstream boaters before encountering still water.

Without knowing the depth of the streambed beneath the surface, upstream of the dam, I used the elevation at the outflow, and calculated an overall gradient of 26 fpm. A truer gradient can be obtained by calculating from the bottom of the Great Falls instead of from Route 115. This measurement reduces the gradient to 24 fpm.

The Lost Mile

Actually, only three-quarters of a mile is lost: one-quarter mile due to the dam structure and water passage conduit, and one-half mile due to blocked accessibility.

In the old days, we used to put-in below the dam in the pool that is located immediately downstream of the outlet. We drove down the dirt service road from the west end of the dam to the water's edge. Since then the Army Corps of Engineers has prevented this means of access by erecting a gate across the top of the road, and keeping it locked. To reach the pool nowadays you have to portage your boat half a mile. Granted that the way is all downhill, nonetheless most people are not likely to want to invest the effort.

This is a shame because a most exciting set of rapids is located immediately below the outlet pool: a hundred yards of rocks and standing waves. Oh, well . . .

Looking downstream along the face of the dam at the outflow pool and the following rapids.

Lehigh River Section 7

Section 7: Francis E. Walter Dam to White Haven   Adversity level 2: Challenging
Distance: 5.8 miles   Flow rate: Needs 500 cfs on the Lehigh (Walter Dam) gauge
Travel time: 1-1/2 to 2 hours   Gradient: 25 feet per mile

The put-in is located on the right bank at the bottom of a dirt road. The road originates at the back corner of a picnic area that is located west of the dam, and west of the Army Corps of Engineers office building. Neither four-wheel-drive nor high ground clearance is necessary. The road proceeds downhill for a mile and a half to a fork: the right tine extends for one block to a riverside parking area; the left tine extends for four blocks to another riverside parking area (under a cable-cross mechanism). I prefer the upstream put-in so as to get a longer ride.

This stretch of water is a short introduction to more difficult whitewater that comprises the following two sections. Paddlers often overlook it. That's a shame, because it has much to offer: in beauty if not in boating challenge.

The area is a wilderness tract that gives the impression of paddling through a remote corner of the world. You'll encounter only two features that mar this impression: a bridge and a house (actually two houses, although the one to the right is difficult to see). Otherwise, the surrounding forest is silent and untrammeled until you reach the outskirts of White Haven: for what it's worth, 5 miles of isolated paddling that is not sandwiched between a railroad and a bike trail.

I recommend this stretch for reasons other than its quiet solitude. It's a great place to try out a new boat, in order to learn about its maneuvering capability and stability characteristics; to break in a new partner; or to test your paddling skills before shooting the more challenging rapids in the Gorge. There is whitewater here, but on a lower scale than you'll encounter farther downstream.

Plus, the distance to the take-out is shorter than the two Gorge sections. If the new boat or partner doesn't work out, or if you determine that your skills need more refinement, there is less paddling to endure. And you're less likely to upset in the mild rapids that exist; if you do upset, the flatwater pools are long enough to enable you to recover yourself and your boat before encountering the next stretch of whitewater.

Granted, this section isn't for hardcore kayakers who are looking for waves to surf. But it's a prime piece of paddling for many others.

From this point to Jim Thorpe, the adversity level depends mostly on the amount of water that is released from the dam – although following a rainstorm, natural runoff from numerous tributaries has an additive effect that might completely outweigh a limited dam release, so be careful.

At moderate levels this section is a fun ride. At high levels it's a *fast* and fun ride. At extremely high levels it washes out for the most part, but creates some big standing waves at certain spots. At no level are there huge boulders and strong hydraulics like you'll find between White Haven and Jim Thorpe. Although the gradient is slightly higher than the next two sections, it's more consistent due to the absence of cascades and pools. In other words, the river flows pretty much like a ramp or sliding board without exposed rocks and sudden drop-offs. This is not to say that there aren't a few boulders and a couple of places with standing waves, but they don't present much of an obstacle.

In short, the ride is enjoyable for paddlers who are more interested in scenery than in wildly thrashing water. By the same token, whitewater enthusiasts might consider the ride tame and lacking in challenge. You can't please everyone. Let's say that this section is a middle ground or transition between the creek-like flow upstream of the dam, and the harsh whitewater rapids downstream.

Except for the turnpike bridge, the barely visible house on the mountain above the left bank is the only sign of civilization until the approach to White Haven.

This stretch of river passes under three bridges: the Pennsylvania Turnpike (a mile from the put-in), Route 940 in White Haven (5-1/4 miles from the put-in), and Interstate 80 (the take-out, a quarter mile later). You can go on either side of the islands that dot the river, including the one under the Route 940 bridge and the following one, but after this last one stick close to the right bank if you don't want to miss the take-out under the Interstate bridge.

For the first half mile after the put-in, you're likely to see anglers during fishing season. At flowrates up to 500 cfs, you might see then standing in the middle of the river, or close to the banks. Avoid their fishing lines. Announce your presence in order to give them time to reel in the line if you can't get far enough away to avoid it, or pass behind them: that is, opposite the way they are facing and casting. Be careful of the backlash if they are using fly rods. At flowrates above 700 cfs, you'll likely see them fishing only from the right bank, because the current is too fast to stand in the water without getting knocked down and washed away. (The left bank is fairly inaccessible from land.) Hug the left bank to avoid entanglements.

A quarter mile later the river is split by a pair of islands. The main flow goes right, but you can take either of the other two channels. If you take the center channel, you'll soon see that the island is split into two islands. The channel between them is impassable. You'll soon merge with the left channel so that now the water is diverted by only a single island. At the bottom of the island (a quarter mile from the initial divergence) the channels merge at a rapids.

A block past the cluster of islands you'll pass under the Northeast Extension of the Pennsylvania Turnpike.

A mile later there's a small island in the middle of the river. The main flow goes right, but at 800 cfs the left channel is passable.

Two miles later you might notice a trickle of water leaking to the right over a narrow patch of stones and grass. Take this route for a change of scenery – but not unless the flowrate exceeds 800 cfs, or thereabouts, or you might get hung up in shallows. This trickle passes around the side of an island that measures three quarters of a mile in length. The channel seldom exceeds 10 feet in width, and in some places is tighter, yet I was able to canoe all the way without running aground.

The canopy of leaves creates a tunnel that is dark and mysterious. After a while you might notice in the woods to your right what appears to be a horizontal division in the foliage, about 10 feet high on the embankment. This is an abandoned railroad bed: an extension of the Lehigh Gorge Trail, which stretches between White Haven and

Lehigh River Section 7   47

This dark and mysterious channel on the right side of a long slender island is passable all the way. It is well worth paddling for a change of pace.

Middleburg Road.

At the bottom of this long slender island you'll pass effortlessly into the main channel. You'll see a small island ahead and to the left. The main flow passes to the right of this island, but the left channel is passable. You are now in the White Haven environs.

The bridge that you see a block downstream is Route 940. The river splits at the island under the bridge. You can go either way: straight ahead or turn right. The division of water is about equal. This island is a quarter mile long. If you go straight ahead you'll encounter another island to the left. The main flow (of this half of the flow) passes between the two islands, but you can take the left channel around the small island. This brings you back into the main flow a hundred yards downstream.

A block downstream there is another island, again splitting the flow about evenly. Take either channel. After passing the island, steer for the right bank if you plan to take-out. The public access is directly under the twin bridges of Interstate 80.

White Haven access during a whitewater release. Boats of all kinds, colors, and persuasions have been carried down from the parking lot and prepared for launching. Note the dual Interstate bridges overhead.

Lehigh River Section 8

Section 8: White Haven to Rockport
Distance: 10.0 miles
Travel time: 2 to 3 hours
Adversity level 3: Very challenging
Flow rate: Needs 500 cfs on the Lehigh (Walter Dam) gauge
Gradient: 22 feet per mile

The White Haven access is located on the right bank under the twin bridges of Interstate 80. It can be quite congested on release days, so either arrive early or be patient. Commercial outfitters regularly run raft trips from here to Rockport. They generally work together so they're not all launching at the same time. You can fit yourself in between groups without interference.

Due to pontoon friction and hull configuration, rafts move more slowly on the water than canoes and kayaks. This means that you're likely to catch up with a group that launched before you. This is not a problem. Outfitter guides in kayaks keep their groups close together; there will usually be a lead kayak and a tail kayak, and, depending on the size of the group, any number of kayaks interspersed within the group. In my experience these guides are considerate of faster boaters. Independent paddlers should be equally as considerate.

The width of the river now averages between 50 and 100 feet, with a few restrictions where the banks come closer together, or where midstream boulders, shore-side shallows, or high standing waves constrict the *runnable* width. Don't try to pass a group of rafts unless there is adequate passing room. It's okay to intermingle with the group while you effect a passing, but give the individual rafts wide clearance; remember that they are not as maneuverable as a canoe or kayak, so if anyone has to execute evasive action, it has to be you.

Also keep in mind that most rafters are not expert paddlers. They are generally non-paddlers who don't know anything about rafting. This may be their first time on the water. Keep your distance from them, and pass the group as quickly as possible. Once you regain open water, you can relax and cruise more slowly. Even without paddling, a canoe or kayak will drift faster than a raft due to the laws of hydrodynamics. You will rapidly outdistance them.

With regard to flow rate, know that from White Haven downstream there are numerous tributaries that add water to the river. The farther downstream, the more tributaries spill into the river. Therefore there will always be a difference between the dam release volume and the actual volume. After a long and heavy downpour this volume differential can be considerable: perhaps so much that the river may be runnable despite a restricted release from the dam. On the other hand, the actual volume may be higher than you care to run.

To gain some perspective on the actual volume, check the streamflow at the Lehighton gauging station. The reading will tell you how much water is flowing past that point. You can then interpolate between the two streamflow readings, and make an informed decision about whether or not to run the river; or between which two points on the river it is best for you to run. The choice is yours.

Having written all of the above, let me remind you – in case you didn't read the statistical sidebar – that in my opinion the minimum dam release rate for this section is 500 cubic feet per second. I am told by experienced kayakers that you *can* run it at 400 cfs without too many hang-ups. Anything less than that may be more trouble than it's worth. You won't just scrape over hidden rocks, you'll come to a grinding halt on them. This is merely annoying if it happens a few times; it's obnoxious if it happens

Lehigh River Section 8

Looking upstream. Railroad track and Hickory Run State Park stretch along the left bank. The bulge or dimple where the river doglegs is Lunch Rock. Christina Young flew me up the river in her Super Cub.

again and again and again. Stranding takes all the fun out of paddling.

One quarter mile after the put-in you'll pass under a railroad trestle.

Nearly a mile after the trestle, an island that stretches for two city blocks splits the river in two. The main flow goes right (and subsequently skirts a couple of small islands that give either-way choices to the paddler), but the left channel is passable at 800 cfs.

A quarter mile past the island you'll pass under the bridge at Lehigh Tannery. The parking lot there is a popular access for users of the Gorge trail, which parallels the river from White Haven to Jim Thorpe. A sign warns that this is not a water access point, and that putting-in or taking-out boats is prohibited. It's not only prohibited; it's practically impossible. I don't know why anyone thought that a warning sign was necessary.

Steep embankments rise nearly 50 feet high on both sides of the river. Tall trees and thick vegetation grow on the slopes despite the nearly vertical incline. The only place that you could possibly launch or retrieve a boat is on the left bank downstream of the bridge, below the foundations of the old tanning factory. And even there you would have to bushwhack through the dense understory.

I don't know – perhaps the land was cleared of vegetation before the access ban was posted.

A quarter mile past the bridge is Maple Island, one of the few islands on the river that is named on U.S. Geological Survey topographic maps. Maple Island measures a quarter mile in length and half of that in width at the widest point. The main flow passes to the right of the island. The left channel is passable, but be aware of a full-width ledge that drops a foot and a half.

You can't miss the next landmark: half a dozen concrete bridge supports for a railroad trestle that was removed ages ago. Black Creek flows into the river on the downstream side of the pier on the left bank.

Shortly afterward, the river water flows around an island on the left; it's shaped like a right triangle. The main flow goes straight past the island. If you turn left into the channel, you can paddle in swift current along the base of the triangle. Prepare to make a sharp right turn, then follow the left leg of the triangle until it merges with the main flow.

The next island – a quarter mile farther along the river – is small and over to the left side. The left channel that passes the island is scratchy at flowrates less than 1,000 cfs. Keep right, in the main channel.

Splashing through the rapids with a guide direction traffic.

Three and a half miles from the put-in is a geological formation that is known to paddlers as Lunch Rock. The name is eponymous. When I paddled this section with the Mohawk Canoe Club, we always stopped there for our midday meal. Although it might seem too early in the trip to eat, you should know that club headquarters was located in Trenton, New Jersey. Most of the members lived not in the immediate vicinity but in a widespread area: either in central and south Jersey, or across the Delaware River in the Philadelphia environs.

For most members it was a 2-hour drive to the Lehigh Gorge. Then we had to establish a shuttle, which meant shuffling canoes from one roof to another, and leaving some vehicles at the take-out while others drove to the put-in. All this took time that required an early morning departure from home. As a result, we were all pretty hungry by the time we reached Lunch Rock, even if it wasn't 12 o'clock noon by the time we got there.

This handy lunch spot is a slab of bedrock about half the size of a football field. It slopes gradually to the water's edge where paddlers can either ram their boats onto the lower shelf or swing into a convenient eddy. If the water is running too fast to effect either of these maneuvers, you can dart behind the protruding lip and dock in the dead water behind it. You can't miss seeing this expanse of bare rock on the left bank, where the river narrows and takes a dogleg around it.

We might have had a dozen canoes hauled up onto the rock, and twice as many people, and still had plenty of room to spare. This was always a great place to chat and laze in the sun before proceeding downstream. Nowadays, raft outfitters use Lunch Rock to let rafters stretch their legs. I've seen as many as a dozen rafts on the rock; that equates to more than sixty people, yet still there was ample space available for other boats and paddlers.

As information, a narrow path at the highpoint of the rock leads away from the river on a perpendicular course to the railroad track, then continues on the other side to connect with the Fireline Trail in Hickory Run State Park.

The long pool downstream of Lunch Rock is followed by what I call unofficially

Lehigh River Section 8

the One-Two Punch. See Lehigh Reflections for the explanation. The One-Two Punch is a double set of rapids that is separated by a short pool. The first rapid is fairly friendly, but the second one is twice as long and definitely hostile: lots of rocks and standing waves that make for interesting paddling.

Major tributaries now dump water into the river: Sandy Run directly opposite Goulds Run, followed by Hickory Run, Leslie Run, and Mud Run. The influx helps to alleviate the scraping problem when the dam release rate is set at bare minimum, but may create challenges for less experienced open-boaters at higher flowrates.

You can pass on either side of the tiny island at Sandy Run. Shortly afterward, a continuous stretch of rapids extends for half a mile. Now you might have to use your bailer for its intended purpose, instead of engaging in water fights and bailer battles.

A mid-size island exists midway between Leslie Run and Mud Run. The main flow goes straight past the island, but the right channel is eminently passable. Then comes another continuous stretch of rapids that precedes and follows Mud Run. Once again you may have to use your bailer to bail.

Pass on either side of the island that's located a mile past Mud Run. From there on it's clear paddling through intermittent whitewater to the take-out at Rockport.

If you have never run the Lehigh River in canoe or kayak, my advice is to learn the ropes by first doing the section from the dam to White Haven at 500 to 800 cfs. This will give you a taste of whitewater without scaring you to death. At that flowrate canoes are unlikely to swamp because the water isn't deep enough, even in rapids, although you might take some splashes over the bow. If you dump, the swim won't be too bad because the current is relatively slow, and won't prevent you from swimming and pushing your boat to the closest bank. You might even be able to stand and walk your boat to shore or to a convenient boulder.

After you feel comfortable with that section, do a trip from White Have to Rockport at the same level. Keep in mind that two of the rapids in this section measure half a mile in length, and the water is deeper and faster. Swimming is undesirable.

Paddlers of all persuasions gathering at Lunch Rock.

Everything changes at higher water levels. How much it changes depends upon the level. The advantages of a dam release of, say, 1,000 cfs, are twofold: (1) you're less likely to scrape over hidden rocks because the ones that were barely hidden at lower levels are now deep enough that you can pass over them without touching (although now you have to watch for rocks that were exposed when the water was lower but are now partially hidden); and (2) because of (1) the runnable width of the river is greater: that is, you have more choices for avoiding the worst of the whitewater.

Higher water is a two-edged sword, because now the standing waves stand higher and extend longer, increasing the risk of swamping an open boat.

After you've mastered running the Upper Gorge at low

Some canoes are filled with so much flotation that they are almost equivalent to covered boats. But they play well in whitewater and are easy to retrieve in the event of overturning. Kayakers prefer this section to the next because it has more "playing" or surfing rapids.

Not to worry! Getting stuck on a midstream boulder happens to rafts all the time. Here a guide helps to shove off the raft against the current.

water, and at successively higher levels, you might be ready for the Lower Gorge.

The work of taking-out and putting-in at Rockport's high embankment has been alleviated by the installation of ramps and staircases. Two people can share the load by each grabbing an end and carrying a canoe up or down a staircase. A solo paddler will have to bench-press a canoe onto his or her shoulders, then climb up or down the steps by him- or herself. A kayakers generally slings the kayak onto one shoulder. The rubberized mats are commonly used by raft outfitters, but there's no reason why a canoeist can't drag a boat up the ramp by the painter, or let it down as the case may be.

Rockport is a busy place during whitewater releases: boats from White Haven are taking-out, boats for Glen Onoko are putting-in.

Lehigh River Section 9

Section 9: Rockport to Jim Thorpe (or Glen Onoko)

Adversity level 3: Very challenging

Distance: 17.1 miles (or 14.3 to Glen Onoko)

Flow rate: Needs 500 cfs on the Lehigh (Walter Dam) gauge

Travel time: 4 hours (or 3-1/2 to Glen Onoko)

Gradient: 21 feet per mile

Before the Lehigh Gorge became a State park, the Glen Onoko landing was inaccessible to vehicles. The train station in Jim Thorpe was the next suitable access below Rockport. Drakes Creek might have been usable, as it is today, but I didn't know about it then. And anyway – beside the fact that the dirt road might have been less unimproved then than it is today – it's only three miles from Rockport: hardly worth the effort to take-out there, unless you want to extend the run from White Haven.

With the creation of the park came improvements. Most of the improvements had to do with the bike trail: laying gravel on the railroad bed from which the rails and ties had been removed, and stamping the gravel to form a consistently smooth surface. A restroom was constructed adjacent to the parking lots in Rockport and Glen Onoko. And the Glen Onoko landing was conceived as a way to reduce overcrowding at the Jim Thorpe train station, especially when the growing number of raft outfitters increased tourism pressure dramatically.

In the old days there was no way for a vehicle to reach the stone beach at Glen Onoko. No public road led there, and the railroad trestles were used only by trains. Extending and paving the road from Main Street, and converting one of the two trestles for vehicular use, produced a new river access that was previously inaccessible. The new site shortened the distance between major access points by 2-3/4 miles.

The Gorge is not only a spectacular sight be behold – with steep mountain ranges on either side of the river rising nearly a thousand feet above the water – but it also contains the wildest whitewater in the drainage system, the largest number of rapids, and the most complex obstacle courses to be found anywhere on the river. Yet there are no waterfalls, high ledges, or sharp drop-offs. Everything is runnable by raft, and by canoes and kayaks in the hands of skilled paddlers.

I reiterate: 500 cfs is the minimum amount of water necessary to make continuous passage without hanging up. This is not to say that you won't rub rocks, only that you can scrape over them without getting your canoe or kayak hung up. Rafts may hang up temporarily, but they can be shoved off with some assistance from the occupants.

A description of every rapid would prove fruitless because their appearance and the way to navigate them are different at every water level. A slight increase or decrease in the flowrate can alter their contours dramatically: sometimes for the better, sometimes for the worse. Different levels may also vary the way some rapids are threaded: near the left bank at one level, straight down the middle at another level, for example.

Standing waves at low water may be washed out at high water – or they may stand higher. At low levels you might want to search for deep water, even if it's rough, in order to avoid shoals; at high levels you might want to avoid standing waves for a calmer route so your boat doesn't get swamped or tipped. In short, you have to attack each rapid on the basis of the way it appears at the moment.

Furthermore, there is seldom only a single route through any particular stretch of whitewater. You may choose one way, and the paddler behind you might choose another. And both can be the right way. In some cases there is no right way or wrong way

– only a way that turns out to be better or worse than another.

I don't think that I've ever run the Rock Garden the same way twice. There are so many boulders and so many channels between them that I carom down the river like a billiard ball rebounding off cushions, banking shots from one side to the other. I simply call 'em as I see 'em. At another level I would run the rapids by a completely different route.

The excitement starts as soon as you depart from land. Here a guide is directing rafters away from boulders and into bouncy whitewater.

Except for the Rock Garden – which is a mile and a half of nearly continuous rapids with multitudinous obstructions – whitewater stretches alternate with pools that give swimmers the opportunity to regain their boats and empty them. I once dumped in the Rock Garden and was thrashed for half a mile before I pulled my canoe and myself onto a midstream boulder. But other rapids are shorter and more merciful, making rescue easier.

So I will simply annotate the rapids and islands, and let you make the call when you reach these landmarks.

Rafters using a commercial outfitter need not worry. The guides know the way; not only are they skilled kayakers, but they are familiar with the river and its vagaries under different flowrates. They will lead the best way through the rapids, or will station themselves at appropriate locations and give directions as you approach.

An island is located right around the bend below Rockport. The main flow passes to the right of the island, but the left channel is passable at 800 cfs.

Another, longer island is located a quarter mile farther downstream. Again the main flow passes to the right of the island, but the left channel, although narrow, is passable at 800 cfs.

Now comes a 2-mile stretch of fast water and low standing waves that do not present any difficulties under any flowrate.

Drakes Creek landing

As I noted above, the first major landmark below Rockport is the confluence with Drakes Creek, which enters from the left. At its normal flowrate, Drakes Creek is a pile of jagged rocks and large boulders over which water flows and plummets: a continuous cascade that doesn't flatten out until near the end. The stream flows under a tall arched railroad bridge and over a boulder field that fans into the river.

To describe this access, the best word I can use without getting an X rating for foul language, is horrendous. I've seen some portage trails worse than this on my wilderness canoe trips in Canada, but not more than a handful. Yet at least one raft outfitter habitually utilizes this access as a take-out and put-in, to the detriment and well-

Lehigh River Section 9

Drakes Creek landing is horrendous whether you're coming or going. And that's not counting the half mile walk for rafters.

being of the customers.

For the purpose of the present volume, so I could write a portrayal from personal experience, I took-out at Drakes Creek and, a week later, put-in there. Never again, except in dire emergency under threat of death.

To take-out, I first had to bang my canoe against a spread of jagged rocks where fast water flowed past the bank. I couldn't step onto shore without getting swept away. I had to step into the water where the rocks were covered with slippery moss and angled sharply downward. I crawled onto a boulder field with one hand holding my canoe. Then I had to drag the boat onto rocks that were loose underfoot. Finally, I was on land – if you could call it that.

I must mention at this point that I had to land amidst a bevy of commercial rafts that were also taking-out. The outfitter's guides tried to warn me away, as if they owned the take-out. (In fact, the river access is part of Pennsylvania State Game Lands Number 141.) Then, they insisted that I get my canoe out of their way as fast as possible; they showed resentment at my presence, as if I had no right to be on a public landing.

I was afraid to portage the canoe on my shoulders because the rocks that fringed the forest tipped like teeter-totters. I dragged the boat a couple of hundred feet uphill, to the stream outflow. The 30-foot embankment to the railroad track is nearly vertical. The only way to reach Drakes Creek Road was through the tunnel under the railroad.

The water in the tunnel flowed thigh deep. The outfitter had negligently blocked the tunnel completely with rafts that were stacked atop each other. I waded into the tunnel, shoved stacks of rafts aside, and pushed my floating boat to the upstream side of the tunnel, at which point I pulled it onto the muddy bank and dragged it forty feet to the base of an almost vertical wall of loose rock, where a loading ramp and a steep staircase stretched up to the roadbed.

The treads of the staircase were narrow and slick with mud. I climbed 28 steps with the canoe delicately balanced on my shoulders. Once on the road, I carried the canoe to my waiting vehicle and put it on the roof. The rest was easy: a mile and a half drive up a steep dirt road to a county road that was tarred.

I witnessed the rafters who had it worse. They had the same difficulty that I had in getting out of their rafts without falling into the river or slipping on wet rocks. They carried only their paddles and bailing buckets along the teeter-totter path, some of them tripping. The outfitter hired stevedores to do the heavy work – and heavy work it was: two young men were left behind to handle a couple dozen rafts instead of a single canoe. The guides carried their own kayaks.

Crossing the stream under the bridge was okay for adults, but I saw children floundering waist-deep in the water. And this was during a drought in which the streamflow was minimum. Some customers clambered precariously onto extruded concrete at one end of the tunnel's foundation. After they climbed up the staircase, where my ordeal ended, their ordeal was long from over.

Drakes Creek Road consists of a bendy single-lane passage. It ends in a cul-de-sac which is wide enough for passenger vehicles, such as cars and pickup trucks, to turn around. If independent paddlers choose Drakes Creek as an access, they should be skilled in driving short distances in reverse. When two vehicles meet, one of them has to back up until it reaches a pull-over.

Buses can neither negotiate the bends in the road nor turn around at the bottom. The bus stop is located three-quarters of a mile up a fairly steep grade. The outfitter's customers are required to walk this distance in order to obtain transportation to the outfitter's parking lot.

Drakes Creek tunnel was completely blocked by an arrogant outfitter who believed that private boaters had no right to use a public access.

Putting-in at Drakes Creek was easier because the portage is downhill. But it still requires wading across the creek and walking on jagged tipsy rocks. Independent paddlers can drive to the bottom of the road but, as noted above, raft customers have to walk three-quarters of a mile from the bus stop to the river. I slid my canoe down the staircase by letting the painter slide through my hands. Then I dragged the boat to the water, floated it amid rafts that blocked the tunnel, and dragged it along the streambed to the river – taking a different route than the one that the outfitter was using.

During my put-in, the same outfitter that I encountered the week before was launching another bevy of rafts. This time the guides and helpers were downright abusive. They never said that I had no right to launch at the landing, but they harassed me to no end, continually telling me to get out of their way. They challenged my ability to run the river, and challenged the seaworthiness of my canoe. I was not abusive in return. I went about my business, and minded my own business.

I must mention also that other outfitters are more respectful, both at landings and on the river.

Back to the Lehigh River

A block-long island exists about a mile downstream from Drakes Creek. The main flow goes right, but the left channel is eminently passable.

Half a mile later, Stony Creek flows into the river from the left bank. If you're not in a hurry, stop here and hike up the streambed for two hundred yards. The 20-foot-high waterfall is well worth seeing.

Next, where the river makes a fairly sharp turn to the right, an island occupies the inside of the curve. Two-thirds of the water passes left of the island. The remaining

Lehigh River Section 9

one-third creates an interesting channel that emerges in a rocky rapids that has already started in the main flow upstream, and which continues for a quarter mile.

Another island splits the water some three-quarters of a mile later. The main flow goes right. The left channel is passable; it empties into a rocky rapids.

A quarter mile later, yet another island appears. The main flow goes left through a series of rocky rapids. The right channel drops the same amount of elevation on a more even keel, then joins the main flow below most of the rocks.

As the river continues westward, a string of about a dozen clustered islands guards the right bank. The main flow goes left. The right channel splits into smaller channels where the water flows between and among the various islands, some of which are only large enough to hold a single tree. None of these channels is passable: not even the main alternative channel along the bank. At 800 cfs, I had to walk the canoe several times over the rocky streambed. Nonetheless, the scenery was pretty and I enjoyed the experience. Not for kayakers, though, for whom getting out of and back into the boat is an onerous task.

For the next mile, as the river makes a sweeping curve to the left, a series of three whitewater rapids are separated by pools. There aren't many boulders to avoid, but there are plenty of standing waves to plow through. The excitement of passing through one rapids after another is a taste of things to come.

Running aground on outcrops is a common occurrence.

Between the second and third set of rapids, a rocky beach stretches along the left bank. This is a good place to stop for a rest, or if you need to bail out your boat.

You can't miss noticing Penn Haven Junction. This is where the railroad crosses the river on a steel trestle, and where Black Creek enters from the west (right bank). There's a lot of interesting history here: an inclined plane for coal cars, a switch in the rails so that trains can chug up Black Creek to Weatherly and beyond, and the remains of a small community from antebellum days. A descriptive plaque at the junction provides some relevant information.

The water at the Junction is flat and calm. This is about the halfway point between Rockport and Glen Onoko. If you want to make a rest stop, keep to the left after you pass under the bridge, and land along the sandy left bank that lies immediately downstream.

Above this landing area is an abandoned railroad bed from which the rails and ties have been removed. If you keep your eyes peeled on the left bank about a mile downstream, you'll see a stone wall that rises 40 feet in height. This is an abutment for a trestle that used to cross the river at what is now called Old Penn Haven Junction.

Shortly afterward, the main flow passes right of an island whose left channel is passable. Two blocks later, the main flow passes left of a boulder field that includes a small island. Rafts should stay in the main flow, but canoes and kayaks can take the right passage for a change of scenery. Either way you have to negotiate a bunch of boulders.

Falling out of a raft is a recreational hazard.

Now comes a long stretch of mostly obstacle-free travel: the calm before the storm, so to speak. The river isn't truly calm, for a pair of whitewater rapids that are relatively free of exposed boulders come one after the other.

So is swimming.

If you're looking for a great place to have a picnic, pull over at Bear Creek. The outflow is delineated by a shoal of rocks that spread into the river from the left bank. The landing is no great shakes, but if you hike uphill for a hundred yards or so – not to the flat spot that you come to first, but another one higher up – you'll find a clearing with a stone fire pit, and a railroad tie and a log for comfortable sitting. This is on the upriver side of the stream.

Then comes the Oxbow: a 180-degree sweeping curve around the Pocono Mountain peninsula. A 6-inch iron pipe crosses the river at this point, supported by a suspension bridge some 50 feet above the water. This pipeline was laid in the 1887 to carry petroleum from the oilfields in western Pennsylvania to Bayonne, New Jersey. Currently it houses fiber-optic cables.

The Rock Garden

Once around the bend you'll encounter standing waves, boulders, more standing waves, more boulders, and very short pools of relief before encountering more standing waves and boulders. This sequence of events continues for a mile and a half of nearly continuous rapids, with one short respite along the way.

Even where no boulders or whitewater occur, the current flows swiftly on a constant descent. To give you an idea of how fast the elevation of the streambed falls along this stretch, the gradient doubles from that given in the statistical sidebar: from 21 feet per mile to 42 feet per mile.

You'll be so focused on avoiding rocks and navigating through waves that you probably won't notice the long sweeping curve to the right, or the high-voltage cables nearly a thousand feet overhead: you need to concentrate on what you're doing and where you're going instead of sitting back and taking in the scenery. That is as it should

Lehigh River Section 9

be. This mile-long stretch of whitewater needs every bit of your attention.

Just when you might think that you're running out of steam, the river turns sharply left: precisely at a spot that offers a makeshift sanctuary.

Almost invariably, current flows strongest on the outside of a curve, while the current on the inside of a curve slacks off or comes to a standstill. In this case just the opposite occurs. The geometry of this river bend is a rarity: an indentation on the outside of the curve allows some of the water to spread sideways off the current line. It doesn't create a true eddy or backflow; instead, it forms a tranquil and shallow pool in which water lingers motionlessly.

This slow-down is the division between the upper and lower stretches of the Rock Garden.

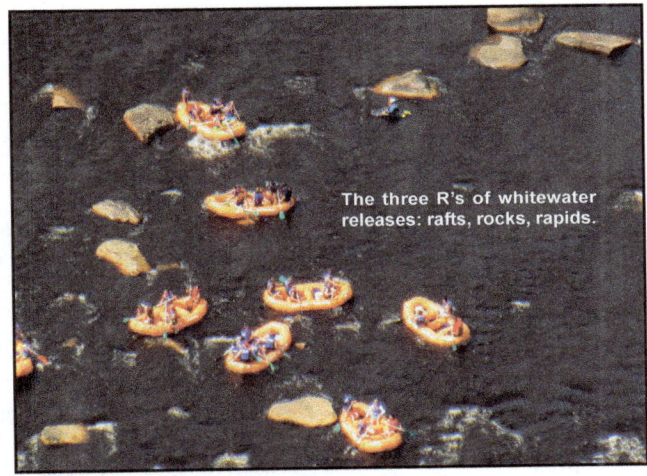

The three R's of whitewater releases: rafts, rocks, rapids.

Rafting groups tend to get spread out in the mile-long rapids upstream, usually because some of the rafts get hung up on rocks and need time to get free. Habitually, outfitters use this indentation as a gathering place to consolidate the flock, and to issue instructions to the customers on how best to proceed through the more challenging whitewater downstream.

Now comes the piece de resistance: the dreaded lower stretch of the Rock Garden. What the next half mile lacks in standing waves it makes up for in boulders the size of automobiles. And by this I do not mean to imply that it lacks standing waves. It has its fair share, and then some, but the greatest obstacle to safe passage is not wave heights, but the preponderance of exposed boulders that block the way.

Threading the Rock Garden provides thrills or chills, depending on your point of view. I cannot tell you the best way to maneuver through this enormous obstacle course, because the "best way" depends on flowrate. This observation is true of any whitewater rapids, but it is exemplified the most in the lower Rock Garden.

For example, at the minimum passable streamflow of 500 cfs, most of the water flows between rocks that are placed so close together that no boat of any kind can fit through the resulting channel. Although the river measures 100 feet across at its widest point, in some places exposed boulders confine passage to a single thin channel. To stray outside this channel is to run aground. Only rarely do other navigable channels exist. This is why outfitters send their rafts through the Rock Garden one at a time. And that is no guarantee that the "best way," or "only way," will remain open. In single file configuration, if a raft gets slightly out of alignment with the only passage, it can be driven onto an adjacent rock in such a way as to partially block the channel. This can spell disaster for everyone behind.

Worse yet, for part of its length the Rock Garden shrinks to only 50 feet across.

This further reduces the maneuvering options. And like the mile-long stretch upstream around the bend, the gradient in the Rock Garden is double the overall gradient from Rockport to Jim Thorpe, to 42 feet per mile.

If you've never run the Rock Garden in a canoe or kayak, you might want to make your first attempt at low water. The slow speed of the current will give you time to maneuver around boulders, will enable you to align your boat with passable channels, and will not have extraordinarily high standing waves that can swamp a canoe or flip a kayak. The downside to low water is that you'll probably scrape over rocks that are fully submerged at higher flow rates.

Canoeists and independent kayakers should never enter the Rock Garden in the middle of a raft group. Canoes and kayaks need maneuvering room. Canoes especially should be backpaddled through standing waves. The last thing a canoeist needs is to be bumped from behind by a raft as he aligns his boat with a channel or reduces speed so he can ride over the waves. In this contest of boats, the canoe is bound to lose.

Odd as it may sound, the Rock Garden is one of those whitewater stretches that becomes *less* challenging at flow rates above minimum, because of two reasons: (1) more channels become passable so you can choose a course that avoids channels with high standing waves, and (2) boats can pass over many of the pillows and barely submerged rocks when the water is deeper . . . but only to a point, after which hydraulics and extremely high standing waves become additional obstacles to avoid. Furthermore, at high flowrates, boats are propelled by the current with such celerity that the amount of time for maneuvering and decision-making is reduced: you have to make spot decisions and make do with the consequences.

I think that the most acceptable flowrate for beginners is 750 to 800 cfs – and that is based on the assumption that the tributaries are not adding materially to the streamflow. Subtract a correction factor if recent rainstorms have flooded the adjacent streams. If the
natural flow rate is high, you would be better served to run the Rock Garden during a minimum dam release.

For more experienced paddlers, I would say that the most exciting level for running the Rock Garden is between 1,000 and 2,000 cfs. At 1,000 cfs, alternative channels begin to become passable. At 2,000 cfs, the single low-water channel may look hairy or scary to an open-boater, but passable side channels will offer alternative ways to avoid the huge standing waves that now occupy the low-water channels; this minimizes the risk of swamping. Also, the number of exposed rocks is fewer: many of them will be submerged so that, in essence, the passable part of the river is wider.

Lehigh River Section 9   61

At 3,000 cfs the situation worsens, especially with regard to standing waves and hydraulics. The water is now roaring, and roaring fast. There is almost no time to maneuver. This doesn't present a problem to rafters, because they'll likely bounce off or ricochet around exposed boulders, or get shoved over top of them by the tremendous force of the current.

800 cubic feet per second.

At this level, kayaks can knife through high standing waves without swamping, but not with utter impunity. They are at greater risk of getting flipped over, especially if they get broadsided.

Canoes can now get swamped with ease. They can also dump if they get slammed at an angle by an exceptionally high roller, and the upstream gunwale dips too low. The force of the current flowing over the gunwale will flip at canoe at nearly the speed of light.

Both canoes and kayaks can get sucked into hydraulics, with devastating consequences.

At 4,000 cfs (the highest level at which I have run the Rock Garden), most boulders are buried and hydraulics are nonexistent. The wave crests are rounded instead of pointed, more like ocean swells, but the troughs can be deep and frightening. I wouldn't necessarily call it a wash-out because considerable rough water remains, but there aren't many nonmoving obstacles, so your primary concern is keeping the boat from swamping in waves that rise higher than the gunwales. At this level you don't have to worry about finding channels. You can paddle almost anywhere because only a handful of boulders will be exposed.

Below left is the only boulder that is exposed in the lower Rock Garden at 4,000 cfs. This is the one that I caught in the incident that I described in the Introduction: the first day of my three-day December odyssey. Below right is the same boulder at the normal water level (300 cfs), surrounded by its smaller brethren.

Lehigh River Section 9

Comin' 'round the bend to the Glen Onoko landing. Below the Rock Garden, rafts take the final turn and land on the broad stony beach where most trips terminate. Note the trucks and trailers that are partially loaded with rafts. Some trucks are waiting to tote rafts away, while others are offloading rafts for a trip downstream.

Back to the Lehigh River

At the end of the Rock Garden the river smooths out so you can catch your breath. It then makes a right-angled turn to the right . . . and there's the beach if you plan to take out at Glen Onoko.

The broad beach that you first encounter is reserved for commercial raft outfitters. They need a large amount of space because they may have a couple of dozen rafts (or more) in a group, and more than one group may land close in time. Also, other groups may in the process of launching. Trucks and trailers will be waiting on the beach to deflate and load the rafts. Buses will be waiting for customers in the parking lot above the beach.

Independent paddlers should pass the broad outfitters' beach and take-out at the narrow beachhead a hundred feet or so downstream, just before the converted railroad trestle. A short trail leads to a nearby parking lot that is reserved for private boaters, so they don't have to contend with throngs of rafters.

A sheer cliff face rises a couple hundred feet above the left bank. It offers a wonderful overlook of the landing area from an outcrop at the top. Several trails reach this overlook from the first parking lot west of the bridge.

As noted in the statistical sidebar, the distance from Rockport to Glen Onoko is 13-3/4 miles. The distance from Drakes Creek to Glen Onoko is 11 miles. The distance from Glen Onoko to the train station in Jim Thorpe is 2-3/4 miles.

For paddlers who continue past Glen Onoko, the whitewater may seem somewhat anticlimactic after the Rock Garden. Yet the river still has scenery and rapids to offer. If you plan to go on, hug the cliffs where the water is deep, pass under the bridges, and paddle through the still water around the turn. Prepare for the penultimate rapids: not many rocks to worry about but an exciting ride through confused standing waves: due to the placement and configuration of boulders on the streambed, waves splash from more than one direction, adding a fillip to the passage through the whitewater.

Lehigh River Section 9

Rafters will love this quarter-mile stretch, especially if they started from Glen Onoko, because it is their first introduction to whitewater. It's just as much fun for kayakers. Canoeists are cautioned to backpaddle if the waves stand too high.

The rapids end after a long sweeping curve to the left. An island on the right is hardly distinguishable from the riverbank until you get close to the inlet. The bulk of the water flows left of the island. If you take the inlet to the right, you'll find yourself in a rockless, fast-flowing channel more than 20 feet wide. This broad island measures nearly a quarter mile in length.

Partway along the channel you'll pass the confluence with the Nesquehoning Creek. If you're not in a hurry, you can stop on the mainland before you reach the creek, or paddle up the creek and land on the left bank. The reason for doing this is to observe the ongoing archaeological dig on the floodplain.

At the end of the island there is another, much small island. Take whichever channel has the most water in order to return to the main flow. Now you'll see a railroad trestle ahead. You can pass on either side of the center pier.

After the trestle the water is fairly flat. If you keep looking to your left, you'll see a pair of cyclopean stone walls: the remains of Lock #2 from the days of yesteryear, when the Lehigh Gorge had been tamed by a system of dams and locks that enabled the transportation of coal in barges.

Another mile downstream are the remains of Lock #1.

A quarter mile past the lock you might notice Robertson Run gushing through an arched stone tunnel above the left bank. This little stream originates high up on Pocono Mountain.

Bad New(s) Rapids

The next immediate landmark is the new Route 903 bridge. The center pier was placed alongside the right bank, where it cut into the river in such a way that it narrowed the channel and restricted the flow of water precisely where a rocky rapids was located. The result of this placement was twofold: standing waves stand higher than they used to stand, and the depth of water has been increased so that exposed rocks became largely submerged. Initially, the overall effect increased navigability. But . . .

. . . during construction, a heavy-duty crane had to be positioned where the bridge was to pass overhead, in order to lift and place the massive steel beams that spanned from the center pier to the left bank abutment. Tons and tons of stone were hauled in, dumped, and graded to create a roadway for the crane and other construction vehicles. Then a riprap peninsula was extended from the roadway nearly all the way across the river. Pipes or culverts were laid beneath the roadway in order to allow passage for some of the water.

Where the river used to measure some 100 feet in width, the navigable passage was reduced to less than 30 feet. Some of the water passes through the culvert pipes, but most of it has been funneled into the newly formed passage. The venturi effect in the restriction increased the speed of the current and raised the height of standing waves. What used to be an innocuous but fun set of rapids that could be easily circumvented became an awesome whitewater channel that grades Class III or IV, depending on the amount of water that is released from the dam.

For rafters, this 100-foot-long sluice is a thrilling ride through big water that has no exposed boulders.

For kayakers, depending upon skill level, it's either a grand place to test your mettle or a fun splash on the troughs and through the crests of tall standing waves. Most kayaks charge straight down the middle and knife through the waves, becoming totally submerged in the process. However, I witnessed more than one kayak getting flipped by the centerpiece whitecap that dominates the midpoint: a 3-foot-deep trough followed by a 3-foot-high permanent wave that stands diagonally to the current, and which sports an upstream curl at the top that tipped over unsuspecting kayakers with the ease of a barefoot bear foot turning over a loose rock in the search for grubs.

There are no hydraulics! Kayaks washed out toward the right bank, and their unseated occupants swam a block or so before finding good footing and slow-moving water in the shallows.

Canoeists beware. It is for you that I have named this the Bad News Rapids. You must have a definite plan in mind before entering this short stretch of whitewater. If the following description fails to allay your fears, stop at the head of the riprap and either portage this stretch or scout it.

The simplest and safest way is to hug the left bank, but if you don't turn into it ahead of time you'll be sucked into the midstream pompadour and swamped or dumped by conflicting waves that rebound off the rock-laden banks and implode through each other in the middle.

As the narrow sluice lies against the right bank, the current angles in that direction because the bulk of the water is turned that way by the head of the riprap. If the angle of your boat is not set when you enter the top of the rapids, you will be propelled away from the left bank. But if you set the angle to the left, and cut over the current line as soon as you clear the head of the riprap, you'll skirt the centerline whitewater and, by continuously drawing to the left, you can slide between the jetty wall and the tall standing waves.

You can also hug the right bank for a more adventurous and challenging passage. The problems with a right bank passage are twofold. The current wants to slam you against the rocks, and the width of the passage between the jetty wall and the confused centerline waves is narrow . . . but it can be done.

Don't let the bow catch the rocks, or the current will grab the stern and thrust it into the waves with your boat turning sideways. You must keep your boat parallel to right bank rocks so the bow doesn't get snagged. Then, about thirty feet downstream from the top, you must clear the rock that stands a foot or so away from the bank. If you hit the rock or get pinched between it and the rock wall, it's game over. If you clear it, you will drop over a foot-high ledge, then immediately drop over another but slightly higher ledge, after which you can squeeze along the bank past the worst of the whitewater into the lower waves downstream.

I repeat: if my description sounds confusing, scout the rapids from the left bank and identify the bulge that constitutes water flowing over a rounded rock, and you'll see what I mean. A canoe can drop over the two short ledges without water pouring over the gunwales.

Now the question that must be posed is: how long will these rapids remain? Bridge construction is slated to be completed in 2017. Will the riprap peninsula remain as a permanent structure for maintenance purposes, or will it be removed and the river returned to its original dimensions? Your guess is as good as mine.

Lehigh River Section 9

The new and possibly temporary rapids under the new bridge.

Past the old Route 903 bridge site, the river curves gently to the right. The take-out is just ahead on the right. The main flow passes to the left of the island. Don't take the right channel unless the flow rate is at least 800 cfs, or you will run aground on rocks.

Beware of the left channel. In the middle of the channel a monstrous standing wave can easily swamp an open boat. At 800 cfs, this wave stands some than two-and-a-half feet in height. Not to fear: there's plenty of room to slip along the right side of the wave.

If you take the narrow right channel, you can beach your boat as soon as you reach the stony take-out beach. If you take the broad left channel, start turning right as soon as you clear the downstream tip of the island. This will put you in the lee. You can then vector to the beach.

To reach the landing by vehicle, enter the parking lot from Route 209 in downtown Jim Thorpe, turn left, and proceed for a hundred yards. Rafting outfitters as well as independent paddlers utilize this access. You are allowed to drive your vehicle from the parking lot down to the water's edge. There are two driveways: the downstream driveway is reserved for commercial outfitters; the upstream driveway is for independent paddlers.

Whether you take-out at Glen Onoko or downtown Jim Thorpe, you can congratulate yourself on having paddled the Lehigh Gorge!

Train station access beach.

Lehigh River Section 10

Section 10: Jim Thorpe to the Lehigh Gap
Distance: 12.4 miles
Travel time: 3 to 4 hours
Adversity level 2: Challenging
Flow rate: Needs 800 cfs on the Lehigh (Lehighton) gauge
Gradient: 12 feet per mile

Whereas whitewater conditions in the Lehigh Gorge may be more extreme than some paddlers are willing to dare, this section offers big water whose rapids are negotiable by all but the most uncoordinated novice. This stretch is a favorite for boaters who want a taste of mild standing waves with a paucity of exposed boulders, in order to build up to the heavy-duty torrents that plague the Gorge.

Do not misunderstand. This section has plenty of whitewater. There are some rapids that extend for a quarter mile. The primary difference between the rapids in this section and those in the Gorge is wave height. Also, because the river is more spread out, the flow rate is slower. Notice, too, that the gradient is lower: about half the gradient in the Gorge, and about a quarter the gradient in the Rock Garden. Furthermore, the gradient is fairly consistent: there are no sudden drops or hydraulics. On hot days, I've seen people put their kids in the water to cool them off. I've also seen people drift alongside their boat on lazy stretches. Some people spend hours drifting slowly down the river on inner tubes, either relaxing and soaking in the sun, or fishing on the fly.

For some of the way, especially downstream of Parryville, the water is so shallow that your blade will touch the streambed most of the time. Whenever this is the case, you can stand in the current without getting bowled over. The downside of shoal water is that there are places on the river where you may run aground on gravel bars, even during whitewater releases from the dam.

Don't think that I am pooh-poohing this stretch of the river. I'm not. Not everyone is a whitewater enthusiast who wants only to experience the heavy-duty challenges that are prevalent in the Lehigh Gorge. Many people enjoy more family-oriented trips in which excitement is not as important as scenery and relaxation.

Note that I have changed the streamflow gauge location from the Francis E. Walter Dam to Lehighton. There are two reasons for doing this. First, when water is released from the dam, it takes so long to flow through the Gorge that this section doesn't become runnable until afternoon. Second, after a heavy rainfall, upstream tributaries may dump so much water into the river that this stretch may be runnable when the Gorge is not, even on days when there is no whitewater release.

The designation of this section is somewhat arbitrary in that the put-in and take-out are based not on restrictive geological criteria as they are in the Gorge. They are my personal preferences. I could just as well have created a section that stretched from Glen Onoko to the stone beach south of Packerton, or from the Jim Thorpe train station to Bowmanstown, because those stretches are commonly paddled by raft outfitters. In fact, because those particular stretches receive so much boating activity as a result of guided tours, the point could be made that I should have sectioned this guidebook in deference to the outfitters' greater usage.

Well, I didn't. I leave it to my readers to refer to the previous section in order to learn about river conditions between Glen Onoko and Jim Thorpe, and to do the math in order to ascertain the length of trips that are tailored differently from the way I have sectioned the river. I apologize to my readers for the inconvenience, but please understand that no river or stream can be divided into neatly defined and commonly traveled sections without considerable overlap.

Lehigh River Section 10

With that caveat, start at the stone beach upstream of the Jim Thorpe train station, below the parking lot, as described in the penultimate paragraph in the previous section. From this section onward, I will adopt the outline format that I employed for the bike trail in the *Lehigh Gorge Trail Guide*. I will denote significant landmarks – bridges, tributaries, access points, obstacles, rapids, and so on – with approximate mile marks, followed by whatever amount of text is necessary to describe the feature. Thus:

.2 – The only *serious* obstacle in this section is a large rounded pillow rock in the middle of the rapids opposite the sewage treatment plant, where the river takes a sharp turn to the left. You can examine this whitewater obstacle from the top of the retaining wall if you feel dubious about the best way avoid it.

At this point the left bank is littered with small exposed rocks that prevent close approach. In fact, I saw several rafts stranded there. As usual, most of the water is pushed toward the outside of the curve. As the water approaches the bend, the main current angles from the left side of the river to the right. A clearly defined tongue is formed by the hidden rocks on either side. My original impression was that the trick to negotiating this obstacle course was in not getting crowded against the retaining wall on the right bank.

Although I first ran this obstacle course blind – that is, without scouting it – afterward I spent some time in watching boaters approach and pass through the midstream whitewater, so as to ascertain the dynamics of the flow. My initial fear was disabused: you don't have to worry about getting shoved against the retaining wall on the outside of the curve, because upstream boulders direct most of the flow away from the right bank and into the standing waves in the middle.

You can force your way to the right bank, but I don't recommend it. The area between the pillow rock and the retaining wall is littered with natural boulders and huge chunks of concrete. I suspect that the concrete rubble comprises remnants of the dam that used to divert the river through the upper canal lock, the location of which is now occupied by the treatment plant. Unless the water is extremely high, a boat will strike this large-scale debris with possibly disastrous results.

Not to worry. As I noted above, the flow naturally turns away from the right bank, and automatically directs watercraft into the standing waves in the center. I watched a host of tubers, who were plying inflatable pool furniture, drift within arm's reach of the right bank upstream of the pillow rock. Without even trying, they were gently and effortlessly angled away from the dam wreckage and pillow rock, and sent through the central whitewater.

My advice to rafters is to stay in midstream, follow the tongue, and

This group was with the guy in the inflatable pool chair on the previous page. If they can make it through this turbulent whitewater without the ability to maneuver, anyone can. The dog in the yellow raft appeared to enjoy the ride. Note the retaining wall on the right, and the pillow rock in the middle bottom. The water level on this day was not particularly high.

punch through the standing waves. The same goes for kayakers, as long as they are prepared to fight confusing waves that will pummel the boat from both sides. The most important thing to remember is to pass to the left of the pillow rock – far left. And you definitely don't want to *hit* the pillow rock.

Rafters and kayakers may ignore the next paragraph. It is intended for canoeists. But let me reiterate: don't hit the pillow rock or you might get caught (rafts) or upset (kayaks).

Canoeists: remember not to get hung up on the left-bank shallows. Stay slightly left of midstream. Approach the tongue cautiously. The speed of the water will determine if you have time to backferry left. If not, point the boat directly at the left bank (broadside to the current) and paddle forward as hard as you can. As long as you get more than half the boat past the rock, the water flowing over the rock will lift the stern around it and straighten the boat in alignment with the current – although you may leave some bottom paint behind you.

However, that maneuver will plop you smack dab in the middle of the standing waves. You need to get left of the standing waves in order to prevent getting swamped or dumped. If you determine that you can't avoid the waves, turn the canoe downstream and backpaddle hard: this is better than going through the waves sideways, because that will certainly flip you over. But the best thing to do is to pass left of the major whitewater, near the left bank, where the waves are shorter and rounded.

If you survive the pillow rock, everything else from this point on is downhill – or downstream. The rest of the trip is fairly smooth paddling all the way to Easton, with a few obstacles along the way. This is not to say that there is no more whitewater. There is. But it's not as monstrous or as challenging as the standing waves at the pillow rock.

1.3 – Train trestle. There are some walloping standing waves under and past the

Lehigh River Section 10

trestle, especially left of the center pier. Pass right of the center pier if you want to avoid the worst of the whitewater. Water flowing between the right-bank abutment and the adjacent pier is overflow from the river, not (as it appears from downstream) outflow from a stream. After the bridge the current is fast but not furious unless the river is flooded after a tremendous rainfall. The rest of this section alternates between stretches of whitewater with short standing waves, and fast-flowing pools. From here to Weissport, you might hear voices emanating from the left bank; the towpath along the canal is a favorite place for hiking, biking, and jogging.

1.8 – The main flow passes left of this 2-block-long island. The right channel is passable all the way to the end, where it rejoins the main flow, but at that point a gravel bar is too shallow to float a boat; you'll have to get out and walk.

2.3 – A set of rapids that extends for a quarter mile passes to the right of this series of islands, the last one of which ends halfway through the whitewater. The left channel is cute and passable.

3.7 – Top of a block-long stretch of whitewater.

4.0 – The broad stony beach on the right bank is a popular river access. To reach this landing by road from Lehighton, turn east from Route 209 onto North Main Lane, and follow the gravel road past the bottling company.

4.1 – This railroad trestle is supported by two piers that divide the river into three channels. The right channel is scratchy and should be avoided for fear of running aground. The center channel is eminently passable, consisting of rolling water much like a washboard with rounded corrugations. Most of the water passes through the left channel, where large standing waves threaten to overwhelm a canoe.

4.2 – The main flow passes left of the island. If you take the left channel under the bridge, you are already aligned for a left passage. The right channel may be passable but look for exposed rocks before going that way; at low water levels the right channel can be a gravel bar.

4.5 – Weissport Bridge (Bridge Street), followed 1 block later by the Lehighton Bridge (Route 209), immediately after which lies what appears to be an island. Stay left! The right passage is pretty much of a backwash. Some water flows over rocks through shallow interruptions in the island. In actuality, the landmass that constitutes a single island at the normal flow rate is flooded at higher flow rates so that it appears to be three smaller islands.

4.8 – Mahoning Creek enters from the right.

5.4 – This is one of several instances on this section in which the main waterway is not the way to go. A gravel bar extends from the top of the island to the right bank, making passage impossible even at high water (although perhaps not at exceedingly high water). Take the narrow channel left of the skinny island.

5.7 – Rapids.

5.9 – The main flow passes right of the island. The narrow left channel is barely passable.

6.2 – The main flow passes right of the island. The left channel is passable if you can get over the entry rocks.

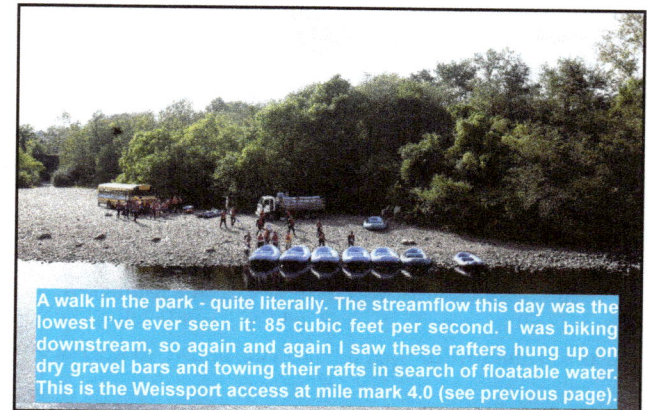
A walk in the park - quite literally. The streamflow this day was the lowest I've ever seen it: 85 cubic feet per second. I was biking downstream, so again and again I saw these rafters hung up on dry gravel bars and towing their rafts in search of floatable water. This is the Weissport access at mile mark 4.0 (see previous page).

6.3 – The main flow passes left of the island. The right channel is barely passable.

6.4 – Twin bridges of the Pennsylvania Turnpike.

6.7 – Pohopoco Creek enters from the left. I have taken-out here without much difficulty. Hug the left bank, round the rocky outcrop, and turn into the creek. Under normal circumstances the stream will hardly be flowing – unless the Beltzville Dam is releasing water. Paddle toward the lock that is the termination point of the old canal. Land on the right shore (or left bank of the canal outflow). Carry your boat up the short slope to the parking lot 100 yards away. You can put-in here, too. For the next mile or so you'll hear traffic noise from Route 248.

7.3 – The main flow passes left of the island. The right channel is passable.

7.5 – A huge gravel bar spreads across the middle of the river. Rafts run aground here even during whitewater releases. The trick is to keep right as close as possible past the peninsula that protrudes into the river, and turn right below the point whenever possible – or drag the boat right when paddling is not possible. Then pass to the right of the island downstream. I tried a different tack by hugging the left bank and working my way through the small rock garden; I had to pole a bit and hump the boat, but I made it through without walking and towing the boat.

7.9 – Landings left and right upstream of the Bowmanstown Bridge (Route 895). The left bank landing is accessible from Cedar Street in Bowmanstown. The right bank landing is accessible from Bowmans Road by turning right at the cul-de-sac into a picnic park known as Marvin Gardens (a $280 property in Monopoly). Raft outfitters habitually use these landings.

8.5 – Lizard Creek enters from the right.

9.0 – Riverview Park landing on the right bank. This is a huge parking lot with a concrete boat-launch apron that extends into the water so that boats can be unloaded from trailers (and vice versa). The parking lot seems to be used more by bikers and picnickers than by boaters. Picnic tables abound, some under a roof. A portable toilet is kept on site. A changing tent is available, harkening back to the early days of the 1900's when similar contrivances enabled seashore swimmers to change into and out of bathing suits while retaining a sense of modesty.

9.1 – The main flow passes left of the island. The right channel is scratchy and might be impassable if the water level is low.

9.3 – You are now confronted by a pair of islands that splits the water three ways, all of which can be scratchy unless the water level is exceptionally high. Neither channel is better than either of the others, so pick your poison. The unnamed island that you reach first is to your left; the next one a couple of hundred feet downstream is called Bowman Island. I've had the best luck in the left channel, I suspect because it is narrow, which helps to bulge the water and increase the depth. The center channel is broad and tends to be scratchier. The right channel is slightly narrower than the left, but because most of the water is funneled between the islands or down the left channel, this channel receives less water; yet it is deep enough to float a boat except near the end, where you have to pick your way between barely submerged rocks. I've never made it through either of these channels without scraping rocks.

9.9 – Another widespread gravel bar. Best bet is to hug the right bank.

10.8 – This is the start of a stretch of whitewater that extends for nearly a quarter mile.

11.3 – Two consecutive islands: the first on the left and the second on the right. The left and right channels are scratchy, so stay in the middle and pass right of the first island and left of the second one.

11.6 – Aquashicola Creek enters from the left, followed by a small island. The main flow passes right of the island, down the broad middle of the river. Although it isn't intuitive, the way to go is not with the main flow but toward the confluence and between the island and the left bank. This is because the main flow washes over a gigantic gravel bar that measures more than two football fields in length. This gravel bar cuts across the river diagonally, so that the water flows nearly perpendicular to the river's direction of travel. This is not to say that you can't find a place to float over the gravel bar; only that unless the water level is extremely high, you'll have to pole and hump your boat across the bar. The water is comparatively deep along the left bank.
You are now entering the Lehigh Gap. After you pass the gravel bar, and approach the bridge in the distance, work your way toward the right bank for the take-out.

12.4 – Pass under the Route 873 bridge and take-out at the right-bank landing 100 feet beyond. To reach this access by road, you first have to find Paint Mill Road, which is unsigned; it's about half a mile south of the bridge: not a perpendicular intersection but a Y-shaped fork. Take the east tine north and turn right when the bridge is directly overhead. The gravel road leads to the landing some 100 yards away. A concrete apron serves as a boat launch.

Lehigh River Section 11

Section 11: Lehigh Gap to Canal Park (Allentown)   Adversity level 1: Not challenging
Distance: 19.6 miles   Flow rate: Needs 1,000 cfs on the Lehigh (Walnutport) gauge
Travel time: 5 to 8 hours   Gradient: 8 feet per mile

Although the parameters that I have established for this section extend for nearly 20 miles, the distance is a measure of publication convenience rather than one of trip length. This section can be separated into shorter segments for which I will provide convenient access points that average 5 miles apart.

The required flow rate applies largely to the upper 60 percent of the length of this section, to the dam between Northampton and Cementon. Below the dam the depth is such that I would call the remainder perennial all the way to Easton, although in times of drought the short segment below the dam in Allentown is probably scratchy... but that stretch can be bypassed.

One might think that the encroachment of civilization downstream of the Lehigh Gap would be extreme. I am happy to report that such is not the case. Both banks are so covered with forest that for most of this section the feeling of remoteness is common. A few houses can be seen where intervening trees have been cleared. Bridges shatter the sense of isolation. But until the river reaches the outskirts of Allentown, straddling vegetation preserves the suggestion of wilderness, if not the actuality. Only occasionally did I hear a tractor-trailer shifting gears far away.

Paddling time is variable and dependent upon streamflow. I canoed this section when the gauge at Walnutport registered 3,400 cfs, which is abnormally high. The speed of the current enabled me to paddle the entire section in less than five hours without once scratching bottom. At flow rates less than 1,000 cfs, the initial segment downstream of the put-in can be scratchy. Also scratchy is the approach to Treichlers bridge and the segment adjacent to the canal between Laurys Station and Northampton (which see). Beyond the dam I could never touch bottom with my paddle.

I encountered few rapids, and those that I did encounter had waves that measured less than one foot in height. I got splashed a few times. Exposed boulders are few and far between. The worst rapid is the stretch below the dam in Allentown, which can be avoided (as you will read below).

The river averages 300 feet in width.

0.0 – Put-in at the concrete boat ramp that lies practically underneath the Route 873 bridge. The water here is deep enough for motorboats, but turns into rapids within a quarter mile, where the watercourse makes a sharp dogleg to the right.

2.5 – Bridge that connects Walnutport with Slatington. Boat access is located on the left bank immediately downstream of the bridge. Trout Creek enters from the right, a block farther downstream; the stream is partially concealed by vegetation on an outflow island.

3.1 – Piers that once supported an old railroad trestle march across the river.

5.3 – The main streamflow passes to the right of the island; the left passage is narrow but passable if the water is high enough.

6.2 – Power lines cross overhead.

Lehigh River Section 11

Most of this section of the river looks as idyllic as the scene in this photograph. The view is looking upstream at Blue Mountain and the Lehigh Gap.

7.0 – Remnants of an old dam that was part of the canal system stretch halfway across the river from the right bank, leaving a 50-foot passageway in which the water swells upward and creates a stretch of descending whitewater. The main flow goes straight ahead. For an extra thrill, turn right before the small island and take the right passage.

7.4 – The right bank under Treichlers bridge is an ideal boat access. The D&L Trail lies 100 feet up the shallow embankment. A parking lot (built for hikers and bikers and other trail users) is located 100 yards away. The river in this area is almost impassable when the water is low.

The river now takes a sweeping curve from north to south: 180 degrees. A long and fun stretch of rapids is located a couple of miles down the straightaway, adjacent to the canal. There's nothing to worry about: it's a rollercoaster ride that gets better the higher the water, and is without exposed boulders unless the water is extremely low.

11.9 – Bridge that connects Northampton with Cementon, followed immediately by a dam. Pass under the bridge between the right bank and the pier, then hug the bank as you approach the dam. The water moves slowly close to shore. Skirt the vegetation until you reach the stony beachhead some 30 feet before the dam, just past the blockhouse. The portage trail around the dam is about 100 feet in length.

This spot can also be used as an access. A jeep road leads for a block or so to a parking lot on Route 329.

14.4 – Coplay-Northampton bridge with no boat access, followed a block later by an abandoned railroad trestle.

15.0 – Hokendauqua-North Catasauqua bridge with no boat access.

The dam below the bridge that connects Northampton with Cementon. Land on the gravel beach to the left of the blockhouse, then portage on the trail behind the trees to the gravel beach below the dam.

15.6 – Catasauqua Pine Street bridge with no boat access, followed a block later by an abandoned railroad trestle.

16.0 – West Catasauqua-Catasauqua bridge with no boat access.

16.8 – Route 22 bridge with no boat access.

17.4 – Abandoned railroad trestle followed immediately by a new bridge which at the time of publication was still under construction. On the left bank between the bridges lies the outflow of a small stream and the unrecognizable end of Lehigh Canal 6 (which see). Paddle 100 feet up the barely moving outflow to a concrete boat ramp and parking lot.

17.9 – Tilghman Street-North Ellsworth Street bridge with no boat access.

18.7 – Dam followed immediately by Hamilton Street bridge. This is a good place to end a trip, but not a particularly good place to start one. Veer toward the left bank when the bridge comes into view. Water that is backed up by the dam hardly flows. Gradually hug the shore until you are brushing vegetation. About 30 feet before the dam you'll see a narrow gravel roadway leading into the river. Land alongside the rocks and step out onto the beach. Drag the boat some 20 feet up the roadway to a clearing.

The parking lot is right in front of you. To reach this lot by vehicle, drive west along East Walnut Street and cross the railroad track. Turn right (north) to head for the dam, or left (south) to go to Canal Park.

Lehigh River Section 11

To continue paddling on the river, portage the boat between the canal and the fish ladder, cross the debris under the bridge, and let the boat slide down the rocky embankment to the water's edge. Crossing the debris and scampering down the rocks isn't easy . . . but it isn't all that difficult, either.

Alternatively, you can launch your boat into the canal beyond the lock (from the parking lot side), and paddle to Canal Park, and farther. See Lehigh Canal 7 for details.

The main reason I suggest terminating the trip here is not to avoid the portage, but to avoid two sets of rapids between the dam and Canal Park, which might not be acceptable for a family oriented trip, or one with small children. Although I got splashed I thought the rapids were fun and well worth the effort of the portage. The mid-river whitewater is pretty feisty, but you can sneak along the left bank through lower wave heights.

The second set of rapids is created by riprap in the middle of the river. These artificially placed rocks force most of the water to the sides. The resultant channels are narrow and filled with standing waves that are not overly challenging to negotiate. Again, I personally would not want to miss this whitewater.

19.6 – Round the bend to the left and pull onto the concrete boat ramp at Canal Park.

The dam at Allentown. The fish ladder is inside the fence next to the right border of the picture. The portage route, such as it is, cannot be seen; it passes between the fish ladder and the canal, then over dirt and debris to a rock pile under the bridge.

Lehigh River Section 12

Section 12: Canal Park (Allenton) to Delaware River
Distance: 16.4 miles
Travel time: 6 to 8 hours

Adversity level 0: None
Flow rate: Almost perennial
Gradient: 3.5 feet per mile

As in the previous section, the distance of this section is a measure of publication convenience rather than total trip length. This section can be separated into shorter segments for which I will provide convenient access points along the way.

You can see by the gradient in the statistical sidebar that the river doesn't drop much in this final section before the confluence with the Delaware River. The amount of drop you will experience is even less. Only the first half this section consists of normally flowing water. The rest is held back by dams: one at Hugh Moore Park, the other at the Delaware River at Easton. Both of these dams created flatwater for the extinct canal system.

I call the flow rate "almost perennial." That's because I paddled over a few places where moving water was shallow, say, little more than a foot deep. At times of extreme drought and restricted release from the Francis E. Walter Dam, it's possible that a boat might scrape bottom at these spots. But I suspect that those times are rare.

This section is similar to the previous one in exhibiting a sense of isolation. A buffer of trees lines the banks for much of the way, reducing most signs of civilization to infrequent bridges. I was pleasantly surprised by the quasi-wilderness experience in so civilized a river that flows through crowded metropolitan areas.

The first mile and a half was attended by noise from the railroad yard that lies beyond the left bank. Miles later I heard a train on the track beyond the right bank. Intermittent traffic sounds congregated mostly near the bridges. Otherwise, the river is quiescent and virtually pristine.

As I noted above, after the midpoint of this section there is not much assistance from current. Padding in the backwash of the dams is like padding on a lake. This means slow going. A few riffles add a change of pace but there are no rapids or whitewater.

The width of the river averages 200 to 300 feet. The navigable waterway is reduced in some places by the presence of islands, where the water splits and flows through narrowed channels. All the islands can be passed on either side.

0.0 – Put-in at the concrete boat ramp in Canal Park. Plenty of parking space is available. I met an angler there who was fishing for muskies (muskellunge, related to pike and pickerel). He told me that he has caught yard-long specimens from shore, or from a kayak around Sterner Island. If you look across the river you'll see the outflow of the Little Lehigh Creek.

1.1 – Sterner Island. Right channel is larger but the left channel is equally passable.

1.8 – The end of Sterner Island. For the next couple of miles the river is essentially isolated from human encroachment.

4.0 – A public boat ramp is situated on the left bank, just before the railroad trestle. This leads to a parking lot on River Street. There's plenty of parking space available because this lot is a major access for the towpath trail that is popular with bikers, hikers,

Lehigh River Section 12

and joggers. One block downstream of the trestle is the Hill-to-Hill Bridge (Route 378).

4.3 – Phillip J. Fahy Memorial Bridge for New Street. At this point the old Bethlehem Steel Plant comes into view on the right. Normally the ruins of abandoned buildings and structures present a blight to the senses. Not so in this case. Rusted it may be, but the structure is so huge, so grand, and so historic, that instead of an eyesore it is a monument to the industrial revolution and the nascent days of steel production that helped to forge a developing nation.

4.7 – Monocacy Creek enters from the left. For the next several blocks you'll have excellent views of the Bethlehem Steel Plant on the right.

Believe it or not, due to largely undeveloped banks and a veneer of trees and other vegetation, the river looks like this for most of the way from Allentown to Easton. Who would have thought?

5.5 – Minsi Trail Bridge.

6.0 – Pass on either side of this unnamed island.

6.7 – Saucon Creek enters from the right.

6.8 – Main Street bridge in Freemansburg. It's possible to take-out under the left side of the bridge, but I don't recommend it because of the difficulties involved. After climbing up the rocky embankment you have two choices: climb up the stairs with your boat on your shoulder(s) then take the sidewalk to the right (northward) to the lot; or portage across the towpath, paddle across the canal, and fight through the vegetation to the same lot.

Carrying a kayak on your shoulder up the reversing staircase is doable; I have my doubts about portaging a canoe up those steps. Walking down to put-in is easier, but there's a better access half a mile downstream.

7.4 – Laubach Island. Either side is passable. The left channel has a short set of riffles and a difficult but doable river access on the left. Turn into the outflow of Nancy Run a hundred feet or so ahead of the riffles. Drag your boat over the rocky streambed to the towpath where the water in the canal is diverted into the stream. At that place a paved road extends 200 feet to Lockhouse Road, like the vertical stroke of a T. This isn't the easiest access but it's better than the one at the Main Street bridge.

Laubach Island is undeveloped, and covered with trees and thick vegetation. It measures 3 blocks in length by 1 block in width. Yet this almost-never-visited mid-river island constitutes an important political boundary. The middle of the island's length separates Lower Saucon Township from Bethlehem Township and Freemansburg; the middle of the island's width separates Bethlehem Township from Freemansburg. I guess boundaries have to be located somewhere.

Now comes 3 miles of untainted river frontage that is bordered by trees and vegetation.

10.4 – Private boat dock for members only. By this time you will have long since noticed that the river current is almost unnoticeable. This is due to the dam at Hugh Moore Park: the so-called Chain Dam.

10.8 – Gene Hartzell Memorial Bridge for Route 33, followed immediately by Turkey Island. The right channel is cute because it measures only 50 feet across, and is dominated by tall trees on either side. Leaves offer shade and a sense of isolation. But if you go this way you'll miss the take-out on the left bank near the middle of the island. Not to fear: the lack of perceptible current will allow you to paddle upstream a block or so if you want to take-out.

11.1 – Public boat landing with a huge parking lot. Motorboats launch here in order to plow deep water both upstream and downstream.

11.5 – The USGS topographic map designates this island as both Island Park and Hugh Moore Park. The island measures nearly a mile and a half in length, and a quarter mile across at its widest point. In the late nineteenth and early twentieth century, the island was the site of a massive amusement park that offered a wide assortment of entertainment activities for folks of all ages and interests: a Ferris wheel, roller coaster, merry-go-round, dance pavilion, swimming pool, theater, casino, picnic areas, ball fields, and playgrounds.

A trolley in Easton used to transport people along the left bank of the river to a bridge that led to the island. Patronage flagged during World War One. After the bridge was destroyed by an ice flow – twice – the park was closed and the structures were dismantled.

I trudged across the island in search of ruins or remnants. I found not a vestige to serve as a reminder of the island's past glory. The island was a tangle of fallen and rotting trees, intertwined thorn bushes, vines, and tall deciduous trees. Nature has completely reclaimed the island.

You can pass on either side of the island. The left channel is narrower and cuter than the right, but be aware that a dam exists a block past the end of the island. This does not present a problem; the water moves so slowly that you can easily paddle to the preferred right-bank portage without getting swept over the dam.

13.1 – Dam portage trail(s). The preferred portage is on the right bank. Land on the stony beach, then drag, carry, or portage your boat along the dirt road past the house and corral (between them and the canal) to the steps that lead down to the water's edge. Clamber over the rocks to reach the river. You can take the narrow channel to the right of the island if you want to avoid the standing waves in the main flow of the river.

You can also portage on the left bank. This looks scarier because you have to approach very close to the dam. As always, the water above a dam moves slowly, so there is little difficulty in attaining the concrete barrier where a rocky path leads to a cleared

Lehigh River Section 12

viewing area (adjacent to the towpath trail), thence past the fish ladder and between the trees to the water's edge. The length of this portage is 200 feet as opposed to 600 feet for the right-bank portage. Take your pick and paddle.

13.7 – Riverview Park Fishing Bank on left bank. On the right bank for the next block (before the bridge) are several spots that you can use as a water access. There is (or are) lots of parking in Hugh Moore Park.

13.9 – South 25th Street bridge.

14.1 – Hugh Moore Park bridge. A separate lane enables bikers, hikers, and joggers to cross the river while remaining on the D&L Trail.

14.2 – Boat landing on right bank in Hugh Moore Park.

15.2 – Take either channel to pass this unnamed island.

15.4 – Abandoned railroad trestle.

16.3 – Route 611 bridge, over which crosses almost perpendicularly an active railroad trestle.

Postcard pictures of Island Park in its heyday. From top to bottom: Roller-coaster, casino, merry-go-round, and boat landing. These are only a few of the activities that were available to visitors.

A tinted postcard picture of the dancing pavilion at Island Park.

16.4 – Take-out on the left bank before the dam (obviously). Don't miss it! The take-out driveway veers off Larry Holmes Drive.

The dam at Easton, where the Lehigh River flows into the Delaware River (at right, looking upstream). The take-out is located to the left of the picture, on the opposite shore. The State of New Jersey is to the right of the Delaware River. Part of the fish ladder is visible in the foreground. The rungs are for maintenance workers, not fish. The Lehigh River watershed is so large that it used to be called the West Branch of the Delaware.

Lehigh Canal Section 1

Section 1: Jim Thorpe through Weissport to Parryville

Adversity level 1: Not challenging
Distance (total): 6 miles   Distance (runnable): about 4 miles (in two stretches)
Travel time: 1 hour per stretch   Elevation differential: 88 feet

The towpath along this stretch of canal is a popular place for hiking, biking, jogging, and just plain walking (and dog walking). The water-filled portion of the canal is an "approved trout stream."

The remains of the entry lock are located at the site of the sewage treatment plant on the east side of the Lehigh River. The original canal passed directly through the area that is now occupied by that plant. The canal is extant on the downstream side of the plant, but it is dry for the first 2 miles. However, the dry stretch is not without interest.

First is a small stone structure that looks like the foundation of a building. It is located between the canal and the river. A couple of hundred feet afterward is a large stone structure on the east side of the towpath (although the descriptive plaque is on the west side). This large structure is a weighing lock: one that was used to determine the amount of coal in a canal barge, so that appropriate tolls could be charged.

Three-quarters of a mile afterward is a lock observation post (on the east side).

Two miles from the entry lock, an inlet lets water from the river flow into the canal through a culvert under the towpath. The canal can be paddled from this point to Weissport. Or perhaps it is more accurate to state that the canal can be paddled from Weissport to that point: a distance of 2.5 miles.

The channel is narrow in the beginning, and the depth of water is constrained by the streamflow of the river. A lock is located a quarter mile downstream, after which the waterway broadens to 20 feet or more: a minimum width that is maintained the rest of the way to Weissport. Thanks to Long Run, which enters from the east nearly half a mile farther downstream, the water here is perennial. Although the water level drops during times of drought, the height (or depth) of water is controlled by two overflow channels between Long Run and Weissport.

Weissport is the obvious access. The Bridge Street parking lot can accommodate several dozen vehicles. For ease in water entry, a pair of wide staircases leads down to the water's edge through the concrete bulkhead. The downside for distance or upstream paddlers is that the segment between the road and the first dam is only 2 blocks, with the first earth dam located less than a block beyond the lock. An earth dam is a barrier that is made of fill dirt; a culvert slightly more than a foot in diameter allows water to flow through the dam into the next lower segment of the canal.

Paddlers who go all the way upstream from Weissport must portage at least 5 times: around 3 locks and 2 earth dams. And that's not counting the portage to the river: a distance of at least 50 feet through woods without a trail. Paddlers who choose to go to the extreme end of the water-filled passageway must portage around another lock in order to enter the final segment where the water depth is marginal.

Paddlers who return on the river face a difficult task to reach their starting point. The Bridge Street bridge lies a quarter mile from the parking lot, and a thick grove of trees bars the way uphill to street level.

The best way to return is to take-out opposite the broad rocky beach that outfitters use to recover or launch rafts. This is where the first earth dam is located, but the take-out is no bargain. The bank has been buttressed by piling huge boulders on a 60 degree slope. I won't say it's impossible to portage a canoe up this embankment, but I wouldn't try it. I would climb over the boulders on all fours with the painter in one hand, and drag the boat to the top. Then it's only a few feet to the downstream side of the earth dam.

Weissport can also be used as a downstream put-in, but only if conditions are right. Water in the segment that lies upstream of the bridge flows through a culvert under Bridge Street. This culvert is wide enough for a canoe to glide through, if you dare. Otherwise, offload your boat in the gravel clearing on the south side of the street.

The canal and towpath north of Weissport present a pastoral vision.

Even then, during times of drought the water in this segment of the canal isn't deep enough to float a boat. You might have to drag the boat for nearly a quarter mile before reaching runnable (or floatable) water – and that is over a weed-filled, muddy bottom.

After the canal freezes in winter, it is ideal for ice fishing.

It's better to launch from Parryville.

A suitable parking lot is located off Route 248 upstream of the Pohopoco Creek. Put-in above the final lock and paddle upstream. You can paddle over the white Styrofoam containment strips without damaging them. It's more than half a mile to the first and only lock. When you portage around the lock, take time to read the information plaque, and examine the double-channel lock with a bypass flume, and the nearby stone hut.

You can then proceed another three-quarters of a mile before you run out of water. Or in times of flood you might be able to paddle all the way to Weissport.

You'll have to portage over an active railroad track if you wish to return via the river. If you do this, take-out at the Pohopoco Creek by turning into the outflow and beaching on the point of land between the creek outflow and the lock outflow. It's a short easy walk up the path. And you can drive your vehicle from the parking lot along the gravel roadway to within 50 feet of the take-out.

Lehigh Canal Section 2

Section 2: Bowmanstown through Palmerton to the Lehigh Gap

Adversity level: Nonapplicable
Distance (total): 3 miles (approximately)
Distance (runnable): None
Travel time: Not applicable
Elevation differential: 45 feet

Almost all of this section has been obliterated by time and urban development. A few hundred feet of the entry channel are extant until it reaches a liquid storage facility and a housing neighborhood that is part of Bowmanstown.

Half a mile away, an obvious stretch of canal extends beyond Bank Street (at the overpass), wedged between the Blue Mountain Plaza and Route 248. Most of this stretch can be seen from the highway, which it almost perfectly parallels. A few inches of water encompass rounded rocks that constitute the canal bed. I suspect that the water may be deeper when the Lehigh River is running high. This stretch extends somewhat less than half a mile. No lock structures are in evidence.

The next obvious stretch exists downstream of the jug handle to Palmerton. Much of the canal is now a vast cleared area that is used for parking, and a dirt road that anglers and picnickers follow to access the river. Four lock structures remain along this half mile stretch. Two of them bracket the Aquashicola Creek; some supporting timbers from the aqueduct are exposed on the streambed when the water level is low. The end lock is located a few feet from the river.

Although this section offers no opportunities for paddling, it is a real treat for canal historians and enthusiasts who like to examine or document lock remains. Those that straddle the Aquashicola Creek, plus the final one downstream where canal boats were lowered to the level of the river, stand in remarkably good condition with very little breakdown. Remnants of the gates also remain: iron frames and wood planks. This stretch is well worth exploring on foot.

Lehigh Canal Section 3

Section 3: Walnutport to Lockport
Distance (total): 4.2 miles
Travel time: 2 hours (roundtrip)

Adversity level 1: Not challenging
Distance (runnable): 2.8 miles
Elevation differential: 40 feet

Walnutport is the approximate midpoint access for this section. The ends are not directly accessible.

The canal stretches upstream from Main Street for 1.8 miles (of which 1.2 miles are runnable), and downstream for 2.4 miles, although at the time of my surveys for the present volume (spaced several months apart), the flooded part of the downstream stretch measured only 1.6 miles below Main Street. The canal was essentially dry below the lock that is located at the bend in the river.

The dirt towpath is favored by hikers, bikers, and joggers: all except for the last quarter mile where the towpath has been obliterated after the confluence with Bertsch Creek. You might see anglers fishing from the groomed towpath. I saw one pull a fair-sized pickerel out of the canal. He told me that he was fishing for bass.

The water entry is little more than a pair of cement conduits from which the overburden of dirt has been washed away, leaving the pipes partially exposed. When the river is low, water barely trickles through the conduits into the upper segment of the canal. I haven't see the entry during whitewater releases, but I imagine that water must gush right over top of the pipes at times when the river is raging. The first lock is located some 50 feet away.

Whether the first segment is runnable is dependent upon influx from the river. In times of drought this segment is a narrow and shallow strip of water that is congested with weeds, and might not be deep enough or wide enough for boating.

After the next lock it's clear paddling to Main Street and beyond (except for portaging around the locks). There is sufficient headroom under the walking bridge north of Main Street. In fact, you can put-in there because there's a small parking lot on North Canal Street. There's plenty of headroom under the Main Street Bridge.

Immediately south of the bridge there is a concrete pad on the river. Paddlers who want to complete a loop on both river and canal can utilize this access to either put-in or take-out. Adventurous paddlers can bypass the boat launch and do the entire loop. Be careful not to paddle beyond the bend in the river, or you might find yourself portaging longer than you wanted.

The first lock below Main Street is less than a block away. You can drive south along Lehigh Street

On Canal Festival day in Walnutport, canoes and instruction on how to paddle them are freely available to all visitors.

Lehigh Canal Section 3

Canal Festival day falls on the third Sunday in October. There are activities and food for people of all ages.

and launch a boat from the parking lot below the lock, so you don't have to portage it if you want to paddle only downstream and back.

A major point of interest is the refurbished lock tender's house adjacent to the lock. The lock has also been artfully restored and modernized, complete with a walking bridge that spans the water-filled canal. After that, the canal is so wide and open that you might think that it's still in use. For the most part it measures some 30 feet across.

Another point of interest is the Poughkeepsie Bridge location. The railroad trestle used to cross the Lehigh River and canal. It has been removed but the piers still remain. An information plaque on the towpath provides some historical perspective.

The gates are missing from the next lock so that water flows straight through the structure under the foot bridge.

After the following lock, which has a foot bridge that leads to a picnic area, the canal is no longer flooded enough to float a boat. Tall weeds sprouting from the bottom indicate accumulated silt. For what it's worth, the final quarter mile may (or may not) have runnable water.

An aqueduct used to cross Bertsch Creek. The aqueduct is long gone. A makeshift wood bridge that is barely holding together enables pedestrians to describe a loop from the previous lock (which has a footbridge).

Most of the aqueduct's center pier is still standing, although some of the stones have fallen down. A lock is located on the downstream side of the aqueduct. The walls appear to be well preserved. The bottom is gridlocked not only with entangling weeds, but with trees (both standing and fallen). The canal terminates a block away.

Visitors should note that the Walnutport Canal Association is active in promoting this section of the canal. The WCA offers guided tours of the lock tender's house, and operates a museum that is dedicated to the memory of the canal system. The museum houses artifacts and photographs of an era long past.

The WCA also hosts the annual Canal Festival on the third Sunday in October – by which time the colors of autumn foliage are at peak. Dozens of vendors offer food, drink, crafts, and exhibits. Canoes are freely available for anyone who wants a taste of paddling on canal waters. There are hayrides on the towpath for landlubbers.

This is a gala event that you shouldn't miss.

Lehigh Canal Section 4

Section 4: Treichlers
Distance (total): 1 mile
Travel time: 1 hour (hiking roundtrip)
Adversity level 1 (for hiking): Not challenging
Distance (runnable): None
Elevation differential: 5 feet

This short stretch of canal is extant for its entire length of 1 mile. There are no paddling opportunities because the canal is dry; or in some places, muddy. Much of the canal is fiercely overgrown with entangled vegetation. Not only are all the locks still standing in good condition, but part of the dam is continuing to do its job.

To see the remains of the dam that extends more than halfway across the river from the right bank, park in the lot that serves as an access for the D&L Trail, on the east side of the bridge. Drive down Cove Road to get there. Walk upstream from the lot for just over half a mile.

Most of the existing dam's concrete lintel is intact. The downstream side of the dam is badly fragmented: enough to expose the bottoms of the cribs, enabling observation of the way the dam was constructed. Much of the rock filling has been washed away by floods, despite the fact that the upstream facing appears to be intact, and is buried under so much accumulated silt and dirt that large trees have taken root over the years – and consequently help to hold the substrate together, especially now that floods are controlled by the Francis E. Walter Dam.

If you look across the river you can see the remains of the dam on the other side of the narrows, plus the stone structure that constitutes the upstream facing of the entry lock.

There is a convenient view of the canal and one of the locks at the bottom of Breadfruit Drive, next to the flour mill. The edge of the road is the top of one lock wall; you can look straight down into the lock. A grated metal bridge enables hikers to cross over top of the canal to the towpath. Note the tree that is growing out of the inside of the lock wall. Also note the connected timbers that served as the upstream gate.

Although the berm that functioned as the towpath is remarkably intact, it is largely overgrown with saplings, tall weeds, sticker bushes, and fallen trees. Despite these obstacles, from the Breadfruit Drive lock a narrow path extends for three-quarters of a mile upstream (south) to the entry lock, adjacent to the dam. The rock walls appear much as they did when the lock was in use, but a huge mound of dirt occupies the location of the entry gate.

A stone bulkhead connects one lock wall with the dam abutment. Atop this wall stands a wooden hut in a state of disrepair.

The end lock is located at the opposite end of the canal, a quarter mile downstream (north) from Breadfruit Drive. The structure is extremely well preserved. Segments of the gates – both wood and metal – lie inside the lock.

Lehigh Canal Section 5

Section 5: Laurys Station to Northampton
Distance: 2.5 miles
Travel time: Not applicable

Adversity level: Not applicable
Distance (runnable): none
Elevation differential: 10 feet

Although half a mile of this canal is filled with water, it is not runnable for a couple of reasons. First, access to the southern terminus, which is the only part that is flooded, is prohibited by a sporting club that does not welcome visitors. Second, much of the flooded part is poorly maintained and fraught with floating logs, fallen trees, dirt fill, and tangled vegetation, all of which conspires to block boating traffic.

The rest of the canal is either dry or pocked with shallow mud puddles, plus deadfall. Not only that, but most of it is in such a bad state of degradation that it couldn't hold water: the confining dirt walls are largely washed away or totally nonexistent. The northern stretch of the old canal bed has the appearance of a flood plain.

However – and this is a big however – the upstream entry lock stands in a remarkable state of preservation, and is perhaps unique as a prime example of the manner in which the lock system was constructed.

Originally, water was diverted from the river along a broad but shallow channel that is now overgrown with small trees and weeds. This channel extends for half a mile before reaching a tall stone structure that is not just one lock, but two. This double lock consists of three stone walls that stand some 20 feet in height. The thick center wall separates the two locks from each other.

An inside view of one of the two locks, looking upstream at the twin sluices where the water would have entered.

The wooden gates are missing but some of the iron guides remain. Soil deposits on top of the walls have enabled weeds, shrubs, and saplings to take root. The overburden and long hanging vegetation are so thick that the locks are almost completely disguised from outside. Only the inside of the walls and the floor of the locks are not totally overgrown. A puddle in the west lock appears to have been formed by rainwater that is trapped in a depression. The bottom of the east lock consists of soft mud.

The view from inside the locks is awesome, and well worth the effort to go there and see them. The dual locks are located opposite Neff Laurys Road (west of the river), next to what appears to be a cove on the left bank.

The best way to reach this amazing edifice is from the river. I paddled my kayak from the right bank, but it was more trouble than it was worth. I kept stranding on rocks because the water was so shallow. Eventually, I got out of the boat and walked the rest of the way. You can't do this during a whitewater release, but most other times the water is shallow enough to hike. I suggest wearing a life vest for safety and using hiking poles for stability. Paddle a canoe or kayak if the water is deep. You won't regret it.

Lehigh Canal Section 6

Section 6: Catasauqua to Allentown
Distance (total): 3 miles (approximately)
Travel time: Not applicable
Adversity level: Not applicable
Distance (runnable): None
Elevation differential: 40 feet

Most of this canal has been obliterated: not as much by development as by new growth in the dry bottom. Fully mature trees occupy a great deal of the old canal bed, along with tangled weeds and sticker bushes.

Two stretches may be wet. The water that fills the upstream end has the color of creamed coffee. Floating in this muddy concoction is loose debris: brush, old rubber tires, and miscellaneous trash. One fallen tree stretches completely across the waterway next to an abandoned railroad trestle. I suppose the water is deep enough to float a boat, but I wouldn't want to paddle in it.

Another water-filled stretch lies downstream of Catasauqua Creek, which looks as if its water was diverted into the canal to aid in flooding. The water is not deep enough to float a boat.

Puddles of rainwater may be found in other areas. Hiking opportunities are limited to the stretch in Hanover Canal Park, where the ruined remains of Lock #37 are found.

There's not much to see or do on what little remains of this section of the canal system, especially when compared to what other sections have to offer. This section's only redeeming feature is easy accessibility to the bedraggled remains of Lock #37. The flooded segment is a channel that is filled with mud and trash, and is difficult to access.

Lehigh Canal Section 7

Section 7: Allentown through Bethlehem and Freemansburg to Hopesville

Adversity level 1: Not challenging

Distance (total): 12 miles Distance (runnable): 6.5 miles
Travel time: Dependent on trip length Elevation differential: 30 feet

This section of the canal system is not only the longest, but also boasts the longest runnable distance. It has multiple accesses so that boaters can choose among a number of convenient locations for starting and finishing a trip, and making loops by paddling down the river.

The canal begins right at the dam and associated entry lock, which are located practically under the Hamilton Street bridge. Parking is available in the adjacent gravel lot. The next 5.5 miles of the canal is flooded and runnable.

If you plan to paddle down the river and return to this point, launch your boat downstream of the dam. For a short trip you can take-out at the concrete boat-launch apron in Canal Park, three-quarters of a mile away. Due to the layout of the park and its numerous parking lots, you'll have to portage your boat a couple of hundred feet to reach the canal. Then you'll find that you're only a few hundred feet below a well-maintained lock that you have to portage.

If you're just out for a short trip, and want to avoid the long portages, you can take-out before the bend in the river that constitutes Canal Park: on the left bank at the gravel beach before the railroad bridge. From here you will have to portage or drag your boat only 75 feet to reach the canal, and you won't have to worry about traffic.

Alternatively, you can start your trip in Canal Park where plenty of parking space is available. The next lock is 3 miles downstream. Thus you can do a 6-mile loop on river and canal without having to portage around any locks.

If you want to paddle farther than that lock, you can go another 2 miles on the river (5 miles in all from Canal Park, or 5 and a half from the dam and entry lock). This will take you to the point at which the canal runs out of water. The return trek on the canal will include portaging around another lock.

I should mention, too, that although there is no deadfall along the canal, some stretches are filled with a species of weed that is rooted to the dirt on the bottom and that reaches the surface. You can paddle through this weed, but the friction will reduce your travel speed.

Just about anywhere along this 5-mile stretch you can drag your boat through the weeds from the river to the canal, so that the possibilities of paddling loops are limitless. About the only place where portaging between river and canal is difficult is the stretch between the approach to the Route 378 bridge and the end of Sand Island Park. Not that it can't be done, but the distance of the portage measures several hundred feet, and crosses lanes of traffic. Furthermore, in the vicinity of Sand Island Park, portaging requires fording or boating across Monocacy Creek: not an exceptional burden as the water is seldom more than ankle deep.

It almost goes without saying that Sand Island Park is a popular access point, with parking available along more than half a mile of canal.

As noted above, the canal goes dry about a mile past Sand Island Park, and it remains dry for the next mile and a half. If you're paddling down the river and plan to do a loop up the canal, make sure you don't pass the end of the water zone or you'll have to portage farther than you bargained for.

The next downstream access is located at Monroe Street in Freemansburg. The half-mile stretch of canal upstream of Monroe Street has water that is barely deep enough to float a boat, and at times of drought may be impassable. I advise scouting this stretch before planning to paddle it. Downstream of Monroe Street the canal is fairly well flooded for nearly half a mile, at which point a makeshift dam prevents water from filling the remainder of the canal. At that point the overflow is channeled through a culvert under the towpath into the river.

To paddle a 2-mile loop, paddle upstream on the canal until you run out of water, portage to the river, and float downstream until you reach the obvious overflow channel: from the river it looks like a creek.

The towpath continues past the makeshift dam for nearly 4 more miles of dry canal.

The inlet gates for the canal are shown to the right. The Lehigh River is in the background. The black fence on the left surrounds the fish ladder. This is the beginning of five and a half miles of continuous waterway.

Below is the worst of the water weed. Most of the canal is free and clear of this frictional obstruction. An aqueduct carries the canal water over Monocacy Creek.

Lehigh Canal Section 8

Section 8: Glendon to Easton
Distance (total): 2.6 miles
Travel time: 1 hour (or 2 hours roundtrip)

Adversity level 1: Not challenging
Distance (runnable): 2.6 miles
Elevation differential: 10 feet

The Emrick Center in Hugh Moore Park houses both the National Canal Museum and the Delaware & Lehigh National Heritage Corridor. The park encompasses this entire section of the Lehigh canal system.

The canal and its locks exist in near perfect condition. Indeed, the canal looks as if coal-laden boats plied its waters only yesterday – or this morning. A pair of mules occupy a barn next to the fully-restored lock tender's house. During the summer, these mules walk the towpath and tow a tourist boat along the canal, giving passengers a feel of what it was like for boaters when the canal was the major artery for the transportation of coal from Mauch Chunk (now Jim Thorpe) via Easton to Bristol (along the Delaware Canal).

The grounds are groomed for picnickers, promenaders, bikers, and joggers. Although the park is located on the right bank of the river, entrance can be gained only from the left bank, over the 25th Street bridge.

The distance between the entry lock at the dam and the lift lock at the end is 2.4 miles. You can paddle back and forth without having to portage because there are no intervening locks. It's two more blocks to the end lock, but not worth the effort to portage and paddle.

If you want to do a river loop, launch your boat below the dam, float down the river, and take-out at the clearing on the right bank where the lift lock is located. It's only a hundred feet uphill to the lift lock, most of the way on a paved trail. Once you gain the canal, it's a pleasant and placid paddle on flat water to your put-in.

The towpath continues along the river for another mile, to the confluence with the Delaware River, at Easton.

MAJOR TRIBUTARIES

As the cliché goes, when it comes to tributaries there's good news and there's bad news.

The good news is that the Lehigh River watershed boasts a wealth of secluded streams that are seldom if ever paddled. Some of these streams can be paddled by canoe; others are so wild and woolly that they can be paddled only by kayak.

The bad news is that none of these streams is perennial. That is, under normal circumstances they don't hold the depth of water that will float a boat of any kind. I think of them wet rock gardens. It takes a severe rain event to flood these streams to the height at which they become runnable. And severe rain events seldom fall on or preceding weekends: the days on which most people are available to paddle. This is one reason that they are paddled less often than the Lehigh River.

Another reason for being less paddled is that very few paddlers know that these streams exist. Or, if they know of their existence, it never occurred to them that they could be paddled.

When I moved to Jim Thorpe, the only waterway that I had ever paddled in the watershed was the Lehigh River, and only between the dam and the train station, and only on the main channels. Subsequently, I made several trips in which I ran the secondary channels, "behind" the islands that dot the river.

But of tributaries I knew nothing. Nor was I acquainted with anyone who did. So I decided to learn about them on my own. Some I scouted; some I ran blind: that is, without knowing what challenges I would face until I met them. With my extensive background in wilderness canoeing, I knew that there was always a way around a stretch of water that was too uncertain to canoe. And I had ample experience in all the avoidance techniques: lining, dragging, carrying, and portaging.

Because I was running blind, and didn't know what obstacles I might encounter around a bend – deadfall, dropoffs, and waterfalls, to name a few – I adopted a policy of caution. Sometimes I decided against paddling a stream during extremely high water, and waited until the flowrate receded. I figured that it was better to scrape a few rocks or occasionally run aground than to get trapped against a logjam or swept over a height by fast current.

It was all a grand adventure of discovery!

Eventually I decided to share my knowledge of local streams with my fellow but unknown paddlers, so that they might learn what they were missing. In this regard I was somewhat mistaken.

Cheryl captured this picture of me portaging around Warnerville Falls on Tobyhanna Creek.

Major Tributaries

Shortly before completion of the present volume, I found that there was a small but select coterie of hardcore kayakers who already knew about some of these streams, and who paddled them whenever the water was up.

This was fortuitous, for they had paddled streams in a kayak that I couldn't paddle in a canoe. Therefore they were able to provide information and personal insights that I could not obtain for myself. My two sources in this regard were Nolan Berlew and Mark Zakutansky (whom I met in that order). Not only did they describe some of their tributary trips, but they informed me about streams that I had not thought were runnable (read: kayakable, not canoeable), and had decided not to assign to a chapter. Thanks to both of them.

What follows are mostly my personal insights with regard to streams that I canoed, or those that I scouted but decided not to run, plus some high-water descriptions from Nolan and Mark about streams that they and their companions paddled in the extreme.

Water's up!

Go Fish!

Fishing in the tributaries in the Lehigh River watershed can be a rich and rewarding experience for occasional and diehard anglers alike. The river abounds with trout, bass, and, below the dam in Allentown, muskellunge. Not to be excluded are fewer caught game fish such as walleye, carp, catfish, suckers, and eels.

The canals and reservoirs are loaded with pickerel, perch, sunfish, and panfish (sunfish, bluegill, crappies, and other species that are small enough to fit in a frying pan).

Native trout can be found in just about every tributary, even in tiny rivulets such as Keipers Run, Jeans Run, and Robertson Run, to name a few with which I have had personal experience. Remember the account that I related in the Introduction, about the trout that skipped across nearly dry land to get from one puddle to another.

How native trout ever got to this and other small streams that are inaccessible from the river, and manage to survive, I don't have a clue. But these hardy trout thrive in places that I would never have suspected until I saw them with my own eyes.

There are so many tributaries to the Lehigh River that I could never name them all. Then there are tributaries to the tributaries, and tributaries to those tributaries . . . I would venture to guess that there are more unnamed streams than those that are named.

Three well-known streams that didn't earn their own chapters are Hickory Run (in the eponymous State Park), Drakes Creek (near Unionville), and Catasauqua Creek (north of Allentown). After scouting them I determined that, for the most part, they were so dry and choked with boulders, logs, tree trunks, and other vegetative debris that only on rare occasions could short stretches become runnable. Yet I've seen streams that carry a fraction of their water and yet have fish living in them. Just a thought.

By way of segueing to the following tributaries, I once saw fish on the Pohopoco Creek leaping up the dam at Parryville. None of them made it over the top, but they reached at least three feet high, swimming furiously, before they were washed down into the pool by the flow. What kind of fish? You got me. All I know is that they were silvery in color. Their appearance was too evanescent for me to capture one on film. Perhaps video . . .

To recapitulate: fish live in nearly every stream. So, go fish!

TROUT CREEK

The water that creates this creek comes from a vast bog that is located north of Brady's Lake: a reservoir in State Game Lands Number 127. Two major streams flow south through this bog: Rauscher Run and Blexley Run. These streams meet at the north end of the impoundment. I presume that prior to construction of the reservoir (in 1907), the stream that results from the confluence of Rauscher Run and Blexley Run was named Trout Creek: this because Brady's Lake was originally called Trout Lake.

Be that as it may, so-called Brady's Lake is now a favorite fishing spot that is known for producing bass of all three species: large mouth, small mouth, and spotted. A concrete boat ramp is located at the south end of the reservoir, by the dam and parking lot. Kayakers and canoeists commonly paddle along the waterway when the air is calm, but most boaters are anglers who propel their craft by means of electric motors. The reservoir is nearly two miles in length.

As an added fillip, you can also paddle up the Rauscher Run bog. How far you can go is determined by depth, streamflow, and deadwood. There might be fish there that avoid the reservoir where most anglers troll.

Section 1: Brady's Lake dam to abandoned railroad bed
Distance: .6 mile
Travel time: 30 minutes

Adversity level 0: None
Perennial
Gradient: 3 feet per mile

You can thank a family of beavers for making this stretch of water deep enough to paddle. A beaver dam is located a handful of feet before the take-out where a railroad bridge crosses over the stream. This isn't the original railroad bridge, but a replacement that enables vehicles to drive across the creek and along the abandoned railroad bed to a parking lot farther north.

There are two ways to reach the put-in. You can portage your boat on the breast of the reservoir dam, or on the concrete extension on the downstream side, to the overflow outlet; in which case you can put-in on the left bank. Or you can launch your boat from

Brady Lake dam. The buoys warn boaters to stay away from the outflow valve.

Trout Creek Sections 1 and 2

Looking downstream at the bog from the lintel of the Brady Lake dam, to the right of the outlet.

the launch apron and paddle around the small island to the far side of the overflow outlet, beyond the fence, over the concrete breastwork, down the steps to the grass, thence to the right bank. The distance by portage is 200 yards; by water a quarter mile.

The lazy half mile to the take-out is a meandering route through a picturesque bog in which the current is too slight to be felt. You can't "go with the flow;" you have to paddle all the way. The water is clear enough to see the shallow, weed-covered bottom. Take note of the beaver lodge about halfway downstream.

Take-out on the right bank to the left of the other lodge before the railroad bed. Then portage or drag your boat through the weeds, into the gully, and up the other side.

The shuttle vehicle can be driven half a mile from the parking lot to the dirt road on the right, thence three-quarters of a mile to the parking lot by the railroad bed. Afterward, you can drive the vehicle on the railroad bed and across the bridge. Finally, you can continue on the railroad bed to another parking lot where you can turn around.

Alternatively, you can put-in at the take-out, then paddle upstream to the reservoir dam (and back) while puttering in a bog that few people ever see close-up. Paddle quietly, and you might catch sight of a beaver or two; or hear their tails slap the water at your approach.

Section 2: Abandoned railroad bed to Locust Ridge Road   Adversity level unknown
Distance: 4.0 miles (approximately)   Needs high water by observation
Travel time: Unknown   Gradient: 18 feet per mile (approximately)

I haven't paddled this stretch because it ends in an exclusive, gated housing development whose treatment of visitors is adversarial. The private community is known as Arrowhead Lake: actually an impoundment which non-residents are prohibited from crossing. Although the water is held in trust by the Commonwealth of Pennsylvania, the dam at the western end and the land that surrounds it are owned in common by the lot holders.

The length of the free-flowing portion of Trout Creek measures some two and a half miles. It passes through a pristine forest and extensive bog that can be accessed only by water. I hiked partway through the forested portion where the water was shallow and rocky but moving right along. The width averaged 20 to 25 feet. The stretch before the bog needs high water to make it runnable.

I spotted one large downed tree that spanned the streambed and would have to be portaged or carried . . . but the biggest obstacle is overcoming the wrath of Arrowhead Lake dwellers who inhabit the banks of the mile-and-a-half straightaway across the reservoir to the dam. Thus a beautiful stretch of water is lost to the paddling public because of a clique of a privileged few who probably don't appreciate it.

Section 3: Locust Ridge Road to the Lehigh River

Adversity level 2: Challenging
Distance: 1.8 miles (plus 4 miles to river take-out)   Needs high water by observation
Travel time: 30 minutes   Gradient: 80 feet per mile

One might be put off immediately by a gradient of 80 feet per mile: a streambed slope that is fearfully steep by anyone's standard. Yet this short stretch of water is eminently runnable because the streambed is almost perfectly flat: more like a swimming pool water slide for kids than a rough and tumble rapids that consists of tall drops and ledges.

The highest drop on the stream measures barely one foot at low water, and mostly disappears when the water is high. One sluice had two drops over a distance of ten feet, with a combined drop of two feet. Otherwise, the water flows smoothly and regularly with low standing waves that are fun to navigate.

The surrounding geological features are rocky and rugged. In some places the stream passes alongside sheer walls that rise twenty feet or more above the surface – but always with a flood plain on the opposite side. Elsewhere, steep slopes give the appearance of paddling through a deep ravine.

There are boulders the size of waste-paper baskets, but because the average stream width is 15 to 25 feet, there is plenty of maneuvering room to avoid them. The most challenging features are four downed trees that block straightforward passage. Yet each fully grown tree that spans the stream has fallen where a flood plain offers a ready-made platform for landing and dragging a boat around the obstacle.

After a mile or so the stream flows through a feature that looks like a bog. Hummocks the size of bushel barrels sport sprouting vegetation that grows to a height of two to three feet. The stream splits into a number of clearly defined channels that carve through the vegetative feature like the tines of a fork. Each channel measures from six to eight feet in width. The ways are clear of deadfall because the trees in the surrounding forest grow far back from the multiple waterways. My advice is to take the channels that carry the most water.

The fun is over all too soon. Trout Creek feeds into the Lehigh River. The previous confines of the streambed yield to open countryside, first of the "bog" and then of the river.

If your aim is to paddle only Trout Creek, hug the right bank of the river and beach your boat about a block past the confluence. If you bushwhack a couple of hundred yards through the forest, you'll find a broad clearing that can be accessed by vehicle along a dirt road that starts opposite the State forest parking lot on Old River Road. *But*, the uphill climb is long and steep, especially with a boat on your shoulders.

I recommend that you paddle four miles downstream to the take-out at Route 115. See Section 5 in the Lehigh River for details.

Trout Creek Section 3

Section 3 pictures

Above: A calm water area where a power line crosses the stream.

Below: One of the more dramatic geological features that makes this stretch worthwhile paddling.

TOBYHANNA CREEK

The Tobyhanna Creek originates in a massive swamp that is located east and southeast of Gouldsboro. The northernmost reach of this swampy region is part of State Game Lands Number 312. Rain that falls into this swamp flows into an area that is designated as Black Bear and Bender Swamps Natural Area.

It's hard to ascertain how far from the source the stream first becomes navigable. Disarticulated sections have a definite watercourse, although some of these may be too shallow to float a boat. Furthermore, these scattered sections are separated by concentrations of dense vegetation that might prevent through navigation.

The first stretch that is clearly navigable extends northward from the upstream end of Tobyhanna Lake: a reservoir in Tobyhanna State Park that is used for recreational purposes. The longest axis of the reservoir measures 1-1/4 miles. Its perpendicular dimensions measure anywhere from 1/8 mile to 1/2 mile. A 5-mile bike trail called the Lakeside Trail circumnavigates the reservoir. Canoes are available for rent for those who wish to paddle in the reservoir or reach fishing holes far from shore.

A dirt road crosses the northern end of the reservoir. The stream flows through a series of culverts under the road. A navigable waterway extends northward from the bridge but I don't know how far. Another stretch of navigable water can be seen from the Range Trail: a hiking trail that can be reached from either the Lakeside Trail or Route 196. I don't know if these two stretches are connected by navigable water; it would be interesting to try to connect them. Some navigable water exists upstream of the Range Trail, but how far is anyone's guess. Navigability certainly depends on the amount of recent rainfall.

Section 1: Route 423 to Route 611
Distance: 2.8 miles
Travel time: 1 hour

Adversity level 1: Not challenging
Needs high water by observation
Gradient: 18 feet per mile

I was pleasantly surprised to learn that this opening section of the Tobyhanna Creek had no deadfall, and that the few obstacles that it did have were simple to overcome.

Tobyhanna State Park is a wonderful place for a family outing. Summer activities include boating, fishing, biking, picnicking, and camping. Winter activities focus on ice fishing, snowshoeing, cross-country skiing, and snowmobiling.

Tobyhanna Creek Sections 1 and 2

The stream winds through some unspoiled and otherwise inaccessible landscape.

I started on the right bank downstream of the Route 423 bridge. The average stream width is 15 to 20 feet; the depth in the first mile was 3 to 4 feet. The water was so clear that I could see the bottom of grass and sunken leaves.

Two rock dams proved not to be an impediment as the drop of each was less than a foot. I hit them hard and drove my canoe right over them. Someone has built a footbridge across the water downstream of the rock dams. The builder created piers by piling flat rocks atop each other, then laying planks from pier to pier. The clearance is less than a foot, so you'll have to lay your boat against the bridge and drag it over the planks to the other side.

The stream curves alternately through closed forest and open bog until it reaches Leonard Lane. Anglers should note that a sign nailed on a tree upstream of the Leonard Lane bridge proclaims that only fly-fishing is permitted.

Afterward the stream broadens as it passes some large back yards, goes rustic, then enters Millpond Number One. (I have been unable to locate Millpond Number Two.) This broad and quiescent stretch of water extends for half a mile to a rock dam and railroad bridge at the southwest corner. The rock dam – or boulder dam, as the case may be – stands half a dozen feet above the water below. I ran my canoe on the rocks in the middle because the ends were broken down and might have carried the boat (and me) over the edge. I had to get my feet wet, but I had no problem in walking down the stepped boulders with my canoe in hand.

The stream then curves through another forested area to an official fishing hole that is reserved for children and handicapped adults. The short log dam past the parking lot looks challenging at low water, but at runnable water heights the drop is only a foot or so. Passage over the middle of the dam is blocked by the catenary of a cable that is stretched over top of it. I sneaked it on the right where the end of the cable was secured high enough to allow sufficient passage.

Pass under the pair of bridges and take-out on the right bank immediately downstream of Route 611. There's a parking space at that point to accommodate anglers.

This section is so close to the headwaters that it almost never has enough water to be runnable. Too bad, because it's a cute trip that I highly recommend for its beauty.

Section 2: Route 611 to Route 423
Distance: 3.1 miles
Travel time: 2 hours
Adversity level 3: Very challenging
Needs 600 % on the Tobyhanna (Blakeslee) gauge
Gradient: 40 feet per mile

I ran this section and the next one when the streamflow gauge in Blakeslee registered 450%. The reading had been higher, but I stuck to my philosophy that it was more prudent to explore an unknown stream when the water was too low than when it was too high; that dragging a canoe over shallows was preferable to being swept over a drop-off by the rush of fast current. In this case my cautious approach was over-careful. The water level was a bit too low for the conditions of the streambed.

I put-in on the right bank downstream of the Route 611 bridge. A pull-over fifty feet away is large enough to park a vehicle. As soon as I rounded the bend I scraped rock. I didn't go much farther when I ground to a halt. From that point onward, getting out of the canoe and dragging it over rocky shoals became an annoying routine. When the water was deep enough to float the boat, maneuvering around exposed boulders was a constant headache. Time after time I had to hump the boat off the rocks, or use my paddle as a pole to push myself free from entrapment.

Barely submerged rocks and large protruding boulders made for a long and laborious trip. Sometimes the shallows stretched from bank to bank – with an average spread of 20 feet – while other times deep water passed between boulders that were not spaced far enough apart to let a canoe fit between them.

The flow was constant but the current was not anywhere close to bowling me over.

About two-thirds of the way downstream I encountered a couple of logjams. I had to lift the canoe over the horizontal trunks. Pools were few and far between: a welcome relief after hard work that consisted of nearly as much poling as paddling: a slight but intentional exaggeration.

Despite the steep gradient, there were no ledges, cascades, or waterfalls. The incline was jagged but amazingly consistent: let's say consistently jagged. The drop in elevation increased over the last half mile. In places the boulders were arranged like steps, so that drops were spread out over suitable distances: I never had any difficulty in walking among the boulders in the middle of the stream with my canoe in tow.

The take-out is at the Route 435 bridge. The flow rate decreases at the approach of the bridge because the stream widens and levels. Headroom is adequate. Plenty of off-road parking is available beyond the shoulders.

This section is for boaters who enjoy the challenge of overcoming obstacles rather than the pure fun of paddling. A higher streamflow would have made my trip quicker and less physically demanding, but there are some stretches that can never be runnable because boulders stand a foot or two out of the water, and are spread haphazardly like a throw of jacks, with the boulders placed close enough to prevent the passage of a boat.

It took me almost as long to do Section 2 as it took to do Section 3, which is twice as long.

This picture will give you an idea of what the streambed is like in Section 2.

Tobyhanna Creek Section 3

Section 3: Route 423 to Route 940
Distance: 6.4 miles
Travel time: 2 hours

Adversity level 2: Challenging
Needs 600 % on the Tobyhanna (Blakeslee) gauge
Gradient: 22 feet per mile

The sole reason for the challenging adversity level is a long cascade or multi-level waterfall that drops around 18 feet over the length of a football field. Expert kayakers will love this stepped passageway; canoeists will have to drag, carry, or portage their boats a hundred yards over bedrock on either bank. The wise paddler will scout this cataract before putting-in at the bridge on Route 423.

On USGS topo maps, the cataract is designated anonymously as Falls. Local names for the cataract are Tobyhanna Falls and Warnertown Falls (the latter after a small community that used to exist on the highway). I favor the latter so as not to be confused with another small waterfall that goes by the name of Tobyhanna Falls in Section 5.

To reach the cataract by land, park in the large lot on the west side of Route 423, half a mile south of the put-in. Follow the trail for three-quarters of a mile to a T. Turn right, and proceed for a block to an X-shaped intersection. Do not take the sharp left or soft right; take the soft left onto what looks like an abandoned railroad bed. This level built-up roadway is actually the breastwork of an old earth and stone embankment which, according to a 1917 government publication, was called Wernertown Dam (spelled Warnertown Dam by other contemporary sources).

The dam measured 650 feet in length and stood 18 feet high. The dam created a reservoir that was 128.5 acres in extent. A summer resort occupied dry land around the reservoir. Rowboats plied the waterway in the summer. Ice was harvested commercially in the winter, by the Tobyhanna Creek Ice Company. Much of the surrounding property was owned by the Lehigh Coal and Navigation Company, which logged the area extensively. The timber was transported down the Tobyhanna Creek to furnish lumber for the construction of arks, or canal boats.

The breastwork extends straight as an arrow to the stream, where you will notice the partial remains of a concrete abutment and hear crashing water downstream to your left. Take the narrow path that follows the left bank for fifty feet to a long slab of bedrock.

The upstream side of this exposed bedrock is one of two portage take-outs. To study the cataract, walk on the bedrock for a couple of hundred feet. This is the same route to take with your boat. Put-in the pool next to the final drop-off. The four-foot drop into the pool makes for a difficult entry, especially for kayakers; you can carry your boat around the edge of the pool to where the drop-off is not as high.

A similar bedrock portage route exists on the right bank; it starts a little farther upstream in a slow-water spot that lies directly opposite the abutment. As you approach the cataract, steer to the right as soon as you hear crashing water or see the abutment, then slide into the slow water and clamber onto the bedrock. I entered this slow water by nosing into it and letting the canoe swing around as I kept paddling forward, thus turning the bow upstream.

The right-bank portage is a slightly longer and a little more difficult than the left-bank portage: to get out of your boat you have to clamber onto the ledge that stands two feet above the water; after you start the portage, you have to climb eight feet to a higher elevation; and you have to take a zigzag route around patches of vegetation. It's not as difficult as it sounds.

Tobyhanna Creek Section 3

This tinted postcard photograph shows how the cascade looked when the dam stretched across the streambed.

A recent photograph of Warnertown Falls. The kid in the bright orange shirt is fishing in the pool.

Warnertown Falls during a mid-winter freeze. The access trail is a great snowshoe trek. The pool could be good for ice fishing.

Tobyhanna Creek Section 3

The same pool that is noted above lies next to the final drop-off on the right side too, where the bedrock slants gradually into the water; this makes it easy to step into your canoe or slip into your kayak.

Don't fret if you miss the right-bank portage take-out; simply steer left and go for the left-bank portage take-out, which lies 50 feet farther downstream. The creek is only 20 feet wide at this point, so you should have enough time to ferry across. Even if you miss the left-bank take-out, the bedrock along the left bank slants toward the water, so you can run your boat aground before you reach the final cascade from which there is no return.

Despite my written instructions, I highly recommend that you scout this cataract from land, so you can visualize the various take-out locations and prepare yourself mentally for the hundred-yard dash around the cataract.

Maneuvers may be more challenging in super-high water.

I don't see any compelling reason why experienced kayakers can't run the cataract. Most of it consists of a long slide over smooth bedrock with a few bulges to make the descent interesting. The final drop ends in a pool of low froth.

After portaging my canoe, I paddled upstream to the base of the cataract and surfed the waves. I found a point of equilibrium where the force of gravity on the upstream side of the wave on which the hull was perched, was exactly as strong as the current that was tugging the hull downstream. In other words, the canoe was "falling" down the upstream side of the wave at the same rate at which the friction of moving water against the bottom of the hull was pulling it downstream. As a result of these equivalent but opposing forces, my canoe sat in the current as if it were anchored in place, without any assistance from my paddle.

The cataract is the only *major* obstacle in this section of the creek. Half a mile from the bridge (halfway between the put-in and the cataract) I encountered a *minor* obstacle that is not a rarity in small streams: a beaver dam. The timber dam stretched across a pinch-point where the banks lay only 15 feet apart. Fresh wood with newly chewed white ends indicated recent construction. I saw no lodges. The disparity in water levels above and below the dam was four feet.

The oddity of this dam was not its existence, but its nonexistence only two years previous. New construction of beaver dams can never be predicted.

I docked against the dam, stepped onto the top layer of sticks and saplings, snapped some photographs, then shoved the canoe over the dam and lowered it into the pool below. I marveled at this feat of civil engineering.

I noted in the previous section that a streamflow of 450% above normal was too low to permit continuous and unobstructed passage. However, although this section has a number of shoals and rock bars, it has no tight-fitting boulder fields like the previous section. I had to drag the boat half a dozen times or more, and I scraped bottom again and again, but for the most part I sped along with very little effort.

The gradient was consistent, the flow of water continuous. The fact that I paddled six miles in less than two hours speaks for itself. In several places the stream splits around large islands. The diversion of water means that each channel has a shallower depth and a slower flow rate.

If the water had been only an inch or two deeper, I could have floated over every shoal, and it would have made this trip a pleasure cruise without any hang-ups other than the beaver dam and the cataract.

The most attractive feature of this section is the sensation of remoteness. Other than an iron bridge at midpoint, and two subsequent powerline crossings, the Tobyhanna Creek carves an infrequently trammeled route through a wilderness tract that imbues a feeling of isolation: more so than many other game land preserves. (This is State Game Lands #127.)

High drop of the beaver dam.

With sufficiently high water, this section can be an incomparable paddling experience for boats of all kinds.

The current stops about half a mile before the take-out at Route 940, where the water is backed up by the downstream reservoir that is known as Pocono Lake. Stay in the middle, paddle through the opening where a railroad trestle used to cross, then steer toward the left overpass. Paddle under the highway and immediately turn left. Follow the narrow channel between the highway and the grassy peninsula until you reach three boulders near the end of the waterway.

The bank is too steep to carry a boat uphill. I climbed 10 feet up to the roadway with the nether end of the painter in hand, then used it to haul the canoe up to the shoulder, outboard of the guardrail. A convenient vehicle pullover lies a few feet away, alongside the eastbound lane.

The flood zone of the reservoir extends beyond Route 940, which cuts diagonally across the picture. Note the opening through the abandoned railroad bed at the extreme left. The yellow circle denotes the bridge over the waterway. The finger of water alongside the road leads to the take-out.

Tobyhanna Creek Section 4

Section 4: Route 940 to Route 115
Distance: 10 miles (approximately)
Travel time: Unknown

Adversity level 1: Not challenging

Probably needs 300 % on the Tobyhanna (Blakeslee) gauge
Gradient: 19 feet per mile (approximately)

I did not survey this section because it is completely surrounded by private property that is owned by unfriendly individuals. Large "No Trespassing" signs are accompanied by threats of prosecution, although such threats constitute rancid intimidation rather than the promise of due process. Nonetheless, the surrounding *property* is private if not the water that flows over it.

This section starts with an arm of a private impoundment that is called Pocono Lake Preserve. The reservoir drowned thousands of acres of forest to provide a hundred or so homeowners with a cloistered place to sail and motorboat without interference from the non-resident public. I tried to obtain information about Pocono Lake Preserve, first by visiting the roads that lead into the housing development, but I encountered the signs that I noted in the previous paragraph. Second, I visited its website. No information was available unless I created an account. When I tried to create an account, I was turned down because of color.

It is illegal in the United States to use racial discrimination to deny goods or services, but perhaps that law does not apply to private clubs or organizations. It's even illegal to ask a person about his or her race. When I spoke with people who lived in the area, I was told that the folks at Pocono Lake Preserve were extremely hostile and abusive toward visitors. Hikers who were found in the vast wooded areas that surround the development were accosted for trespassing.

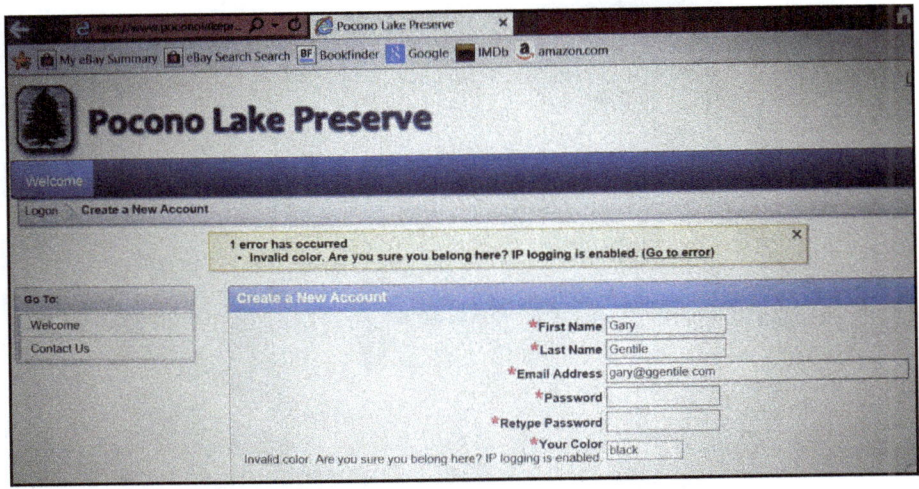

To create an account I was asked to provide my color. I was nonplussed because this had never happened to me. I typed "black" in the box. I received an error notice that read "Invalid color. Are you sure you belong here?"

Notwithstanding the above, boaters are within their rights to boat on the reservoir as long as they access the Commonwealth's water without crossing Preserve property. This can be done by launching from the Route 115 bridge, which is public property. However . . .

Tobyhanna Creek Section 4

By dragging an opisometer (map walker) across a map I ascertained that the shortest paddling distance from Route 940 to the dam that impounds the water measures 7 miles. The dam stands more than 20 feet high. A boat must be portaged across property that belongs to the Preserve. Portaging could pose a problem, which will be explained in full in Section 6. The bridge above the dam does not interfere with portaging.

Flowing water commences at the bottom of the dam, then twists and turns through verdant forest for 3 to 3.5 miles to Route 115.

Obviously there is no gradient on the reservoir. The gradient downstream of the dam to Route 115 is about 19 feet per mile. The streambed measures more than 50 feet in width, so that obstacles such as boulders and logjams do not present a problem for boaters.

This postcard picture of the dam is undated, but was likely taken early in the history of the Pocono Lake Preserve.

This recent aerial photograph of the dam shows the bridge that was built on top of it. Note that a narrow pedestrian walkway is separated from the vehicular roadway by a railing.

Tobyhanna Creek Section 4

A recent aerial view of the impoundment that is known as Pocono Lake Preserve.

An undated postcard picture of the Tobyhanna Creek downstream of the dam.

A recent photograph of the placid waters of the Tobyhanna Creek, a couple of miles downstream of the dam, and adjacent to a new housing development that is under construction and that welcomes visitors.

Section 5: Route 115 to Route 940
Distance: 1.7 miles
Travel time: 30 minutes

Adversity level 1: Not challenging
Needs 300 % on the Tobyhanna (Blakeslee) gauge
Gradient: 24 feet per mile

This section is short but fast and fun, and well worth paddling several times in one day. If you establish a shuttle with two vehicles, it's an easy matter to run this stretch, pack up your boats, and run it again – as many times as you want. The distance by road between put-in and take-out is only one tenth of a mile longer than the distance by water.

The put-in is located at the parking lot of the Austin T. Blakeslee Natural Area, which is conveniently situated next to the stream at the Route 940 bridge. At this point the banks stand about 40 feet apart. At a flowrate of 300 % you can see the rocky bottom but you can pass over it without scratching paint off the hull. And you can easily avoid any boulders that may be protruding.

A cascade is located slightly more than half a mile downstream. Hug the right bank and pull into the still water that precedes the cascade, then disembark. Caution: at flow rates above 500 %, the still water pool flows so fast that you might not be able to disembark before being swept away. Scout it first.

Drag your boat over the bedrock, then launch it into flat water some 40 feet downstream. The height of the cascade is about 8 feet.

This is a favorite hangout for those who hike the trails in the Area. I've watched people – that is, kids and teenagers – jump off the left bank into the top of the cascade and glide down the sloped rock as if they were on a sliding board. They did it over and over, and were having a great time.

I doubt that a canoe can survive the cascade without tipping over or swamping. Expert kayakers can probably run it, but in my opinion they should scout it first. At certain flowrates, there appears to be a protruding ledge off-center to the left that might present a problem.

One block downstream lies another cascade: one that is lower and longer than the first one. Kayakers: plunge straight through it. Canoeists: if you're uncertain about whether you can run it, pull into the pool on the right bank and either determine the best route to take, or drag your boat over the dry rock and launch it into the shorter rapids downstream. I found this cascade runnable at 300 %, but dicey above 600 % because the standing waves stood taller.

After this it's pure fun. Stay left of the island unless the water is high enough to cover the rocks in the right channel. The confluence with Tunkhannock Creek is located at the halfway point, a quarter mile downstream from the island. The additional water increases the flowrate, but not by much. The main flow passes between the next two islands (which lie side by side), but you can also take either the left or right channel. The left channel is narrow but unobstructed.

Avoid large boulders after the island, then pick you way through nearly continuous whitewater along the most favorable route, until the water flattens out after a couple of hundred yards. The last half mile is flat.

Keep left as you approach the Route 940 bridge. Pass under it, and take-out at the adjacent gauging station on the left bank. There's enough room to get a vehicle into the stub of a clearing for loading boats.

Then run it again!

Tobyhanna Creek Sections 5 and 6

Tobyhanna Falls

Section 6: Route 940 to the Lehigh River
Distance: 7.8 miles (plus 6.3 miles to the dam)
Travel time: 2 hours to the confluence (plus 2 hours to dam)
Adversity level 1: Not challenging
Gradient: 14 feet per mile
Needs 600 % on the Tobyhanna (Blakeslee) gauge

    This stretch would be a wonderful family outing were it not for the hostile and abusive harassment from members of a fishing club that owns some of the adjacent land: members who actively curse and threaten paddlers who pass through the area. Before you contemplate running this beautiful stretch of water, make sure to read the addendum that describes my personal experience with the Dream Mile Club.
    Put-in at the USGS gauging station on the left bank, downstream of the Route 940 bridge. This is the very streamflow gauge that is cited in the statistical sidebar. At this point the streambed is more than 50 feet wide. When the stream is minimally runnable, the water flows smoothly but not forcefully, and is so clear that you can see the rocky bottom as if you were sitting in a glass-bottom boat. It was this clarity that enabled me to see and recognize three ancient weir dams upstream of the club dam. At least half a dozen other submerged weir dams, all built of local rock, lie downstream of the dam. At low water, I saw all of them from the air when Christina Young took me flying over the Lehigh River watershed.
    This entire area was timbered in the 1800's, when it was owned by the Lehigh Coal and Navigation Company. At that time the weir dams raised the water level so that barges and log rafts could navigate the stream to the Lehigh River. Most of the wood was used on the canal system that existed on the river before the Civil War. Because the vast forest was clear-cut, all the trees in sight constitute second growth.
    Pass under the suspension walking bridge that spans the stream just shy of the 3-mile mark. A block beyond the bridge, carry around the low dam on either side. The rest of the way is clear paddling with no obstructing boulders or standing waves – just

fast flowing water that requires little more effort than steering.

The Tobyhanna Creek joins the Lehigh River at the Boy Scout camp known as Acahela. From there it's six miles to the Francis E. Walter Dam. See Lehigh River Section 6 for details. This would be a dream trip if it were not for the . . .

Dream Mile Club

As Cheryl and I paddled down this beautiful stretch of water, we were met with obnoxious stares and shouts of derision from two club members who were fly-fishing in waders near the right bank. We hugged the left bank so as to give them plenty of room. Nonetheless, both of them yelled that we had no right to be on this stretch of the creek. We didn't speak to the first one. He reeled in his line, turned toward shore, and hollered over his shoulder like a grade-school tattletale, "I'm gonna call the warden."

The second angler was even more hostile. He screamed that we weren't allowed here, and insisted stupidly that we go back upstream.

I said calmly, "We have permission to paddle here."

He wanted to know who gave us permission.

"The Pennsylvania Fish and Boat Commission."

"Well, you can't be here. I'm calling the warden."

By "warden" they didn't mean a fish, game, or prison warden, but a privately hired bouncer who had no official government affiliation. He was nothing more than a glorified gatekeeper whose only weapon was harsh language and intimidation, which, I was soon to learn, he wielded with uncommon abuse.

A few minutes later we saw a small group of men who were waving from the right bank. I smiled and waved back as I always did with sideline greeters. But they weren't waving to say hello to a fellow human being. As we got closer we saw that they were waving for us to come toward them. We did so naively. When we got to within shouting range, a man in a beige uniform (with short sleeves and short pants, looking more like a Boy Scout than a sergeant at arms) barked that we were trespassing on private property.

That wasn't true. We had entered the stream from a PennDOT bridge, and had not touched land anywhere along the way. We had stayed strictly on the public waterway.

The so-called warden motioned for us to land. As this was an invitation, I felt that the best thing to do was to accept and explain the lawful circumstances of our passage. What followed was a one-sided harangue that was overburdened with language that I cannot repeat in a family book, including words that pertained to perverse forms of baby making and avoidance. The warden was the loudest and most outspoken, but several the others carped at a lower decibel level.

The first thing they threatened to do was to call the police. They argued among themselves about who would have the honor. While I discoursed with the warden and one who happened to be a board member, about canoeing activity, they kept saying to each or one of the others, "Have you called the police yet?" No one reached for a phone.

I showed them a printout from the website of the Pennsylvania Fish and Boat Commission (which I always carried with me for just such an occasion, so I could show it to belligerent anglers and law enforcement officers who were not familiar with the law). I will discuss this matter more fully below, but in the instant case the relevant Frequently Asked Question was this: "Can a riparian landowner prevent the public from boating or floating in a non-navigable water?" (In this sense, "non-navigable

Tobyhanna Creek Section 6

water" referred to rivers and streams that had not been designated as commercial waterways; more on this later.) To which the authorized answer was, "No, because there's a 'navigation servitude' that gives the public the right to use the water for purposes of navigation only. This servitude does not extend to fishing."

They could see that there was no fishing gear on my person or in the canoe.

The warden went apoplectic, shouting at the top of his voice, "That's bullshit! That doesn't apply to us."

This holier-than-thou attitude was adopted by all the club members who were present. I mentioned that we had not trespassed on club property, but had only exercised our rights under the law of navigation servitude.

Throughout this "conversation" they kept threatening to the call the police and have us arrested. Now they added that they were going to prosecute us. At that point in my survey of seldom paddled Pennsylvania streams I was not as conversant with the finer points of the law as I am now. (Again, more on this below.)

Understand that I never raised my voice or used foul language. It's not my style. (My friends used to call me nonchalant Lamont.) I remained as calm as if I were conversing with reasonable, rational people, and not a pack of misguided stooges who thought that their wealth entitled them to benefits that "poor folk" like Cheryl and me didn't deserve.

We kept waiting for the police to arrive, but apparently no one ever called them, even though they kept reiterating, "We're calling the police," and "Did you call the police yet?" The overzealous warden kept ranting and raving, but it was all a bluff, straight out of Robert Ringer's book, *Winning Through Intimidation*, which I read in the 1980's to great personal advantage. The threat of arrest was nothing more than hand-waving.

Besides, even if trespassing were proved in court, it wasn't a felonious offense unless the trespasser damaged property or had intent to commit a crime. Otherwise it was nothing more than a minor violation, much like a traffic ticket, that resulted only in a fine. Of course, there was the inconvenience of appearing before a magistrate who, in all likelihood, would throw out the case on the grounds of navigation servitude.

In the meantime, despite the warden's constant maledictions and overt posturing, I discussed the situation in gentler language with the aggrieved board member. He explained that boating was against club rules, even for club members. So why couldn't I ask for special permission, I asked? He said that the board would never approve it. After further discussion of club rules, he and I decided that it would create less trouble for all parties concerned if Cheryl and I were to terminate our trip here and now. So that is what we did.

The outspoken warden was tasked by the board member with conducting the shuttle. The warden then became even more vocally violent, stating that club members paid a lot of money to have the convenience of fishing without intervention from underprivileged outsiders. The board member shrugged. As far as he was concerned, the situation was settled.

As information, the Dream Mile Club is a private organization whose assets are worth more than a million and a quarter dollars, and whose annual income exceeds one hundred thousand dollars. An Internet poster noted (verbatim with grammatical errors):

> "I have two friends that belong to the Dream Mile Club ,on the Tobyhanna Creek
> "$25,000.00 deposit ,$500.00 a year dues
> "Waiting list to get in !"

There Oughta Be a Law . . . And There Is

After the trip, I submitted a written report of events to the Pennsylvania Fish and Boat Commission. A Regional Supervisor of the Bureau of Law Enforcement confirmed in writing, "A term called 'Navigational Servitude' applies to this situation. A landowner cannot prevent a boat from floating through his property, but if you have to ford or walk on the stream bed you could be trespassing.

"This would be different for the Lehigh River which has been ruled navigable by the courts. Here a person can walk or boat between the high water marks of the river and not be trespassing. The Tobyhanna Creek may meet the same criteria, but has not been ruled on by a court of law.

"You must understand that even though you were not considered trespassing under the conditions of 'Navigational Servitude,' you could endure being cited, arrested, harassed or sued and have to defend yourself in a court of law."

The officer, whose name I must protect, also initiated a telephone conversation in which we talked at length not only about my incident with the Dream Mile Club, but about other situations with which the PFBC had to deal. With regard to the Little Juniata River, for example, the PFBC received so many complaints from boaters about being harassed by anglers of the Spring Ridge Club, which claimed that a mile-and-a-quarter section of the river was privately owned by the club, that the PFBC (among others) filed a lawsuit on the public's behalf against the Spring Ridge Club – and won. The court found that the waterway was navigable and therefore open to the public: all the public, not just those members who belonged to the Spring Ridge Club.

He told me that in most other instances in which riparian landowners called the police to arrest boaters on public waterways, the police refused to respond to the call, or to arrest alleged trespassers if they did respond. The reason: judges threw every case out of court. What was the point of arresting someone only to have the person found not guilty? (Understand that "arrest" in cases of trespassing doesn't mean shackled in handcuffs and carted off to jail. It means verifying a person's identity and sending him a letter in the mail, with information about when and where to appear in court.)

One thing that the officer made clear to me, by his attitude if not by specific wording, was that the PFBC advocated freedom of the waterways for the fishing and boating public. The law of navigation servitude is equivalent to federal aviation laws. An airplane is permitted to fly over private property as long as it doesn't land on it. By the same token, a boat may drift over a privately owned streambed.

The way the officer explained it to me went like this: although a streambed may be owned by a riparian landowner, the water that flows over it belongs to the Commonwealth of Pennsylvania. Therefore, the water is public property, and is held in trust by the Commonwealth for the enjoyment of all citizens.

This means that the Dream Mile Club had no legal right to prevent me from paddling next to or over club property. It's like walking past private property on the shoulder of a road. Trespassing doesn't occur until or unless you step on the actual property; being several inches away from private property doesn't constitute trespassing.

But . . .

There is a fly in this particular ointment. A couple of blocks downstream of where Cheryl and I took-out, there is a short dam that is topped by a road that enables club members to drive vehicles across the creek. Because the club owns the dam road, carrying a boat over it *could* constitute trespassing. I wrote *could* because this is a gray

Looking upstream at a weir dam (at the top of the picture), the walking bridge, the dam and roadway, and another weir dam.

area in Pennsylvania law: a case of conflicting laws – the law of navigation servitude versus the private property law.

The PFBC has no authority to arbitrate over such a situation. According to the officer, a decision on which law supersedes the other can be made only in a court of law, and perhaps on a case to case basis. So, although the warden had no legal right to stop us where he did, he might have had such a right when we carried over the dam road.

This begs the questions: What constitutes trespassing? And when is trespassing legitimate? You are trespassing every time you walk up someone's driveway or sidewalk to knock on the door. But you can't be arrested for it, or sued by the property owner. The courts might well view portaging the dam as a non-invasive action.

In follow-up correspondence, the PFBC officer wrote, "The dam on Tobyhanna Creek was placed there many, many years ago and therefore we have to live with it until it is gone. Dams and other water obstructions must now be permitted through DEP [Department of Transportation] and therefore those issues stated in your letter would be addressed through the permitting process. Any obstructions that are placed without permits would be dealt with through the 'Cleans [sic] Streams Law' and others for removal and possibly penalties provided by law. For clarification of the 'Clean Streams Law' please contact DEP."

Note how the dam has been constructed in such a way that water flows through pipes so small that they prevent the passage of boats.

This is not a case of passing the buck. Although the PFBC endorses freedom of Pennsylvania waterways, its authority is limited. Witness the Little Juniata River case. To obtain a ruling, the PFBC had to take the Spring Ridge Club to court.

So there you have it. Or do you?

Navigable Waterway

Now for a wrinkle in the fly's ointment.

I delved farther into pursuant legalities than the PFBC has possibly ever gone. And I unearthed an interesting fact that perhaps is little known. Or unknown. Or forgotten. Or ignored. Or suppressed.

First, to set the stage. According to one FAQ of the PFBC, "What makes a river, stream or lake navigable for legal purposes?" the answer is, "Waterways must be regarded as 'navigable in law if they are navigable in fact.' According to the United States Supreme Court in *The Daniel Ball* in 1870, waterways are 'navigable in fact' when they are used or susceptible of being used in their ordinary condition as highways for commerce over which trade and travel are or may be conducted in customary modes of trade and travel on water."

FAQ: "Does that mean that a waterway must currently be used for commercial purposes in order to be navigable?" Answer: "No. The test for navigability is not a contemporary test. It's a historic test that goes back to when William Penn was granted charter to Pennsylvania. Pennsylvania courts place particularly [sic] emphasis on a waterway's use during the late 18th and early 19th centuries – prior to the invention of modern modes of transportation and at a time when the only significant routes of travel, trade and commerce were on waterways."

FAQ: "What if a water that was used for commerce during the late 18th and early 19th centuries is no longer used for commercial purposes today?" Answer: "It doesn't matter. The test of navigability is rooted in its historical use."

Through research, I discovered that the 1915 edition of the Commonwealth of Pennsylvania's *Report of the Department of Fisheries, From December 1, 1913, to November 30, 1914*, published a list of "Free or Public Waters." That is, rivers or streams which, due to their use for commercial purposes, were declared public highways by an Act of the State legislature. Among them is the "Tobyhanna Creek, in the county of Monroe, from the river Lehigh to the junction of the Tunkhanna" (as the Tunkhannock was then called).

The property of the Dream Mile Club is located along this stretch. If you recall the Andrejewski case that I discussed in the Introduction, you will know that the streambed of any waterway that was declared a public highway is owned by the Commonwealth.

Understand, too, that the Tobyhanna Creek was used for commercial purposes by the Lehigh Coal and Navigation Company: the original owner of the property that is now owned by the Dream Mile Club. In fact, during my conversation with the club board member (and during the warden's histrionics), he talked about the history of the area and mentioned that club property had been commercially logged. Remember, also, that I saw weir dams as my canoe floated over them.

The Tobyhanna Creek was declared a public highway in 1838.

On non-navigable waterways, the public's rights extend only to boating and floating. But on navigable waterways, "The rights of the public in public waters are quite broad and extend to fishing, boating, wading, floating, swimming, and otherwise recreating."

Furthermore, "The Commonwealth's ownership extends to the ordinary low water mark, and the adjacent riparian landowner owns above the ordinary high water mark. An easement exists in favor of the public between the high and low watermarks. That easement includes the right to fish."

The PFBC advises "the public to stay as close to the water as possible or if they want to be safe [from trespassing] to stay in the water. If they don't venture on to upland properties, they'll be OK."

Now you have it.

The lower eight and a half miles of the Tobyhanna Creek have been designated by law as a public highway over which riparian landowners may not exercise control. The streambed between opposite low water marks is entirely open to the public. The dam and the roadway over it are an extension of the streambed. These facts are documented and can be presented as evidence in a modern court hearing. These precedential facts cannot be overlooked by a judge.

If the Dream Mile Club ever takes anyone to court, they're in for a rude awakening. Afterward, threats and intimidation will be nothing more than pointless harassment from disaffected club members who will be barred by court order from pestering boaters and anglers, all of whom have a legal right to recreate in the vicinity of the club's property.

The Club's dream mile will then become a nightmare for sanctimonious members, and an aspiration for the tax-paying public who will obtain a double benefit: unfettered access to a beautiful stretch of water, plus a way to paddle a section of the Lehigh River without having to portage around the Great Falls.

A page from the 1915 edition of the Commonwealth of Pennsylvania's *Report of the Department of Fisheries, From December 1, 1913, to November 30, 1914.*

DATE OF THE ACT.	RIVER OR STREAM DECLARED A PUBLIC HIGHWAY.
1815, March 13. Law Book XV, p. 314, P. L. 181.	Tioga river, from the line of the State of New York to Peter's Camp, in the county of Tioga.
1838, April 16. P. L. 591, ...	Tobyhanna creek, in the county of Monroe, from the river Lehigh to the junction of the Tunkhanna.
	Toby's (or Toby) creek. See Little Toby's creek.
1798, March 21. Law Book VI, p. 245.	Toby's creek, from the mouth of the second fork.
1851, April 14. P. L. Vol. 39, Appendix p. 716.	Tomb's run. Slate or Tomb's run, in the county of Lycoming from its connection with Pine creek, six miles up said run.
1859, April 11. P. L. 506, ...	Tomb's run emptying into Pine creek, in the county of Lycoming, to its sources.
1816, March 19. Law Book XV, p. 572, P. L. 182.	Tombicken creek, a branch of Cattawissa creek, from its mouth to the line of a tract of land patented to Jeremiah Warder, Jeremiah Parker and Richard Parker, called Turn Hick.
1813, March 26. Law Book XIV, p. 1, P. L. 189.	Towanda creek, in the county of Bradford, from the mouth thereof up the main branch to Spalding's mills.
1826, April 10. Law Book XX, p. 412, P. L. 343.	in Bradford county, from the mouth thereof up to the mouth of Roger's creek.

UPPER TUNKHANNOCK CREEK

More of this stream's length is impounded than free-flowing. The name is applied downstream of a reservoir known as Stillwater Lake, which is fed by Dotters Run and Hawkey Run, both of which originate in a large tract of forest to the north. The land that surrounds Stillwater Lake is a Boy Scout camp known as Camp Minsi.

After the dam at the southwestern corner of the reservoir, the stream flows for a mile through a heavily treed housing community into Lake Naomi: a huge private impoundment that measures nearly two miles in length. The dam at the western end stands some 10 feet in height. Water that flows over the dam then becomes an unbridled stream. About 100 feet downstream of the dam, the creek flows under Route 423.

Only section: Route 423 to Route 940 (or beyond) Adversity level 3: Very challenging
Distance: 1.0 mile (approximately)
Needs 500 % on the Tobyhanna gauge
Travel time: 20 minutes or less
Gradient: 77 feet per mile (approximately)

This stream is for kayakers only! When I first saw this creek it was during its normal flow rate. I scoffed, and struck it off my list of runnable streams. It looked more like a wet rock garden than an actual stream. Yet after a significant rainfall it becomes a raging torrent that presents a short but thrilling ride for kayakers.

I walked partway downstream from Route 423. I saw enough to convince me that the creek was not for canoeists: not because of boulders but because of huge standing waves and deep engulfing troughs.

I can't really describe a stream that I haven't seen except from intersecting roads: Church Road, Old Route 940, and Stoney Hollow Road. Yet the view from these intersections gives a fairly accurate picture of the stream's remarkable whitewater. Intermittent events, such as a dam upstream of Church Road, and a 2- to 3-foot drop downstream of Old Route 940, enlarge the picture. The dam appears to be about 5 feet in height, with enough water flowing over the lintel to carry a kayak over the lip.

Take-out at Route 940. There's another half mile of exciting whitewater, but then the stream flows into the backwash of Pocono Lake: a private reservoir that impounds Tobyhanna Creek. After the whitewater subsides in the flatwater of the reservoir, you would have to paddle about a mile and a half to the Tobyhanna take-out at a different spot on Route 940: a high price to pay for a short amount of enjoyment.

Upper Tunkhannock Creek Only Section

Above: Put-in below the bridge next to the rocks on the left bank (bottom left of the picture).

Opposite page: Looking upstream at the dam from the Route 423 bridge.

Below: A kayaker's delight: rough water, ledges, and barely submerged rocks.

TUNKHANNOCK CREEK

This stream is not to be confused with another one of the same name northeast of Scranton: one which flows into the Susquehanna River in the borough of Tunkhannock.

This stream originates in an unnamed swamp. Accumulated water strains through marsh weed until a narrow passage is formed. The upstream portion of the swamp is inaccessible. Some dirt roads exist in the area, but none approach the water's edge, and all are gated to prevent vehicular passage.

The Tunkhannock Creek is a tributary of the Tobyhanna Creek. The former joins the latter less than a mile from the take-out on Route 940. See the Tobyhanna Creek chapter, Section 5, for take-out-details.

Section 1: Hypsie Gap Road to Kuhenbeaker Road Adversity level 2: Challenging
Distance: 0.9 mile Perennial
Travel time: 20 minutes Gradient: 6 feet per mile

I am separating this short stretch from Section 2 only because it contains some deadfall and a small dam that prevent clear and unobstructed passage: obstacles that some paddlers might prefer to avoid. The attraction of this stretch is that the stream flows through a pretty pristine area that is seldom if ever seen.

The water is flat and possesses a slight flow throughout the year. Hypsie Gap Road passes over the stream on a cute and quaint stone bridge that is double-arched. A hundred feet from the left bank is a dirt road that extends a quarter mile to a dam and associated brick building. Park at this intersection on the edge of either road but do not block the gate in front of the dirt road. Put-in on the left bank upstream of the bridge.

If you are put off by the minimal hindrance that is presented by deadfall, ignore this section and go straight to Section 2. (Do not pass Go, do not collect $200.) I ran this section when the streamflow gauge near Long Pond registered 750%. The water was high but the current was mild: the latter situation occurring because the downstream area is a marsh in which the excess water overflows the narrow channel and submerges the adjacent marsh weed. This was fortuitous: the high water enabled me to paddle around a downed tree by passing over the bank that would ordinarily not be deep enough to float a canoe; otherwise, I would have had to fight my way over the tree: an act that would have been difficult due to the depth of the water, which was 3 to 4 feet. The depth would have prevented me from standing and obtaining firm purchase on the bottom for lifting the canoe over the tree; plus it would have made it difficult for me to get back into the boat. At normal depth these issues may not present a problem.

Several fallen saplings also stretched across the channel, but I was able to push through them. At one point I had to force myself through a phalanx of encroaching alders. These deadfall antics increased the workload but were not otherwise obstructive.

The dam proved not to be an obstacle. It was a fat metal pipe that was laid perpendicular to the current. I floated right over it; the drop was only a few inches.

I paddled under the bridge at Kuhenbeaker Road, then took-out on the left bank immediately after I emerged from the overhead. This is the put-in for Section 2.

Tunkhannock Creek Section 2

Section 2: Kuhenbeaker Road (SR 4001) to Long Pond Road   Perennial
Distance: 7.1 miles   Adversity level 0: None
Travel time: 2 to 3 hours (more if you dawdle or fish)   Gradient: 5 feet per mile

If you look upstream from the bridge on Kuhenbeaker Road, you will see a stream of water that measures some 5 feet in width. When the stream reaches the bridge, it broadens to 15 to 20 feet, and from that point onward is seldom narrower and never unnavigable. The banks are indeterminate due to the thick edging of marsh weed.

Park in the fire-lane entryway a hundred feet south of the bridge but do not block the gate. Put-in on the left bank on the downstream side of the bridge, partially under the bridge. Proceed downstream over marsh weed which is bent over by mild current. This twisting narrow passage is the gateway to the aptly named Long Pond.

I call the Long Pond section of the Tunkhannock Creek perennial because I first paddled it during a time of extreme drought, when all the other creeks in the Lehigh River watershed were walkable but not runnable, including Tunkhannock Creek downstream of Long Pond. Flow may be moderate or barely perceptible. Water depth is several feet: never shallow enough to touch bottom with keel or blade.

An open water channel snakes through bordering marshland like a short-frequency sine wave. In addition, thick marsh weed that is barely awash clots the banks. In some places weed, water lilies, and small pond lilies stretch completely across the waterway so that passing over the mass of vegetation is unavoidable; in other places a narrow but clear channel winds from side to side between the banks, like a channel inside a channel. You can easily paddle over the vegetation but the friction will reduce your speed and efficiency. It is less tiring to follow the clear channel.

Because of all these squiggles within squiggles, the straight-line distance from put-in to take-out at Long Pond Road is significantly different from the actual paddling distance. The straight-line distance from bridge to bridge is 3 miles; the northern road route is 4 miles; the paddling distance is 7 miles.

The Uncle Wiggly route to Long Pond. Watch out for the Skeezicks!

Peninsulas of foliage extend from tree-lined banks of high ground into the watery expanse. Mats of vegetation create islands. Keep following the clear (or clearest) channel through this green fairyland. You can't get lost despite the broad width from bank to bank.

Beaver dam in the middle of a squiggle.

About one-third of the way downstream lies the only permanent obstruction: an active beaver dam. When we approached the dam, one beaver slapped its tail loudly against the surface of the water as it dived out of sight. Immediately another one surfaced from beneath the downstream side of the dam, clambered over the top, and slunk into the pond of its own making.

A small rivulet of water was passing over the right side of the dam. We rammed it hard and got hung up. We "humped" the canoe forward. I had to crawl to the bow of the boat and hump, while Cheryl poled against the dam. We slid free without damaging the wooden structure. The dam was less than a foot in height.

The channel continues southward, turns toward the west, then turns north as it enters the broadest area of the pond. At this point the trees that grow on the surrounding landmass are more than half a mile apart. The waterway between standing marsh weed is very broad, but again it is easier to proceed along the cleared and convoluted channel that is relatively free of marsh weed but which may harbor stands of lily pads and small pond lilies, whose multicolored leaves and either white or yellow blossoms contrast sharply with the lavender hues of tall pickerel weed.

A pair of eagles ignored us as they soared on thermal air masses in their endless quest for prey.

After a while the cleared channel grows so wide that you might wonder which way to proceed. Rule of thumb is to look into the dark water and go where the submerged marsh weed points. Even without any noticeable flow, the individual blades have assumed a permanent "bend," pressed downcurrent by the constant passage of water. These pointers will lead you around and through the floating islands of vegetation.

The grandstands of the Pocono International Raceway will come into view, will be blocked by the forest on the horizon, then will come into view again before passing out of sight for good. Keep following the circuitous route as it approaches the right bank. About three-quarters of the way from the put-in you will pass some backyards and see the boats of homeowners. After veering westward the channel turns north and the Long Pond Road bridge will come into view.

If you plan to terminate your trip here, take out on the left bank before passing under the bridge. This service road is used by county fire engines of the pumper variety to fill their tanks from the creek. Note the tall white standpipe whose nether end is submerged. A closed and locked gate keeps unauthorized vehicles from driving to the

Tunkhannock Creek Sections 2 and 3

Long Pond with the race track in the distance.

water's edge. Either portage your boat 500 feet along the road, then lift it over the fence, or drag the boat up the steep embankment to Long Port Road and a waiting vehicle.

We did a single-vehicle shuttle by leaving a bicycle at the take-out – I cabled the bike to the utility pole adjacent to the standpipe – then I pedaled 4 miles along the northern route to the put-in and retrieved the vehicle.

Section 3: Long Pond Road to Tobyhanna Creek   Adversity level 3: Very challenging
Distance: 8.2 miles (plus .8 mile to take-out)   Needs 500 % on the Tobyhanna gauge
Travel time: 3 hours (less for kayaks)   Overall gradient: 36 feet per mile

I can best describe this 8-mile stretch as a 3-hour adrenalin rush.

This stretch of the Tunkhannock Creek can look deceiving if you see only the put-in or take-out, where the water flows fast but appears flat and calm, with a surface that's as smooth as a baby's butt.

When I first set out to run this section after a storm dropped 3 to 5 inches of rain, I stopped at Hemming Road on my way to the put-in. Good thing I did, because what I saw made my stomach flutter, and made me beg off the trip. The Tobyhanna Creek streamflow gauge was registering a flow rate that was 1,100 % above normal. At that level, the water was racing so fast along the banks above the 4-foot wooden dam downstream of the condemned bridge that it would have been impossible to land and portage around the raging drop-off without getting swept over the lip to my doom.

And the creek was still rising! By the next day it was up to 1,600 %! Great for kayaks; death for canoes. Let me 'splain.

This section should actually be two sections: one half from Long Pond Road to Hemming Road, and one half from there to the Tobyhanna Creek (thence to the take-out three-quarters of a mile downstream). But "no trespassing" signs are posted all around the condemned bridge and the left bank of the stream. I don't know if the signs refer to the land on the other side of the bridge, or to water access. I paddled straight through this halfway station.

Note that the overall gradient in the statistical sidebar is 36 feet per mile: accurate but deceiving. The upper section (which I will call Section 3a) has a gradient of 28 feet per mile, while the gradient for Section 3b is 44 feet per mile. The difference is interesting but does not materially affect the navigability between the two sections.

In fact, Section 3a is much more frustrating to paddle than Section 3b. Here's why:

Section 3a starts at Long Pond Road where the stream is wide and inviting. Within a couple of hundred yards the width shrinks to an average of 15 feet for the rest of the way to the Tobyhanna Creek. In some places the width expands to 20 feet, and rarely to 25 feet, but it also decreases in many places to barely 10 feet. The reduction is partially due to rhododendron thickets that grow inward from the banks so that water flows under the branches but the actual navigable width is restricted by those branches.

Section 3a measures 4.2 miles. Along that length are several downed trees, two logs, two low walking bridges, and two steep ledges or drop-offs. At a streamflow of 578 % above normal, I was barely able to duck under the downed trees and low bridges by curling flat over the center thwart. This would not have been possible had the water been higher. Kayakers take note.

I was able to get over the logs with difficulty. The water was so deep that I couldn't touch bottom in either case.

The first log was fat enough for me to balance on it as I dragged my boat over top of it. The second log was so thin that I had to straddle it with my legs in the water as I hefted the canoe onto it. The fast current was a hindrance as it swung the nether end sideways against the log. Dense brush on the banks prevented carrying around the logs. At higher water, these logs would have been submerged.

The ledges that could have been run by kayak had to be lined by canoe. The first ledge was bordered by rock banks on either side. I stepped out of the canoe into knee-

Forgive me for showing only the ledges in this section, instead of the pristine beauty of the stream, but this is information that paddlers need to know. This is ledge number one.

Tunkhannock Creek Section 3

deep water near the left bank, and held onto the boat as I pondered my options. The ledge did not consist of a sheer drop on the downstream side. it was sloped at about a 45 degree angle. And the water was shallow because the ledge was so wide.

Although it was counterintuitive, the best place to climb down the ledge was in the middle of the stream. Nor did I have any trouble in walking the canoe through the shallows: the force of the current was mitigated by the spread of the water. I then walked down to the midstream pool.

A hundred yards later I reached the condemned bridge and the succeeding drop-off. The bulk of the current flowed along the left bank, so I backpaddled along the right bank under the bridge to the top of the drop-off. A kayak could have charged right over the ledge. I stepped into the water and precariously walked and lined the boat into the lower level water.

End of Section 3a; beginning of Section 3b.

The drop-off at Hemming Road. At low water you can see that this drop-off constitutes the remains of an ancient dam that was made of timbers which resemble railroad ties.

Despite the much steeper gradient, Section 3b is less challenging and a lot more fun than Section 3a because it lacks deadfall. The only downed tree on this section I was able to avoid by passing left and ducking under an overhanging branch. You can't duck under the branch at higher water, but the left-bank gravel bar will be flooded enough to enable a boat to pass six feet beyond the end of the branch.

This section is a 4-mile straight shot for paddlers of all kinds. There was one ledge that I had to portage that a kayak can run right over. Its downstream side is sloped; water cascades into a hole and through a tall standing wave that would instantly swamp a canoe. I dragged my boat through the woods for 30 feet, along the right bank.

My most daunting issue was the apprehension, perhaps even anxiety, which I felt in facing the unknown. The whole stream sashays like the proverbial drunken sailor, with few straight stretches where you can see what's coming. There were a number of sharp, blind turns where rhododendron thickets blocked the view downstream. My level of disquiet rose at each blind turn; I wondered if I was charging into a logjam or drop-

Ledge number 3 doesn't look like much from this perspective, but at this flow rate it appeared to me that the bow of my canoe might be overwhelmed by the standing waves at the bottom of the drop. Because I was alone I let caution be my guide . . . but I really wanted to run it.

off that would spell disaster. None did. But that knowledge came only in reflection of past events.

Every once in a while I could see a hundred yards downstream. Then I could actually observe the steep incline: it was like looking down a slanted board. I took comfort in beholding continuous whitewater with waves no higher than a foot or so. All I had to do was to pass through them on the perpendicular and backpaddle slowly. The boat bounced more than a roller-coaster. It was exciting.

Occasionally I could spare a moment to look away from upcoming waves, and absorb the splendor of a pristine forest that was seldom seen by human eyes. Great hemlocks and thick oak trees provided shade for the moss and ferns that grew sparsely on black topsoil. One deer was startled by my approach.

The streambed eventually flattened out. I spotted some paths and ATV trails, even a few picnic benches. They denoted the end of the outback. Then came the twin bridges of Interstate 80. Half a mile later I reached the Tobyhanna Creek. Avoid the right channel at high water because there might not be sufficient space to duck under the tilted log. The left channel is wider and unobstructed.

I was back in civilization. Sigh . . .

Some final words about streamflow. The only time my blade touched bottom on Section 3a was at the first cascade, where it spread across the bedrock and enabled me to stand in the mild current. Thus a flow rate less than 500 % is not only runnable, but for canoeists perhaps welcome.

I ran aground a couple of times near the end of Section 3b, upstream of the Interstate. I was able to hump the boat off the gravel bars with ease, but at a lower flowrate I would have had to drag the boat to deeper water – but not more than a few feet. Other gravel bars might appear at a lower flowrate: perhaps a small price to pay for reducing the speed of the current and enjoying the trip and the sights more fully.

BEAR CREEK

Bear Creek starts its long winding course in a vast tract of wilderness terrain that is tucked into the northern quadrant of the Lehigh River basin: an area that is part and parcel of Pennsylvania State Game Lands #91. The height-of-land encloses three sides of the headwaters: Bald Mountain to the west, Big Shiney Mountain to the north, and Little Shiney Mountain to the east.

A number of named tributaries feed into Bear Creek: Red Run, Mud Run Creek, Meadow Run, Little Bear Creek, Tenmile Run, and Shades Creek. Scores of unnamed tributaries also contribute water.

Bear Creek is dammed twice along its way to the Lehigh River. The uppermost dam is located only half a mile from the stream's first appearance, where water seeps through the ground into a bog. At first glance the dam appears to have been built by beavers. Two lodges and numerous beaver-chewed trees surround the impoundment. From a distance, tall grass on the dam obscures its construction features. But close examination reveals a metal grate in the middle, and an outlet culvert below the earthworks. Thus what is mistaken for a quarter-mile-long pond is actually an old reservoir with a circumference of nearly a mile.

After flowing through forest for a couple of miles, the stream enters a broad bog that measures more than a mile in length. Four miles later, after twisting and turning through unreachable woodland, the stream flows into a second reservoir where water is backed up for nearly a mile. This reservoir is called Bear Creek Lake: the centerpiece of a housing development. It is after this dam that Bear Creek occasionally becomes runnable.

Only section: Route 115 to the Francis E. Walter Dam
Distance: 6.4 miles
Travel time: 2 hours
Gradient: 32 feet per mile
Adversity level 2: Challenging
Needs 400 % on the Lehigh (Stoddartsville) gauge

First let me state that this is an absolutely beautiful stream. The first half of its length is reminiscent of an artist's painting of hinterland America in Colonial times. Trees of all species line moss-covered banks to provide shade as well as a pristine forest whose black topsoil is covered with ferns. The surrounding land is practically devoid of civilization.

Put-in on the left bank downstream of the bridge, behind the utility pole, by pushing through the weeds down to the water. In the first quarter mile you'll see a restaurant and several houses. After that, the only sign of human habitation is a walking bridge with plenty of headroom, at the three-quarter-mile mark.

Three downed trees and three sharp ledges mar the way, plus one potential catastrophe lies in waiting. Note that the overall gradient is punctuated by sudden drops between long stretches of fairly level water.

At a water level that is convenient for canoes, you can duck under the first tree by skimming along the left bank. You can pass over the second tree limb in the middle of a dogleg. And you can squeeze through a narrow right-bank channel at the third one. Then come the ledges. The first one lies a hundred feet beyond the utility easement: a 4-footer that you must hit perpendicular to the direction of flow. A 3-footer lies three-quarters of a mile farther downstream, followed closely by a 2-footer.

Then comes the big mama: the largest, longest, most vicious cascade in the entire Lehigh River watershed, consisting of a series of identifiable ledges at low water, or tremendous combers at high water, with two large trees that are caught on the rocks and that make passage more interesting. Only a picture can describe it with justice.

Canoeists are strongly advised to carry over the dry ledges that extend from the right bank. You can see this cascade from the bridge on White Haven Road.

After the bridge there's another mile or so of flowing water (and exciting rapids) before Bear Creek meets the backwash of the reservoir when the water is stored at the summer level. Take care at the ledge on the curve to the right, a block beyond the bridge. It might be wise to carry around it.

Note the left entrance of Shades Creek a quarter mile below the bridge.

At the lower winter level, you might get an extra mile or so of flowing water.

Take-out on the right side of the dam. The paved road is reserved for boat trailers. Pass the road and go another 50 feet to the gravel beach where there is room to park a dozen vehicles. In wintertime, cross to the other side of the reservoir and land on the long stony beach where vehicles can drive practically to the water's edge.

That's Bear Creek in a nutshell, but there are some things you should know in order to have a better understanding of this fun-to-paddle stream. First the streamflow. It is possible to run Bear Creek when the Lehigh River gauge at Stoddertsville registers 400 %, but it's better at 500 % because you won't scrape any rocks. At that level the water doesn't move so fast that you can't stand in the shallows. This makes self-rescue a matter of wet routine.

At super high levels – say, over 1,000 % – canoeists need to be truly expert paddlers. Even though the ledges wash out, the water flows fast so that the downed trees become hazards unless the water is deep enough to go over them. In this case, Bear Creek is best left for kayaks and covered boats.

The overall gradient in the statistical sidebar is somewhat misleading. I couldn't obtain a whole-creek gradient because one third of the streambed is normally impounded. When I used the dam outflow as the end elevation, I calculated an inclusive gradient of 52 feet per mile. This implies that the steepest gradient exists in the part of the reservoir that is always inundated.

I calculated two other gradients. From the put-in to the bridge at White Haven Road the gradient is 28 feet per mile. Much of the water drops suddenly over ledges, so that the rest of the water flows comfortably at less of an incline. From the bridge to flatwater the gradient is 47 feet per mile – yet, except for the 4-foot drop at the right turn below the bridge, the water flows smoothly and consistently through thrilling whitewater.

I heartily recommend Bear Creek for canoeists who enjoy a few obstacles on an otherwise secluded trip. And I just as heartily recommend it for kayakers who wish to

Bear Creek Only Section 127

Practically dry. Do not try to paddle Bear Creek when the water is this low, or you'll spend most of your time towing your boat over exposed rocks.

Medium high (540 % on the Stoddartsville gauge). I ran Bear Creek at this level, and carried my boat over the dry ledges along the right bank (on the left side of the picture).

Super high (1,100 % on the Stoddartsville gauge). This is what the cascade looked like two days before I ran it. I didn't know about conditions on the upper stretch; plus it looked as if I might have trouble doing the carry. Better safe than sorry.

Where fast water meets slow, where the banks spread wide, and where the streambed is buried by backwash. This is the typical summer level of the reservoir. Note the jeep road at the bottom left of the picture: a perfect place to take-out if you want to avoid most of the flatwater. Except at super high water levels, boatless anglers can cross the stream where the water is still flowing, if they wish to fish from the opposite shore.

challenge themselves in big water that requires constant attention and great expertise.

It's possible to avoid some or all of the two-mile stretch of flatwater. A path of sorts exists at the point where the water ceases to flow (in summer). I warn you, however, that this path was groomed by an imported mountain goat who didn't have to carry a boat on its shoulders.

White Haven Road closely follows the northern portion of the banks of the reservoir. Shortly after the road veers away from the reservoir, you'll note a gravel jeep road to the east, where the land bulges into the impoundment. This is an excellent take-out if you don't want to paddle all the way to the dam. This take-out knocks off about a mile and half of flatwater.

Originally the jeep road was intended to lead to a boat launch, but the projected launch site and parking lot were never constructed. It's two blocks from the take-out to the highway, but you can drive a vehicle down the gravel road, turn left, and drive down to the flat area where you can turn around and park. Now you have to carry your boat only a hundred and fifty feet from the water's edge to the flat area.

A quarter mile farther downstream there's another take-out on the right. The portage trail is not steep but it's more than a block in length. A parking area is located at the top of the trail on the other side of the road. Be careful when crossing the road with your boat.

You might not recognize either of these take-outs from the water. It's best to scout them in advance from the road, then walk down the trails in order to see what they look like from below.

Bear Creek – put it on your to-paddle list. You'll be glad you did.

TENMILE RUN

This little stream drains a bog some two and a half miles upstream of the put-in (but only a mile and a quarter as the crow flies). It's little more than a runnel when it passes under Laurel Run Road. In fact, it's not much more than that at the put-in, on Route 115 (Bear Creek Road), unless flash flood warnings are in effect.

I would never have included a chapter about this stream if Mark Zakutansky hadn't told me that he had paddled it. So for all you expert kayakers out there, I walked it in order to log the distance from which to calculate the gradient. Canoeing is a possibility that I have considered but not yet done.

Only section: Route 115 (Bear Creek Road) to White Haven Road

Distance: 2.1 miles
Travel time: 1 hour

Adversity level 3: Very challenging
Needs very high water (by observation)
Gradient: 97 feet per mile

The put-in is located two miles northwestward along Route 115 (Bear Creek Road) from the take-out at the T junction from which White Haven Road extends southward from the dam that creates Bear Creek Lake. Put boats in the water downstream of the tunnel.

The average width of the stream is 15 to 20 feet. The streambed is largely flat bedrock with no large boulders and few loose rocks to obstruct passage. Those rocks that do exist are scattered, and are small enough to be submerged by only a foot of additional water. The rocky banks are unusually clear of vegetation. Only two logs stretched across the stream, at which points the banks were low and without vegetation to block a carry on either side.

A waterfall that provides excitement for kayakers and a headache for canoeists.

A long series of stepped ledges downstream of the waterfall.

The only major obstacle is a 10-foot-high waterfall about a quarter mile below the put-in. The next hundred yards consists of a series of stepped ledges. A canoe can be portaged left around the waterfall, then either run over or lined down the ledges. From there on it's clear paddling except for a 10-foot slide under the third of three walking bridges a mile from the put-in. Otherwise the slope of the streambed is amazingly consistent. The last half mile tends to be rockier, but the rocks should be submerged at high water levels. The stream is curvy but without blind hairpin turns, so you can always see what's coming in time to maneuver.

The most unusual feature is the increasing height of the right bank after the waterfall. The land remains largely level for half a mile or so while the streambed and left bank trend downhill, until a nearly vertical rock wall rises more than a hundred feet above the water.

Tenmile Run meets Bear Creek where the creek is a narrow channel but the water is part of the backwash of the reservoir. It's a mile and a quarter to the dam, which is where Mark told me that he took-out.

The narrow strip of water is the combination of Tenmile Run (entering farther upstream from the left) and Bear Creek (entering farther upstream from the right). Bear Creek Lake is in the foreground.

Shades Creek Only Section

SHADES CREEK

Shades Creek and Little Shades Creek originate in a highland that is designated as State Game Lands #91. Both streams drain bogs down the gentle south-facing slope in an area that encompasses only about 8 square miles. Because of this small drainage area, the stream seldom receives enough water to cover the bed of boulders.

Little Shades Creek flows freely, but Shades Creek has been dammed to create an impoundment called Indian Lake, which is surrounded by a housing development. About a mile downstream of the reservoir, a tributary known as Pocono Springs adds a bit of water to Shades Creek.

Half a mile later, Shades Creek and Little Shades Creek merge, about a block south of Route 115.

Only section: Route 115 to Bear Creek
Distance: 3.1 miles
Travel time: 1 hour (plus another hour on Bear Creek to the Francis E. Walter Dam)
Adversity level 3: Very challenging
Needs very high water (by observation)
Gradient: 82 feet per mile

When I started paddling Lehigh River tributaries, it never occurred to me that Shades Creek was runnable. So it came as a complete surprise, when I hiked the streambed simply out of curiosity, that I discovered its true nature and challenging runnability.

South of Route 115, Shades Creek flows through Bear Creek Preserve: a conservancy that is held in trust for public enjoyment by the Natural Lands Trust. The Preserve consists of 3,412 acres of pristine forest that provides habitat for mammals and birds, and boasts more than 20 miles of woodland trails.

One trail follows Shades Creek for most of its passage through the Preserve, all the way to the confluence with Bear Creek. Anglers can hike this trail to reach distant fishing holes. However, much of the streambed veers away from the trail, so that anglers who stick to the designated path will miss many of the pools where fish are likely to congregate. I saw inch-and-a-half to two-inch fingerlings in several places; I think of them as pencilfish because their girth approximates that of a graphite-filled wooden writing instrument.

I spotted a five-inch native trout on Little Shades Creek, downstream of the bridge. I must assume that they inhabit the rest of the waterway where food is abundant.

Despite the extraordinarily steep gradient, Shades Creek can be paddled in an open boat. This is because the incline is somewhat flat: like an iron beam with one end elevated. However, the streambed is corrugated like the teeth of a saw blade. There are pools where the water is level, yet there are no big waterfalls or high drop-offs, only two 4-foot ledges (which can be carried), and a few downed trees (which likewise can be carried).

Between the level pools and ledges are numerous chutes and cascades where the streambed slopes precipitously: less of a gradient than the incline of a playground sliding board, and usually spread over a distance of 20 to 30 feet. The length of the chutes and cascades is what makes them runnable in a canoe. The overall drop may be five to six feet, but the difference in elevation is spread over a long enough distance to make the stream acceptably runnable.

When the two streams pass under Route 115 they are located less than two blocks apart. Guardrails and steep embankments that are covered with dense vegetation make water access difficult for either stream. Additionally, the first block of both streams is narrow and fraught with deadfall and encroaching vegetation.

The best place to start a paddling trip is midway between the stream crossings, at the underground pipeline easement. Park in the south clearing, then portage your boat a hundred yards down the dirt service road to Shades Creek. If the water downstream of the pool is deep enough to float a boat, you're probably good to go. As an extra measure, hike a hundred yards or so downstream to test the fast-running water.

For the first quarter mile or so the stream is confined between banks that stand 6 to 8 feet apart. Exposed rocks abounded when I hiked the streambed at low water. With a depth increase of a foot or so, most of the rocks were covered enough to enable clear passage. Take special note of the words "most" and "enough."

I paddled Shades Creek during what I call medium high water: a level that I think kayakers would abhor. I scraped over so many rocks that the hull needs to be repainted. Yet at a higher level I would have been moving so fast that I might not have had time to avoid boulders, or to maneuver between them, or to make required hairpin turns.

The worst obstacle is this pair of boulders that form a double switchback.

Kayakers need super high water.

The problem with adequate water is the smallness of the watershed which, as noted above, I estimated at about 8 square miles above the put-in. Shades Creek does not have a streamflow gauge. Although the closest gauge is located only 6 miles away, at Stoddartsville, the Lehigh River drainage area above that station is 92 square miles. The Stoddartsville gauge can be used as an indication of recent rainfall in the vicinity, but it cannot be relied upon to accurately gauge the amount of water that is flowing down Shades Creek. As information, the Stoddartsville gauge was registering 450 % above normal when I ran Shades Creek.

From a canoeist's standpoint, one good thing about Shades Creek is that the streambed does not lie at the bottom of a narrow ravine with high rock walls on either side: the kind that makes escape extremely challenging. Instead, the banks seldom stand more than a foot or so above the water, and usually one side or the other is nearly level with the surface. This low-relief geology aids and abets rescue in case a kayak flips or a canoe swamps or dumps. Kayakers note: the water is never deep enough to execute an Eskimo roll.

Shades Creek Only Section

The second "waterfall" at low water. Cheryl and Teeny hiked a mile to get here, on a marked trail from White Haven Road. This is an idyllic spot for a picnic.

As noted above, there are several downed trees. A couple have created logjams while the others lie high enough to let water pass underneath (but not a boat). Each is located next to a low bank or broad flood plain; this makes it a simple task to run the boat aground, step out, and drag it around the obstacle.

There is a wooden walking bridge that connects trails on opposite side of the stream; the low water clearance is 3 feet, less at high water. If you can't duck under it you'll have to carry around it. At medium high water I was able to pass under it.

I did a lot of walking and dragging for the first quarter mile, neither of which was trying or demanding: partly due to the paucity of water, and partly due to logs. The water was never more than knee deep, and the current did not have enough force to make standing a problem. It is interesting to note that the two streams intertwine before they actually merge. Little Shades Creek forks into an overflow channel that allows some of its water to drain into Shades Creek. Then, as the relative elevations change, some of the water in Shades Creek flows into Little Shades Creek. I seldom needed to drag my boat after the ultimate merging of both streams.

The combined stream splits half a mile from the put-in. Both channels are choked with debris and have to be carried. After that point, and despite the aggregate of water, the streambed seldom measures more than 10 feet across. This restricted width inhibits maneuvering. Not only that, but in a few places vegetation, mostly rhododendron, grows low across the waterway so that I had to haul in my paddle, lie down flat, and let the force of the current shove me through the thicket.

Another split occurs at 9 tenths of a mile. Both channels were blocked by debris when I reached the fork. I carried over the logs in the left channel because it looked less cluttered than the right channel; plus it was straight instead of making a sharp right turn. The division of water made the channel too shallow to float my canoe. I dragged it partway down the left channel, walked a few feet across the intervening land to the right channel, then dragged it downstream to the point where the channels merged and floatable water depth resumed.

At 1.2 miles, a pair of offset car-sized boulders create an interesting obstacle and 4-foot drop. Most of the water passes left of the first boulder, dumps into a whirlpool, immediately flows right between the boulders, and finally turns left to pass to the right of the second boulder. A short stubby whitewater kayak can negotiate this passage, but my 15-foot  Dagger couldn't make the turn unless it was flexible like rubber or hinged in the middle. I stepped out onto the edge of the whirlpool, then dragged the boat across the pool and over dry rock on the left side of the second boulder.

The Preserve map marks a waterfall at this location. Because of the configuration of another marked waterfall farther downstream, you might be led to believe that this Z-shaped zigzag or double hairpin turn, and the sudden drop at the end of the third leg, refer to these boulders. However, it might refer to the waterfall on the tributary that enters Shades Creek only a handful of feet after the second boulder. Chances are, you'll have your attention pinned to the water and will be moving too fast to notice it. If you can manage eyes right, you'll see a gushing flow of water that drops 10 to 12 feet into a small pool that overflows into Shades Creek.

The stream crosses another pipeline clearing at 1.9 miles.

The other waterfall is located at 2.7 miles, and this one is definitely on Shades Creek. To me it looks more like a ledge than a waterfall. A drop of 1 foot is followed by a drop of 4 feet. Kayaks can paddle over it without any trouble. Canoes should be beached on the sloped bedrock to the right, dragged a couple of boat-lengths, and lowered over the downstream lip into the pool. This is a beautiful spot to sit and ponder if you're looking for a rest stop; a trail from White Haven Road leads to this waterfall.

Bear Creek is located short of half a mile away, past a stretch of smooth bedrock plains. From the confluence it's 3 miles to the take-out at the dam, or a mile and a quarter to the jeep road take-out. You'll have almost a mile of nearly continuous whitewater on Bear Creek before you reach the backwash of the reservoir (at its summer level; in winter you'll have moving water at least as far as the jeep road).

Shades Creek is an awesome piece of water with continuous fast flow from beginning to end. Sure, the upper stretch has a few obstacles that require wading, but once you get past the first half mile, the paddling never lets up. My biggest problem was the length of my canoe. A shorter one would have been more maneuverable. Higher water would have been nice because it would have covered more rocks, but it also would have made the trip more dicey, especially where the narrow channel twists and turns like a sleeping snake.

The best word to describe Shades Creek is "tricky." It's a hardcore trip that is well worth the effort. "Est quod est," as the Romans used to say; it is what it is. And it is not to be missed by adventurous whitewater paddlers.

Sandy Run Only Section

SANDY RUN

This short stream originates in a mountain plateau that lies east of Freeland and a huge strip mine. After flowing downhill, the water enters a vast marsh in which soggy channels intertwine like a complicated network of submerged filaments. At the end of the marsh, Sandy Run is joined by Mill Hopper Creek. The combined waterway then flows over a fairly level woodland tract along the northern edge of Buck Mountain until it reaches Lehigh Gorge Road, some 5 miles from its origin.

Only section: From Lehigh Gorge Road to the Lehigh River
Adversity level 4: Extremely challenging
Distance: 2 miles (approximately)
Needs high water (by observation)
Travel time: 30 minutes (plus more than 1 hour on the river to Rockport)
Gradient: 100 feet per mile (approximately)

I included this stream mostly for anglers, but some expert kayakers dare to give it a shot.

When I first observed the streambed at Lehigh Gorge Road and at its passage under the Lehigh Gorge Trail, I had visions of canoeing the run at high water, because it looked fairly flat. After observing the run from the Lower Railroad Grade I began to have doubts. Finally, I hiked downstream from the halfway point, which was not visible from the abandoned railroad bed – and disabused myself of ever attempting to run this stream by canoe.

I won't go as far as to say that canoeing Sandy Run is impossible. But I will say that, at the minimum running water level, it would require dragging the boat over rocks for at least half the distance, where couch- to car-sized boulders predominate, and where the pools in between them are shorter than the length of a canoe. The middle mile con-

At low water Sandy Run resembles a wet boulder field.

sists of a continuous series of short drops and ledges which are mostly not negotiable because the only passageways between confining boulders are through sluices that are narrower than the beam of the average boat.

High or super high water broadens the sluices and buries many of the rocks, in essence widening the navigable streambed, but the accompanying speed of the current is frightening – that is, it's frightening to me. This puts running the run in the category of whitewater kayaks only. Even so, I heartily suggest that kayakers scout the most challenging central stretch before making the attempt: say, for half a mile downstream of the pier that marks the crossing of the Upper Railroad Grade.

The worst hazard is a two-wire cable cross about a block below the pier. Anglers will find this helpful in crossing from one side to the other when the water is running high. To kayakers it's a potential death trap. The bottom wire stands about two and a half feet above the streambed. At low water, a kayaker can duck under this wire; but at low water the stream isn't runnable. At high water, a kayaker might get guillotined by the wire. Because of the reddish brown rust color, I had trouble seeing the wires when I was standing only 20 feet away. A rampaging kayaker might not see it until too late; or he might run into it without ever seeing it.

Nonetheless, extreme kayakers do paddle down Sandy Run when the water is high enough cover the obstacles. Mark Zakutansky has kayaked down Sandy Run; he told me that he knew about the cable cross and had to carry around it. I reiterate: this stream is for extreme kayakers only.

Mark Zakutansky took this picture when he paddled Sandy Run in flood. Note that the boulders are submerged.

It's another 5 miles from the confluence to Rockport.

The adversity level in the statistical sidebar refers to kayaking. Anglers will find the adversity somewhat less challenging, but still challenging. You'll have to climb down steep slopes from the railroad bed to reach the water. And the banks are blocked by rhododendron thickets. In low water you can skip along the boulders without getting your feet wet. But watch out for slimy, slippery rocks.

There are lots of fishing holes near the downstream end, where the streambed levels somewhat, and the rocks are smaller and fewer.

MUD RUN

Mud Run originates in an obscure highland swamp that is surrounded by housing developments, northeast of Pohopoco Mountain and east of Route 115. In the first 4 miles of its existence, the tiny stream's water is siphoned off no less than six times to create recreational reservoirs for local residents. These impoundments might make Mud Run the most dammed stream in Pennsylvania (pun intended).

After another 4 miles the run flows through Albrightsville. By this time it has accumulated water from a number of tributaries, some of which are also dammed. Then 2 miles later it enters Hickory Run State Park, at the confluence with Keipers Run.

The only part of Mud Run that I have surveyed are Sections 1 (the 2-mile stretch between Routes 534 and 903) and 3 (the 4-mile stretch that passes through the park, in an area that is designated as the Mud Run Natural Area). The adjacent stretches, both upstream and downstream of the park's boundaries, are posted by outdoor clubs that are hostile to non-members, even to those who are not fishing or hunting. I surveyed the park's section on several occasions by hiking down the streambed when the water level was normal, as well as in winter on snowshoes when the stream was frozen and blanketed with snow.

The park stretch of Mud Run is one of the most picturesque streams in the Lehigh River watershed, perhaps rivaled only by Stony Creek. If I had to describe it in one word, I am torn between whether that word should be "quaint" or "breathtaking." The difference will entail some explanation. For that reason, I have split the park portion in half: one half from the upstream border to the Pennsylvania Turnpike bridge, the other half from the bridge to the downstream border. I did this because of the great geological disparity between the two sections.

Furthermore, although this chapter is intended largely for anglers, I have included information (as well as my opinion) that will enable potential paddlers to make an informed decision about running this run before they find themselves trapped in circumstances that might be beyond their ability to overcome.

Section 1 (Route 534 to Route 903)
Distance: 2 miles
Travel time: 1 to 2 hours

Adversity level 3: Very challenging
High water level (by observation)
Gradient: 34 feet per mile

If I had known what I was getting into before I paddled this section, I would have started banging my head against a tree instead of putting my canoe in the water. That's because I could have stopped banging my head any time I wanted, but once I was committed to the stream there was no turning back. Anyone who follows in my keel wash should be committed.

I would never have attempted to canoe this stretch had it not been for kayaker Nick Fitzsimmons. He posted a video on YouTube in which he showed footage of his solo trip down part of this section of Mud Run after a 3-inch rain. By way of explanation, he wrote, "Put in below lake in Towamensing trails."

I'm not sure what he meant. Towamensing Trails (with a capital "T") is a "private residential lake community;" Towamensing Trail (with a capital T minus the final lower case "s") is a road within the housing development. The "lake" is a reservoir that was created by impounding Wolf Run: a Mud Run tributary.

Squeezing the canoe through the first barricade, after which the barricades got more interesting.

In any case, his video camera recorded a wild and woolly trip down a raging torrent that had no exposed boulders. Twice he had to carry through the woods around downed trees, but he did so without evident difficulty. The surface rolled like a corrugated tin roof, punctuated by stretches of high standing waves and deep troughs that might have spelled doom for an open boat.

In view of the flow rate that was running that day, and absent access from Towamensing Trails, I launched my canoe at the bridge on Route 534 after a 1-inch rain. The stream looked inviting from the bridge: broad, clear, and flowing nicely. But first looks can be deceiving. As soon as I passed around the bend I ran into a fork in which both tines were blocked by deadfall. I lifted my boat over, under, and through fallen trees on the right tine. Fifty feet away I had to drag the boat over another cluster of fallen trees. Then the going got worse.

The two tines converged then split into three tines, or channels. Thus the original 20-foot width of the streambed was reduced to narrow waterways that were choked with debris and low-hanging rhododendron that I had to fight my way through. I did more poling than paddling. Often I pulled my way over the water by grabbing thick rhododendron limbs. Mostly I walked and dragged the canoe behind or alongside of me.

The influx of water from Wolf Run, a quarter mile downstream of the bridge, did nothing to alleviate the situation.

The channels continued to divide into other channels that intertwined like tendrils. Some channels were not as wide as the beam of my boat. When I dragged the canoe into an adjacent channel that was wider, I immediately saw that this other channel was either blocked by debris or living vegetation, or that it soon split into more channels. At times the vegetation grew so thick that I couldn't see more than a dozen feet in any direction.

There was no main channel, just a series of runnels that split and merged, split and merged, like water flowing through a colander. The area was a swamp in which the water was strained through the cluster of tiny islets that supported ancient trees and rhododendron thickets. In some places the entanglements were so thick that I had to

Mud Run Section 1

back up and try another "channel." In one place the passageway was completely blocked – not by deadfall but by tree trunks and rhododendron limbs. In order to fit through the barriers, I had to roll the canoe onto its side, lift it over my head, then get behind and push it over top of a muddle of branches. I was not having fun.

After I performed this feat, I noticed that my spare single-bladed paddle was missing. I had stowed my double-bladed paddle because there wasn't enough space to wield it. So the single-bladed paddle became my primary instead of my backup, and therefore was not secured to its bungee. I walked back the way I had come, expecting that it fell out when I flipped the canoe onto its side. I tramped through the water and made crisscrossing circles, but never found it.

Then I lost the canoe. By that I mean that the swamp was so dense and visibility was so limited that I couldn't determine which way I had struggled through the forest. I didn't panic. I hadn't walked more than 50 feet, and a 15-foot canoe couldn't stay hidden for long. I kept slipping and sliding on the muddy bottom and moss-covered rocks, and had tripped or fallen into knee-deep water several times; I was completely soaked up to my chest. Despite temperatures in the upper 80's, I was wearing rugged clothing with long pants and long sleeves for protection against scrapes and thorns: my normal attire in untested waters.

I found an 8-foot-wide channel that extended for more than 30 feet before it split into as many as six blocked channels. I followed this for a bit, then skipped sideways into a smaller channel, and ultimately described a circle back to my canoe, which I had left high and dry on top of rhododendron limbs. I then crawled and hauled the canoe through the shrubbery until I regained a flowing channel, and continued the trip through the entwined vegetation of the swamp in which paddles of any kind were superfluous.

Here the stream filters through a tangle of weirdly growing trees and their intertwined root systems. Iron in the water has stained the bottom dirt orange, which reflects light brightly when struck by sunbeams.

Finally I reached open water where several channels merged and extended as far as I could see: about 50 feet. I hoped that I had finally reached the end of the swamp, so I marked a waypoint on my GPS receiver. I had traveled a mile and one tenth. Some of this recorded distance must have been erroneous, such as the track of my wanderings in search of my paddle and canoe. Other route logs could have been sideways tramping. But pretty much I stayed in the flow as the multiple waterways wound through the swamp. Therefore, for the record and the statistical sidebar, I deducted a tenth as being duplicated travel.

Then I glanced to the left and spotted a road that paralleled the waterway, with a 40-foot driveway that led down to the stream. I supposed that this was Nick's starting point. Hurray! The road is Whitman Lane.

The next mile was pure fun. I got hung up on a short cascade with a total drop of 4 feet. As I always say, better hung up than swamped by the huge waves that were shown in the video clip. After I passed a power line easement, I encountered the two downed trees. The first one was an ordinary carry, the second a little more challenging. In some places the encroaching vegetation reduced the navigable width to 6 to 8 feet. But the water was fast and boulder free.

I encountered another cascade a quarter mile before the take-out. The long, low-angled slope enabled me to run it without taking on water. After a wide left turn the stream paralleled Route 534. From there on it was smooth coasting to Route 903. I took-out on the left bank upstream of the bridge.

In retrospect, the best way to run the flowing part of this section is to obtain entry permission from a Towamensing Trails resident, and forget the upstream stretch.

Section 2 (Route 903 to Old Stage Road) Adversity level 2: Challenging
Distance: .9 mile   High water level (by observation)
Travel time: 20 minutes)   Gradient: 46 feet per mile

I delineated this short stretch as a section for those who don't want to start at Route 524, and who don't have access to Towamensing Trails. If you put-in above Route 903, it makes sense to keep going past it for another fun mile. Or you can start here. Put-in on the left bank upstream of the bridge.

The steep gradient is fairly consistent except for three rock dams less than two feet in height. Two steel cables are stretched across the stream but you can pass under them without ducking. There are some boulder fields that require quick maneuvering. The sole fallen tree does not reach across the streambed; hug the left bank.

Pass Henning Road at .6 mile. Take-out on the left upstream of Old Stage Road.

Section 3 (Old Stage Road to Keipers Run) Adversity level 4: Extremely challenging
Distance: 1.0 mile   High water level (by observation)
Travel time: 30 minutes (approximately)   Gradient (overall): 63 feet per mile

Don't be fooled by the overall gradient in the sidebar. It is horribly deceiving. Broken down into quarters, the first two quarters have a gradient of 23 fpm. The last quarter is 36 fpm. The middle quarter is a whopping 120 fpm; this means that the middle stretch drops 30 feet in one-quarter mile, courtesy of high waterfalls and connecting cascades.

This section is for extreme kayakers only because portaging is next to impossible.

The awesome ruggedness of the middle stretch cannot be exaggerated. It must be seen to be believed. It rivals the Great Falls of the Mud for extremity.

Mud Run Section 3

They say that a picture is worth a thousand words. Here are three thousand words worth of pictures, amply showing why canoeists should avoid this section like the plague. I call it the Lost Mile for canoeists. This section cannot be canoed without pushing the canoe over waterfalls and down sluices, then jumping into the whirlpool and swimming after it.

Each waterfall, sluice, or ledge drops as much as 10 vertical feet. Some of the drop-offs have adjacent shelves on which a boat can be dragged or portaged, but some are bordered by sheer rock walls or wild cascades that prevent portaging, carrying, or lining.

Extreme kayakers can run these ledges with caution, as long as they have the necessary experience and expertise.

As you can see, this Lost Mile is not for the squeamish. It is important for boaters of all persuasions to understand the vicissitudes that await them on this turbulent stretch of water.

The top photo shows the initial waterfall, which is located immediately around the bend past a series of left-bank log buildings that have the appearance of a lodge. In the middle photo you can see this waterfall in the distance from downstream, as well as intervening boulders.

Other, worse boulder fields exist farther downstream. At the end of this awesome obstacle course, you can look up and see the back of a modern building that, judging by its immensity, could be another lodge or the home of a wealthy individual. It stands some 75 to 100 feet above the water.

At this point the stream flatten into a long pool whose fast current is without whitewater.

Downstream, a huge area of giant toppled trees forces the water into a pair of narrow but navigable channels.

I reiterate: this section is for extreme kayakers only. Warning to others: abandon hope all ye who enter here.

Mud Run Sections 3 and 4 (Upper Part)

The portage distance up Keipers Run is slightly more than a quarter mile. There's no trail and the streambed is steep and rocky, especially near the road where the stream passes through a tunnel underneath, and you have to climb uphill through the forest to the level of the road.

You might be better off paddling another quarter mile to the pipeline easement. This isn't much better because of the steep initial slope and the following half-mile of dirt-road portage to Route 903, but the way is clear and the footing is much better. I have hiked both routes but not with a canoe on my shoulders.

By the way, don't be confused by the Keipers Run road sign on Route 903 near the intersection with Route 115. The USGS topo map shows Keipers Run between the pipeline crossing and Weiler Road. The stream where the Keipers Run road sign is posted is unnamed on the topo map. I think the sign was put there by mistake. It should have been placed a hundred yards south of Weiler Road.

Section 4 (Keipers Run to the Great Falls of the Mud) Adversity levels vary
Distance: 4 miles Normal water level (by observation)
Travel time: 5 hours (hiking) Gradient (average): 54 feet per mile

Because this description is geared more toward anglers and hikers than boaters, the adversity levels refer to hiking rather than paddling. Ironically, kayakers might find that the adversity level for paddling is not challenging at all.

I have divided this section into two parts: the Upper Portion and the Lower Portion. I did this largely because of the difference in gradients, but also because of the great dissimilarity in adversity levels due to ruggedness of the streambed. I suppose I could have split this section into two sections instead of parts, but I didn't because this entire stretch is walkable at normal water levels. Furthermore, there are numerous intermediate accesses that people can use to reach this 4-mile stretch.

Also, and perhaps more important, this whole section lies within the boundaries of Hickory Run State Park. And in some places paths parallel the stream.

In case you don't know it, hiking on a streambed is slow-going and slippery. One mile per hour is par for the course. Submerged rocks are covered with algae or moss that have the friction coefficient of ice. Hiking poles are strongly recommended; mine saved me from more than one dunking. In fact, at the end of each long trek, the muscles in my arms were sore while my leg muscles were not.

Upper Part (Keipers Run to Hawk Falls) Adversity level 2: Challenging hike
Distance: 2 miles Normal water level (by observation)
Travel time: 2 hours (one way hiking on streambed) Gradient: 34 feet per mile

The upper portion reminds me of Paul Detlefsen's idyllic paintings of nineteenth-century rural America: all that's missing is the watermill or covered bridge.

The banks are lined with hemlocks and rhododendron thickets, and occasional hardwoods that add vivid colors in autumn. Rugged rock cliffs border the banks here and there. There was almost no place where I could not hike through water that did not come higher than my knees, and mostly the water was only ankle or shin deep. I saw a couple of holes that looked to be six feet in depth. The deep spots were avoidable thanks to adjacent shallows. Atypically, sometimes the depths crowded the banks, and the shallows stood in the middle of the waterway.

The streambed consists almost entirely of bedrock, with only a few loose stones

Mud Run Section 4 (Upper Part)

to trip the unwary wader. Large boulders dot the watery landscape, but they are generally situated far enough apart to enable clear passage. The banks are separated by a distance of 15 to 20 feet, so there is ample space to avoid boulders and deep holes.

On one trek a 9-inch trout leaped completely out of the water in front of me. I spotted other trout rising to the surface, perhaps snapping at bugs. From this I gather that the stream is amply stocked. Signs posted on trees along the bank proclaim that Mud Run is a Delayed Harvest stream. I don't know what "delayed harvest" means, but the sign went on to explain that only artificial lures may be used, and that any form of live bait is prohibited.

Despite the somewhat steep gradient, the streambed is so gently sloped that it almost appears to be level, and can readily be negotiated without extensive clambering. Ledges are few and far apart, and for the most part they are low: say, 1 to 3 feet. Dry rock always lay adjacent to water-filled runnels. I saw only one tree that had fallen across the stream.

A slide in the upper portion of Section 3.

I hiked down Keipers Run from Route 903 but other ways to reach the left bank are less demanding. A pipeline crosses Mud Run about a quarter mile downstream of Keipers Run, and a path on the left bank connects the two. The half-mile-long right-of-way leads from Route 903 to the water's edge, and beyond on the other side; a huge gravel parking lot is located a block or so north of the trailhead. From the same parking lot you can take the Panther Creek Roadway to Panther Creek, then hike parallel to Panther Creek to the confluence – but the roundtrip hike is 3 and a half miles.

I interrupt my access descriptions to mention that I saw a school of three trout in Keipers Run: a rivulet that is seldom more than a yard or two wide. How they got there, and how they survive, is a mystery to me.

Two trails lead to the right bank from Route 534: the Orchard Trail and the Hawk Falls trail. (See the *Lehigh Gorge Trail Guide* for details and descriptions.) One leg of the Orchard Trail parallels the stream for three-quarters of a mile.

I have hiked all the way up Panther Run to the dirt road and, while I didn't see any fish, I saw pools where they might live. The same goes for Hawk Run. Also, while Hawk Run is known largely for the waterfall that precedes the confluence, Panther Run has two waterfalls, one of which stands 25 feet high; the other stands 10 feet high. They are located three-quarters of a mile upstream, or one-quarter mile downstream from the dirt road.

Note that the Hawk Falls trail meets the stream a block upstream of the waterfall.

Lower Part (Hawk Falls to the Great Falls of the Mud, thence to Route 534)
Adversity level 3: Very challenging   Gradient: 74 feet per mile
Distance: 2 miles, plus 1 mile to the highway   Normal water level (by observation)
Travel time: 3 hours (one way hiking on streambed, plus the climb out)

Again this description is geared more toward anglers and hikers than boaters. In this case, however, the adversity level is ascribed to all comers. Canoeists should read the final paragraphs in which I render my opinions about the paddling potential. Extreme kayakers should consult with other extreme kayakers who have run this stretch and beyond.

This lower half is a totally different stream, with a gradient that is more than double that of the upper half. You can reach it from the bottom of the Hawk Falls Trail, and from an unnamed path that leads downhill from the large dirt parking lot immediately west of the

Much of the lower portion of Section 3 is as rocky as the stretch shown in this picture, but not always as steep.

turnpike. Anglers and hikers who have walked downstream from an Upper Portion access should know that the path at the bottom of the aforementioned dirt parking lot is the last means of manageable escape before encountering the gorge.

If you contemplate bushwhacking, be aware of the rugged geology that permeates this stretch: the stream lies at the bottom of a steep-walled gorge whose nearly vertical sides are overgrown with rhododendron thickets so dense and entangled that you can't walk through it – you have to crawl, squirm, or slither.

The one place where I found the descent (or ascent) doable was located along the downstream border of Hickory Run State Park. Park in the dirt lot that I noted in the previous paragraph, walk northwest on Route 534, and turn left onto the tree line at the edge of the open field. This is the park border. Follow the dogleg around the farm field, then turn southwest along the border (or take the shortcut through the grassland part of the woods). Signs on some of the trees delineate the border.

A trail of sorts parallels the border for half to three-quarters of a mile. It disappears when the largely level land starts to slope downhill. Now you have to bushwhack wherever you can find openings between groves of rhododendron. The slope is encumbered with lots of loose rock, so be careful. Keep going downhill across the boulder field until you reach the water's edge. Look upstream . . .

. . . at what I call the Great Falls of the Mud (after the Great Falls of the Lehigh).

Forget Detlefsen, and instead imagine John Wesley Powell boating down a miniature Colorado River that is fraught with car-sized boulders and precipitous drops and dramatic cataracts. What you are witnessing at the border is the worst of running water.

Mud Run Sections 4 (Lower Part) and 5

Kayakers take note. Now let's return to the turnpike bridge, and hike downstream.

On the good side, deep, fish-laden pools abound. Most of these pools can be circumvented because the streambed may measure up to 30 feet in width, and you can jump from rock to rock to attain shallow passage or the opposite bank. However, in some places the deep water spans from bank to bank, forcing anglers and hikers to either swim or climb on rock faces that boast little more than fingertip ledges. And that's at low water!

Take my word that this is not a stress-free hike. Whereas the upper half is close to level and the rocks are mostly flat, here the streambed consists of nearly continuous ledges and boulder bars that are sloped and extremely slippery. Once your shoe soles get coated with moss and algae, they become slippery even on rock that is high and dry. Instead of walking heel-to-toe, you'll be high-stepping through deep water and climbing up and down car-sized boulders. This is an exhausting trek.

But it's also spectacular!

Vertical rock faces line much of the waterway. Where breakdown exists, the banks are thickly overgrown with rhododendron that makes wading in water the most viable passage. Yet there are fish in the pools that separate the boulder bars.

I suppose the reason that the deep pools are fish-laden is because this stretch is so challenging to reach. Determined anglers take note that this lower half might well be worth the effort to get there. Hikers should note that the area possesses a pristine beauty whose rugged isolation adds an enchanting fillip.

Section 5 (Great Falls of the Mud to the Lehigh River)

Distance: 8 miles (approximate)
Travel time: 2 to 3 hours (boating only)
Adversity level 4: Extremely challenging
High water level (by observation)
Gradient (approximate): 54 feet per mile

Forget canoeing this stretch of Mud Run unless you paddle a boat that is completely filled with flotation bags. From the air I saw an almost endless number of places where canoes would have to be carried or portaged over or around drop-offs, pinch points, cascades, and long fields of boulders. I think a canoeist would spend more time out of the canoe than in it. And that says nothing about the Great Falls.

I wouldn't state categorically that portaging the Great Falls is impossible by canoe, but I wouldn't want to try it. After a rock-strewn streambed that precedes it, the first major hurdle to overcome is an 8-foot sheer drop through a 5-foot-wide notch that is split with rocks which divert the flow into a raging pool of whitewater, which almost immediately pours over a 10-foot drop onto a series of similar but smaller ledges that extend for more than a hundred yards downstream.

Getting a canoe through this rampaging obstacle course without losing it or getting your person severely smashed against rocks by fast-moving water is a scenario that I tried to imagine . . . and failed.

As for kayaking, some chaps on the American Whitewater website wrote about kayaking Mud Run from Route 903 in Albrightsville to the Lehigh River, a distance that they gave as 8 miles (although I estimate that it's closer to 12). For what it's worth, they gauged the degree of difficulty as Class IV+ with portages likely. They also declared that paddlers have been harassed by fishing club members.

I had the great good fortune to meet expert kayaker Nolan Berlew when I gave an underwater slide presentation to the Lehigh Valley Dive Club Regulators in Nazareth,

Pennsylvania. He had run Mud Run from Albrightsville. He told me that the stream is normally kayaked at extreme high water. The high streamflow drowns many of the boulders, thus increasing the effective width of navigable water. He also ran the Great Falls without scouting or portaging. Properly handled kayaks can handle the drops and succeeding cascades.

Downstream of the Great Falls the water is just as challenging as it is upstream; perhaps more so. The streambed consists of high ledges and large boulders with some cascades and sudden drops. A dam has been constructed across the stream about two miles from the Lehigh River. Nolan assured me that he paddled over the left side of the sloped dam without difficulty.

Perhaps the greatest challenge was in fending off harassing shouts and jeers from club members, who didn't seem to understand (or who didn't want to acknowledge) that flowing water was owned by the Commonwealth of Pennsylvania, and was therefore available for all users to paddle (but not to wade). This despite the fact that anglers couldn't fish when the stream was in flood stage.

As a result, Nolan said that kayakers prefer to paddle Mud Run in the winter when trout were out of season.

Later I met Mark Zakutansky. He had kayaked the Mud Run gorge on numerous occasions. He confirmed everything that Nolan told me.

I don't doubt that other kayakers can run the Great Falls successfully. But I humbly suggest that it might be a good idea to hike down the boundary line and survey the waterfall and cataract before they make an attempt to do so.

Anglers should note that you can also reach Mud Run from the Lehigh River. In the absence of a whitewater release from the Francis E. Walter Dam, you may be able to ford the river from the Lehigh Gorge Trail: if not precisely at the confluence with Mud Run, then certainly nearby. If you're paddling the river, like many anglers do, you can pull into the outflow under the railroad bridge. Property of the Lehigh Gorge State Park extends a quarter mile upstream from the river. This stretch is eminently fishable.

Gradients

I am pretty sure that my calculation for the stretch between Keipers Run and the turnpike is fairly accurate. The hiking was straightforward because the gradient was consistent and the water was shallow. I walked steadily without interruption.

On the other hand, I had to make interpolations or judgment calls on the gradient for the lower half. Too many times I had to halt and determine how best to proceed, or skip sideways from rock to rock, or wade slowly through hip- or waist-deep water, or inch along rock faces while clinging with my fingertips, or go back upstream and try another route, or crawl through rhododendron thickets that lined the banks. All of this means that my GPS distance log was somewhat inaccurate. I made adjustments by correlating my logged track with calculated distances taken from topographic maps.

The actual gradient may not be precisely 74 feet per mile for all of the above reasons. The streambed is very uneven: more like saw teeth than a sliding board. This may not be a particular hindrance to anglers and hikers, but boaters take warning.

Both distance and gradient for the stretch downstream of the Great Falls of the Mud are approximate, but close enough for boaters to make an informed decision about whether or not they should attempt to run this stretch. If in doubt, don't.

Mud Run Section 4

I took the picture above from the bottom of the cascade when the water was low. The splash of white that you see at the top is the first of many drops in the Great Falls of the Mud. I have Mark Zakuntansky to thank for the dramatic picture below, taken when the water was high. Note the snow on the rocks. It goes without saying that this stretch and others that follow are for extreme boaters only. If you flip at the top, you might have a long bumpy swim ahead of you.

STONY CREEK

Only section: Trail bottom to Lehigh River
Distance: 3 miles
Travel time: 1 hour (plus 2 on the river to Glen Onoko)
Adversity level 4: Extremely challenging
High water level (by sight)
Gradient: 95 feet per mile

This stream is included primarily for anglers, but I can't totally discount kayakers. Anglers can hike two-thirds of the way along the adjacent trail, for which the adversity level is 0, for none. The adversity level in the statistical sidebar refers to kayaking.

Judging by the way the dirt on the path is compacted, I would guess that this is a favorite fishing stream. The water is deep enough to support native trout, which I've spotted in streams far smaller than this one.

When I hiked the trail for the *Lehigh Gorge Trail Guide*, I kept thinking about how canoeable the water looked. For two miles the gradient was fairly mild and consistent. Boulders were minimal, and the few that were exposed were avoidable, despite a narrow width of 10 to 20 feet: or would have been had the water been at a level higher than normal. Then the trail ended, and I had to bushwhack for the final mile to the river. Near trail's end, the gradient increased dramatically and the stream became a boulder-laden obstacle course which for a canoe would be a mile-long portage. Mentally I put the kibosh on attempting to run it.

The only reason I even allude to kayaking is because, first, an anonymous poster on the American Whitewater website mentioned in passing that he had paddled it. I say bravo for audacity. Second, expert kayaker Nolan Berlew assured me that, although he had not run this stream, he knew from being part of the extreme kayaking community that kayakers did indeed run it.

Once the gradient increases, it stays that way – then gets worse. Numerous ledges, cascades, and boulder fields make for an interesting slalom at mid-high levels. At super high levels the boulders are buried but the waves they create are mountainous: the kind that extreme kayakers love to challenge. The denouement is a 20-foot-high waterfall that is located a quarter mile from the Lehigh River, and which is followed by boulder-strewn rapids that are worse than the ones that precede it.

I had a difficult enough time climbing over house-sized boulders and slipping through crevices and climbing down narrow chimneys to get past the waterfall. I can't imagine how difficult it must be to portage a canoe around it – and I have a tremendous amount of experience in portaging, from my wilderness canoe trips. Perhaps the anonymous poster flew his kayak over the waterfall into the pool below; he neglected to mention anything about it. He also neglected to state where he put-in: at the bottom of the trail, or a mile upstream at the power line easement.

In any case, Nolan assured me that extreme kayakers have paddled over the waterfall into the pool below. Expert kayaker Jerry McAward explained to me that a long, pointed river kayak would plunge so deep into the shallow pool that it would likely strike bottom, but that a stubby whitewater kayak could "boof" safely into the pool. Boofing, he explained, is a technique whereby a kayak slaps the surface not nose first but nearly flat so that the bottom of the hull makes an onomatopoeic sound like boof.

I doubt that the stream can be runnable very often: only after a rainfall of Noachian proportions. The watershed is uncommonly small. Stony Creek drains from a swamp a couple of miles past the power line easement, or 6 miles in all from the Lehigh River,

Stony Creek Only Section

and is fed by only three unnamed tributaries, none of which measures more than half a mile in length. I don't think that anglers have much to worry about accidentally snagging a passing kayak.

To reach Stony Creek from Route 903, take Unionville Road to the intersection with School House Road (on the right), and turn left onto the dirt road at the power line easement that lies directly opposite School House Road. On the left side of the entryway you'll see a small yellow sign that denotes game land parking. Ignore the private property sign on the right (north); it refers to land on the north side of the sign. Follow the dirt road as it curves to the left and proceeds under the wires. After two hundred yards you'll see a parking area on the other side of the steel-frame tower. Park there.

The denouement.

The trailhead is in the forest at the far end of the parking area. A gate prevents the passage of motor vehicles onto State Game Lands #141. Walk around the gate and follow the jeep road past a house, at which point the road turns from west to southwest. Turn left at the farm field on your left (east). After this the jeep road shrinks in width as a result of encroaching vegetation. Keep going downhill as the road curves to the right and, about a mile from the parking lot, ends at the stream. It's a long carry that cannot be avoided.

I don't recommend it, but if you want to see what the water looks like farther upstream, from the parking lot walk southeast along the power line easement for nearly half a mile – first on a hard dirt road, then on a grassy two-wheel track. You'll know when easy-going ends, at the last left-bank tower. From there it's only a block or so to the stream, but what a block! You'll have to bushwhack down an extremely steep rocky slope through rhododendron thickets. Keep going until your shoes get wet. I don't think it's worth the effort for an extra half mile of paddling . . . although I must admit that, except for a few downed trees that span the banks, this part of the stream is eminently runnable – even canoeable.

If you want to be really brazen, put-in at Stony Creek Road. This is the easiest put-in because you can drop your boat straight into the water on either side of the bridge. Notice the fallen tree 30 feet upstream of the bridge, and the other one 30 downstream of the bridge; these are only two of several obstacles that bar clear passage unless the water is flowing over them: a rare condition that I have yet to see.

I haven't walked this stretch so I can't give any personal guidance, but I see no reason why the streambed should be any different than the stretch from the power line crossing to the game land trail (which I have walked). Average width is 10 to 15 feet. Although my estimated gradient is 100 feet per mile, the half mile that I walked was remarkably consistent: almost like a board with one end tipped upward. Of course, the in-between mile might consists of pools and waterfalls, but I doubt it.

Expert paddlers: go for broke. But watch out for fallen trees.

BLACK CREEK

As noted below, this stream is formed by the combined waters of Hazle Creek, Beaver Creek, and Quakake Creek. Hazle Creek flows down the south side of Spring Mountain northwest of Weatherly. Beaver Creek starts in an old strip mine area west of Beaver Meadows. Quakake Creek originates in a flat wooded area south of McAdoo and east of Route 309.

Two streams named Black Creek flow into the Lehigh River. The other one is located farther north, on the left bank (east side) between White Haven and Hickory Run State Park. The latter is little more than a trickle by contrast: nice for fishing but not for paddling.

Only section: Black Creek Junction to the Lehigh River
Distance: 4.5 miles (plus 1 mile or 2.5 miles on approach streams)
Adversity level 4: Extremely challenging   Needs very high water (by observation)
Travel time: 1 to 2 hours (including approach streams)   Gradient: 67 feet per mile

Four words come to mind in describing this stream: "For expert kayakers only." To that I should add four additional words: "An expert kayaker's delight."

Because I am an open-boater and not an expert kayaker, after surveying the stream and photographing its major ledges and sluices, I determined that the likelihood of a canoe making it through the numerous boulder fields without coming to grief on at least half a dozen of them was slim to none, and Slim left town. This is not to say that a canoe can't possibly pass through these waters without dumping, only that I – with stress the singular personal pronoun – don't think *I* can do it without dumping. Take that statement for what it's worth. If you *must* canoe, do it at mid-high water.

As a wilderness canoeist I have always said that there is no rapid, drop-off, or waterfall that a canoe cannot go around: either by lining, carrying, or portaging. Yet this isn't necessarily true with respect to Black Creek. The reason is that some of the rapids and drop-offs occur in tight sluiceways where no true banks exist. In some of these places the streambed is shaped like an old-fashioned porcelain bathtub, with sloping rock walls that offer no purchase for a paddler to step onto in order to walk around a killer set of rapids.

Yet I have no doubt that an expert kayaker can negotiate these wild-water restrictions, and be thrilled by the experience. In fact, I have been told by two such kayakers (Nolan Berlew and Mark Zakutansky) that people kayak down Black Creek when the water is high (or super high). I believed them – more so after seeing a video clip on YouTube, one that was shot from a helmet-mounted camera.

Before I describe Black Creek itself, I must describe the approaches: that is, the streams that must be paddled in order to reach the designated origination of the name Black Creek, at a confluence called Black Creek Junction. Two streams merge at this junction: Quakake Creek from the west, and a technically unnamed stream from the north. First I must explain about the unnamed stream from the north.

Three major streams flow down the mountains northwest of Weatherly. Hazle Creek and Dreek (or Dreck) Creek flow from the northwest, while Beaver Creek flows from the west. They are duly designated on the USGS topo map. When Hazle Creek and Dreek (or Dreck) Creek merge, the combined stream is called Hazle Creek and

Black Creek Only Section

Dreek (or Dreck) Creek is named as a tributary.

Then Hazle Creek and Beaver Creek merge in the wilderness that lies west-northwest of Weatherly. On the same map, the name Black Creek is applied to the stream that flows eastward (downstream) of Black Creek Junction (after the confluence with Quakake Creek). But the map assigns no name to the stretch of water between the confluence of Hazle Creek and Beaver Creek, and the confluence of that combined stream with Quakake Creek. Because I rely on topo maps for geological appellations, I don't know whether the stream that flows through downtown Weatherly is called Hazle Creek, Beaver Creek, or Black Creek, or whether it has ever been given an interim name.

Furthermore, I have a "Stream Map of Pennsylvania" that was published in 1965 by the Pennsylvania State University College of Agriculture. This map measures 2-1/2 feet by 4-1/2 feet, yet neglects to assign a name to that connecting stretch of water. Certainly I could ask the local citizens what they call the stream, but that kind of naming convention is somewhat unofficial and is not in keeping with the endorsed nomenclature of the United States Geological Survey. So there you have it.

However, both kayakers I mentioned above told me that they ran this stretch of water, and that it was commonly called Hazle Creek. I am forced to accept that. See the chapter on Hazle creek for additional information about the upstream stretch.

The shortest distance between a put-in and Black Creek Junction lies on Hazle Creek where it flows through Weatherly. See that chapter for detailed information.

Another put-in is on Quakake Creek in Hudsondale, where Route 93 crosses over the stream. The distance from here to the junction is approximately 2.5 miles. See the Quakake Creek chapter for additional details (including the alternate put-in on Wetzel Creek).

In order to obtain the length by means of my GPS unit, I biked along the abandoned railroad bed that closely parallels the stream for most of its length, and I walked the

The stretch of Black Creek between Black Creek Junction and the midway railroad trestle is wide and bordered by low flat banks. The lack of high drop-offs makes it canoeable when the streamflow is middle high.

This pair of cables is located downstream of the midway railroad trestle. It allows anglers to cross the stream, but it's a garrot for paddlers at certain water levels. Kayakers beware.

arc or curved stretch of the first half mile.

The gradient is about 40 feet per mile. On the 90% of the stream that I could see from the railroad bed, the slope was almost perfectly consistent, much like an inclined board with no major ledges or much in the way of protruding boulders that couldn't be avoided because of the 25-foot width of the waterway. This stretch is eminently canoeable – if only it didn't lead to the extremely challenging Black Creek.

A third put-in exists on the arc of Quakake Creek, where Wetzel Creek flows under Station Lane (a few feet from Brenkman Drive). Wetzel Creek is only 5 to 6 feet wide, extends for about a block, then merges with Quakake Creek about a quarter mile downstream of the put-in at Route 93. It's not much to look at during a dry spell, but sometimes after a very hard rain, enough water swells the stream to float a boat, and to propel it at faster-than-light speed to the confluence.

Now on to Black Creek itself. The stream races along the bottom of Hinkles Valley for four and a half miles: from Black Creek Junction to Penn Haven Junction, where it flows into the Lehigh River. The active railroad that plies through the Lehigh Gorge has a switch at Penn Haven Junction, enabling trains to proceed either up the gorge or the valley. The left tine enters Hinkles Valley, proceeds westward, turns north at Black Creek Junction, and passes through Weatherly to points north and west.

At Black Creek Junction there used to be a spur that proceeded due west alongside Quakake Creek to Hudsondale and beyond. No matter which way you go to reach Black Creek Junction – from Weatherly or from Hudsondale – the first major obstacle occurs at the junction: immediately downstream of the confluence of Quakake Creek and Hazle Creek. The trestle has long since been removed – as well as the rails and ties along Quakake Creek – but two supporting piers remain. In the channel between these piers is the biggest logjam I have ever seen.

A couple of years ago, adequate passage existed between the right-bank abutment and the adjacent pier, but recently this narrow channel was closed by accumulated dead-

Black Creek Only Section

fall. Then the only way past this logjam was along the left bank, between the left-bank abutment and its adjacent pier. Immediately prior to publication, the right channel was open and the left channel was partially obstructed by a tree that a paddler could duck under at low water but not at high water. The center channel remains blocked. Which passage will be open tomorrow is anyone's guess.

The logjam against the piers at Black Creek Junction.

Although the gradient in the statistical sidebar reads 67 feet per mile, this is an average from beginning to end. Now I would like to refine that measurement by breaking it in two, in order to give the paddler a better understanding of the challenges that lie ahead.

Two miles downstream from Black Creek Junction, the stream makes a dogleg and passes under a trestle, while the railroad tracks keep going straight. Upstream of this trestle the gradient is 63 feet per mile: extreme to say the least, but actually canoeable because the streambed has maneuvering room (pretty much maintaining a width of 25 feet), the ledges are short (1 to 2 feet), and, most important, exposed boulders are small, the drop-offs are perpendicular to the streamflow, and the tongues are not blocked downstream by badly placed rocks.

After the trestle, the gradient increases to 72 feet per mile. Cascades are nearly continuous with only a few short pools in which to recover a paddler and his or her swamped boat before they are sucked into the next cascade. Boulders are numerous, large, and badly placed, so that in order to squeeze between any two of them, there is likely to be another one in the middle of the streamflow immediately downstream.

My faithful 17-foot Old Town Tripper could never maneuver through such an obstacle course, and neither can my recently acquired 15-foot Dagger – not unless the hulls were flexible and could bend in the middle like a snake.

When Black Creek is runnable, the current gushes so fast over or around the boulders – whose presence have the effect of reducing the effective width of the stream, and thereby increasing the speed of the current – that it is impossible to stand in it. And, as I noted above but must emphasize by reiterating, walkable banks are often nonexistent.

Worse yet, some drop-offs are angled to the direction of the current, are punctuated by rocks, and are followed by strong hydraulics. One 3-foot diagonal ledge in particular must be approached in such a way that a boat is likely to go over it sideways and get flipped by a full-width hydraulic. At other places that water is funneled through restrictions fraught with rocky drop-offs that require radical maneuvers.

If it sounds as if I am trying to scare you, that is because I am. This lower section of Black Creek is not to be taken lightly. The only saving grace is that the streambed is exceptionally straight, with no blind curves to block the view of what you will encounter downstream. Canoeists should attempt this stream only at a medium high level.

My sage advice is that you hike or bike along the service road into order scout the stream. Ascertain the present status of the passageways past the logjam at Black Creek Junction. There's no real reason to scout the section upstream of the midway trestle, because that section is fairly straightforward: not without its challenges, but not with anything that will upset an expert kayaker or canoeist.

Unless you have the utmost confidence in your ability, you should definitely scout the two-and-a-half-mile stretch after the midway trestle. Plot your course through the various cascades, nearly continuous boulder fields, angled ledges, and strong hydraulics. There is no deadfall to worry about. That is, there wasn't the last time I biked alongside this stretch.

Also, choose the right kayak for this stream. You don't want a long pointed hull that is designed for speed, but a short stubby one that is designed for maneuverability in whitewater. In a whitewater kayak, after passing between a pair of boulders, you can turn sharply away from a boulder that lies directly downstream and close to the upstream pair. All too often, this distance is so short that a canoe cannot make such a turn without running into the downstream boulder.

I highly recommend wearing a wetsuit, even in summer heat. Nowhere is the water deep enough to perform an Eskimo roll. Except at super high levels, you'll be scraping over rocks for most of the way, except in the few shallow pools where the water is calm. If the boat tips over, you'll be coming out of it – and you be banging and grating over rough rocks until you manage somehow to claw your way to the sidelines. Without the padding of a wetsuit your skin will be abraded and lacerated in the process.

Having written all of the above, I must now report that every obstacle that I noted above – except for the logjams at Black Creek Junction – vanish under the deluge when the water is super high. In the video clip I watched kayakers drop into cavernous holes and plow through monstrous waves that an open boat could never survive. When the kayaker/videotaper reached the Lehigh River, it was calm by comparison.

Black Creek has no streamflow gauge, nor is there one on any other stream that can be used as an assessment. Direct observation is your only guide. If the water depth is adequate for Hazle Creek in Weatherly, Black Creek is doable – for extreme kayakers and crazy canoeists.

After reaching the Lehigh River, you have six more miles to paddle to the closest take-out, at Glen Onoko.

Quakake Creek is wide and wide-open. Boulders are buried when the water is high, and the normally flat and placid surface becomes a torrent of high rollers.

QUAKAKE CREEK

This stream has a long but narrow watershed that originates south of McAdoo, at Route 309, some 8 to 9 miles west of Hudsondale. Much of this upstream stretch is wide enough to be navigable, and looks appealing from the bridge crossing on Quakake Road, but upon close inspection downstream of the road, it is an ugly jumble of downed trees and logjams, one after another. Parts of the stream are visible from Grist Mill Drive, especially where it passes under the bridge. A boat could be forced down Quakake Creek but only by making a great number of arduous carries.

Only navigable section: Route 93 in Hudsondale to Black Creek Junction
Adversity level 2: Challenging
Distance: 2.8 miles
Needs high water (by observation)
Travel time: 1 hour
Gradient: 33 feet per mile

Despite the fairly steep gradient, the streambed is so evenly sloped that the water flows smoothly as if it were pouring down a tilted board. This is not to say that there aren't a few rocks and riffles at low but runnable flowrates, only that they don't present obstacles to laidback navigation. I would call this a family paddling trip if it led to a readily accessible take-out instead of to very challenging whitewater, when Quakake Creek merges with Hazle Creek at Black Creek Junction to form Black Creek. The only way to avoid Black Creek and the Lehigh River is to portage your boat along the railroad service road to Weatherly: a distance of nearly a mile.

At high flowrates, the stream becomes a raging torrent that isn't visible from the road. Farther downstream, where exposed boulders are usually little more than an easy obstacle to avoid, parts of the stream turn into large standing waves that no longer qualify as a family paddling trip.

The most obvious put-in is at the Route 93 bridge. If you can't see exposed rocks a hundred feet downstream, then the stream is good to go.

In 2006, posters on the American Whitewater website noted that the homeowner on the right bank downstream of the bridge was openly hostile. He claimed that the creek was privately owned, he threatened to call the cops and have boaters arrested, and he intimated that he would damage their vehicles after they embarked. I don't know if the same person still lives there, but I can guarantee that the stream isn't privately owned.

This individual even harassed boaters who put-in on the left bank downstream of the bridge, on municipal property. No one who worked in the municipal building made a fuss, so I would think that it's safe to ignore the abusive homeowner and launch there, but you might want to park elsewhere.

It's also possible to launch on the upstream side of the bridge, although it isn't as convenient as the gently sloping grass on municipal property.

One poster suggested launching on Wetzel Creek, which is located a block away. From Quakake Creek, drive northbound for a hundred feet, bear right onto Station Lane, and stop at the intersection with Brenkman Drive (which leads to Weatherly). Wetzel Creek doesn't look like much when the water is low, but it becomes eminently runnable at high flowrates despite a width of only 5 to 6 feet.

Wetzel Creek merges with Quakake Creek about 200 yards downstream. I saw one problem on this route: a thick tree that spanned the banks and that lay only a couple of feet above the streambed at low water. I don't think it's possible for a kayak to pass beneath it so you'll have to portage . . . unless the water is more than 3 feet high: an unlikely event that will enable you to paddle over it.

After the log the stream takes a short dogleg, then the banks become crowded with rhododendron: mostly on the left side where the current will propel you. Perhaps I am making this sound more difficult than it is, but forewarned is forearmed. Just tuck in your paddle, duck your head, and go with the flow.

Wetzel Creek joins Quakake Creek near the middle of a fairly sharp 180-degree arc in the latter stream. After the arc the stream turns the other way, makes a long shallow arc, then proceed on a fairly straight or slightly undulating course that mostly parallels the abandoned railroad bed above the right bank. (If you had started on Quakake Creek at Route 93, you would have passed under a bridge that used to support trains. Headroom is sufficient.) Sit back and enjoy the ride. The real fun starts at Black Creek Junction.

The upper stretch of Hazle Creek as it flows down the mountain into Weatherly.

Boulders and drop-offs like these are typical on the lower stretch of Hazle Creek between Weatherly and Black Creek Junction. Not for canoes.

HAZLE CREEK

This narrow stream originates on the eastern outskirts of Hazleton, hence the unusual spelling of its name. It flows for three miles through a working strip mine before starting its descent from the highlands. Along the way it picks up water from Dreek Creek, as the name of the stream is spelled on the USGS topo map; or Dreck Creek, in accordance with modern convention. Dreek or Dreck Creek also commences on the eastern outskirts of Hazleton, a little farther south.

Hazle Creek then picks up a bit more water from Beaver Creek, which originates a mile and a half west of Beaver Meadows. Thus the water that falls between an unnamed mountain to the north, and Spring Mountain to the south, is funneled between the eastern slope of Spring Mountain and the western slope of Round Head Mountain, then plunges steeply downhill into Weatherly, eventually merging with Quakake Creek to form Black Creek.

Section 1: Railroad trestle to Black Creek Junction   Gradient: 129 feet per mile
Distance: 1.8 miles   Adversity level 4: Extremely challenging
Travel time: 30 minutes   Needs very high water (by observation)

Two extreme kayakers have told me that they have run this mean stretch of water. The first one who provided information was Nolan Berlew. He told me that in the old days, they were able to drive up the railroad service road from Weatherly to the Hazle Creek railroad bridge. Since then the railroad company has placed a gate across the service road where it begins in Weatherly. Mark Zakutansky added confirmation.

Hazle Creek bridge is where the stream passes under the railroad. It is also the intersection of the active railroad with an abandoned railroad bed that leads north to Buck Mountain Road. Plus, a hundred yards uphill there is an intersection with another abandoned railroad bed that leads west to Beaver Meadows. Both of these abandoned railroad beds make nice trails for hiking and mountain biking.

Nowadays, the way to access Hazle Creek is to drive up Plane Road for a distance of 1.1 miles from the vehicle bridge in Weatherly. Park on the right (north) side of the road, on the other side of the speed limit sign and the orange post with a white reflector. Unload your boat(s). There is better parking a hundred feet or so farther along the road where the shoulder is wider.

What looks like a stony path is a runoff bed for rainwater that flows out of the culvert at the edge of the macadam. Put your kayak on your shoulder and head in the direction in which the "path" points. This quasi-path peters out after a few feet. From this point continue downhill in the same direction through the forest for a couple of hundred yards.

If your angle is right, you'll meet Hazle Creek a block or so downstream of the bridge. If you veer too far to the left (west), you'll meet Beaver Creek. Don't be distressed by what appears to be a wet boulder field; this is not the stream that you will be paddling. Follow the right bank of Beaver Creek to the confluence with Hazle Creek.

Nolan assured me that a canoe could not navigate the narrow, boulder-filled stream. I confirmed this by hiking along (or in) the stream and surveying the bed. I can hardly believe that people have paddled this section, but I have no reason to doubt either Nolan or Mark. In fact, I would go as far as to say that this section of Hazle Creek is a kayaker's delight when the water level is high enough.

The fall of the streambed is consistent; that is, it consists of a nearly continuous series of ledges and sluice drops, one right after the other, punctuated by short, intermittent flat stretches. Most of the ledges measure one to two feet high, although I saw several three-footers. The most challenging hurdles to safe navigation are not the ledges but the sluices. Large boulders funnel water through narrow channels that limit your passage options; or worse, offer only one way to pass between boulders to the next obstacle.

There are hardly any breathing spaces along the way. Yet, when the observable water level reaches the right depth, the obstacles disappear under crashing waves and constant whitewater.

The worst is over shortly after the direction of the stream turns from easterly to southerly. Or perhaps I should say that the most challenging fun is over. The gradient is lower for the rest of the way to Weatherly.

Take-out at the train station or thereabouts.

If you want to know what extreme kayaking is all about, view Mike Stewart's awesome video on YouTube: from the top of Hazle Creek to the Lehigh River. Wow!

Section 2: Weatherly to Quakake Creek
Distance: .9 mile
Travel time: 15 minutes
Adversity level 4: Extremely challenging
Needs very high water (by observation)
Gradient: 86 feet per mile

Access along the main thoroughfare in town looks difficult at best, especially for kayakers, because the stream is confined like an aqueduct between two vertical stone walls that rise as high as six feet above the streambed. While it might be possible to lower a canoe into this aqueduct and have someone hold it in place while a paddler climbs or jumps down into it, I think it might be difficult for a kayaker to perform such a feat as easily – especially when you consider that the current has to be ripping before the aqueduct becomes runnable.

Nonetheless, Mark assured me that he has put-in at the train station. There are spots in the aqueduct where boulders rest against the left bank wall, providing places to embark without too much trouble.

In any case, if the train station entry doesn't appeal to you, you can also put-in either upstream or downstream of town, where there are no stone walls to hinder boarding. I think the best put-in in this regard is at the end of Yeakle Street, where the cul-de-sac lies within sight of the stream and where you can push your boat through the fringe of vegetation to the water's edge. From that point the distance to Black Creek Junction is half a mile. But what a half mile!

The stream looks very much the way it does in the center of town: like a field of boulders that are the size of beach balls, and for the most part no more than 15 feet wide. This obstacle course is a continuous cascade that drops 40 feet from the cul-de-sac before it reaches the Black Creek Junction, with some drop-offs that measure several feet in height, and with a few rocks that are the size of Volkswagens. I don't think it's possible to maneuver through this stretch without bumping into or scraping over a multitude of highly exposed rocks unless the water is high enough to submerge some of them so you can fit between their rounded tops.

This section merges with Quakake Creek at Black Creek Junction to form Black Creek.

BEAR CREEK

I would never have included a chapter about Bear Creek had Mark Zakutanski not told me that he and a few of his extreme kayaking friends had paddled it after an exceptional rainfall. It cannot be run under normal circumstances; even under abnormal circumstances. This stream requires an enormous amount of water to cover its boulder fields. It is a rarity that can seldom be run, and then only by expert kayakers.

The spring from which it originates has been dammed to create a reservoir known as Bear Creek Lake, which is surrounded by a housing development. The outflow dribbles through a culvert under Behrens Road about three-quarters of a mile below the dam, next to the intersection with Bear Creek Drive. The stream looks more like a drainage ditch than a named creek.

Even after a torrential downpour, Mark told me that it can't be run from Behrens Road. He had to carry his kayak downstream until he found sufficient water to float it.

Only section: Behrens Road to the Lehigh River   Adversity level 4: Most challenging
Distance: 3.5 to 4 miles   Needs very high water (by observation)
Travel time: 1 to 2 hours   Overall gradient (approximate): 234 feet per mile

Note that the distance and gradient are estimates. Although I hiked the streambed to take photographs, and to be able to describe the geology, the 5-mile distance that my GPS receiver calculated was wildly exaggerated. Near the beginning I got bogged down in a deep marsh and had to retreat and cross the stream to where the footing was dry and solid. Walking in the shallows and through the forest that lined the banks was devious and slow going. In some places I had to crawl through rhododendron thickets and climb 100-foot cliffs, or both. In other places I had to bushwhack circuitously in order to avoid treacherous ledges.

Compounding the errors of the route worse taken was inaccuracy of signal reception caused by steep ravine walls that blocked near-horizon satellites: those that triangulate position with the greatest degree of accuracy.

As a result, I was forced to rely on multiple map-walker measurements which I averaged, then added 10% for twists, turns, and curves that cannot be shown on paper.

The spread in mileage affected the calculation of the gradient, which also needs additional explanation. The gradient in the statistical sidebar is the *overall* gradient. At about the halfway point the streambed steepens. Above this point the gradient is approximately 149 feet per mile; below this point the gradient is approximately 346 feet per mile.

At the halfway point there is a 50-foot drop over two spectacular 25-foot waterfalls. The pool that separates the waterfalls measures some 75 feet in length: hopefully offering enough recovery time for a flipped-over kayaker.

Now for some description. Start from bridge on Behrens Road where usually only a trickle of water flows along the streambed, like the outflow of a garden hose. As noted above, Mark told me that when he ran it, he had to carry or push his kayak a little ways until he reached water that was deep enough to float it.

The upper half – above the waterfalls – has a relatively steady gradient with few ledges and no high drop-offs. Small boulders abound but will be buried by high water. Several tree trunks span the narrow banks – which are mostly not more than 10 feet

Mark Zakutanski snapped this action shot of the upper waterfall.

apart. I don't know if these will be buried by high water. In many places, rhododendron limbs and lower tree branches hang right down to the water level, or not more than a foot or two above it. These face-hitters can also yank a double-bladed paddle out of your hands if they (the paddles) aren't stowed flat against the deck on these partially blocked passages.

Line-of-sight is short due to vegetation and numerous sharp turns.

After the waterfalls the gradient increases dramatically. Boulders the size of pick-up trucks are sprinkled here and there and almost everywhere, although from my observation the high water will create suitable passageways around them. These boulders, plus ledges and high drop-offs – are nearly continuous from this point onward.

Additional water is added by Little Bear Creek, which likely will be gushing as much as its larger brother. Occasional pools look like rich fishing holes. A wide and open path extends along the right bank from the Lehigh River to the twin falls. It's blocked by downed trees in a few places, and doesn't exist in a couple of spots where huge boulders intervene. Otherwise, it's an easy hike that doesn't require ducking.

Surviving paddlers have to go a little more than 3 miles on the Lehigh River to reach the nearest take-out at Glen Onoko. Anglers who paddle down the Lehigh River from Drakes Creek or Rockport can land on the gravel beach at the confluence, then hike upstream. Anglers who either hike or bike on the Lehigh Gorge Trail can swim across the river; the water here is slow. I have swum across without difficulty.

Little Bear Creek

I was curious about Little Bear Creek, so I surveyed two miles of it above the confluence with Bear Creek, to see how it compares with its big brother. It turned out to be an identical but scaled-down version of Bear Creek, with long pools inhabited by native trout that dash away and hide under rocks as soon as they spot an interloper.

Route 93 crosses the height of land. Rain that falls east of the highway enters the

Little Bear Creek

watershed of the Pohopoco Creek. Rain that falls to the west of the road moistens the ground in an untrammeled forest and becomes Little Bear Creek. At high elevations the streambed is gently sloped; it measures some five feet across. The width gradually increases but is never more than ten feet wide for its entire length.

I started bushwhacking from the end of Bluebell Lane.

The stream is remarkably clear of deadfall. The worst obstacles are rhododendron thickets, whose stout limbs encroach from the sides and droop down close to the water. At first the gully is U-shaped with a fairly flat bottom. As the slope increases, the gully takes on the contours of a steep-walled ravine with a V-shaped bottom. The smooth flow of water is interrupted by short drops or ledges than stand less than a foot in height.

After the first half mile the sidewalls of the ravine become more vertical, although in places off the right bank the slope is angled at only forty-five degrees. At the same place the streambed becomes more rugged. A six-foot-high waterfall is followed by ledges and drop-offs that stand two to three feet in height. Some series of ledges assume the aspect of slides. Slides become sluices where car-sized boulders constrain the width of the stream. The gradient increases dramatically. The left bank is lined by sheer cliffs that rise a hundred feet or more above the water.

One mile from my starting point an unnamed stream joined Little Bear Creek from the left. This increased the flowrate substantially. The streambed now consisted of narrow saw-toothed bedrock. There were no more loose rocks or gravel bars. Half a mile farther downstream stood a ten-foot-high waterfall, followed closely by another one in which the water was bifurcated by a car-sized boulder in the middle. Now I had to do some hairy rock climbing in order to descend past those and other waterfalls that stretched between rock faces on both sides of the stream. I waded through knee-deep water from side to side in order to find that best way down past the obstacles.

In this picture, Mark Zakutanski shows the ruggedness of another stretch of Bear Creek.

Now the streambed became a constant series of ledges, drop-offs, sluices, and huge boulders. Finally I reached the confluence with Bear Creek, 1.9 miles from my starting point. I calculated the overall gradient as 163 feet per mile. This breaks down to 151 feet per mile above the confluence with the unnamed stream; 176 feet per mile below it.

Paddling is for extreme kayakers only. Anglers will find more deep pools above the unnamed stream than below it, where drop-offs come one after the other.

NESQUEHONING CREEK

Make no mistake about it: this stream is for heavy-duty whitewater paddlers only.

For those who possess the experience and expertise, this normally dry watercourse becomes exciting and extremely challenging whenever a heavy downfall turns the barely perceptible flow from a wet rock garden to a thrilling whitewater adventure.

Nesquehoning Creek emerges from high ground at the west end of Broad Mountain. Water trickles down the south slope through a steep-walled ravine to the bottom of the mountain, then turns east. Immediately the water is trapped behind two successive dams that create a pair of reservoirs known as Greenwood and Hauto. The Hauto spillway funnels the overflow into a natural marsh that is dotted with lily pads and filled with fish. The stream proper becomes fast-moving water when the gradient increases downstream of the marsh.

About 80% of the water that washes down the south side of Broad Mountain – that is, 8 linear miles of mountain slope – ends up in the Nesquehoning Creek. The other 20% flows directly into the Lehigh River.

It's possible to put-in at Tippets Road but there is nearby parking for only two vehicles. Worse, the initial entry is clogged with encroaching vegetation that you might have to force your way through. After the first 50 feet, the streambed widens and the vegetation on either side recedes.

I think it's just as well to put-in a quarter mile downstream at Tonoli Road, where a gravel clearing is conveniently located next to the railroad tracks; it can accommodate a large number of vehicles. Launch your boat on the left bank downstream of the bridge.

From that point the paddling distance to the confluence with the Lehigh River is 8 miles; then it's 2 more miles to the take-out at the train station in Jim Thorpe. Although I once ran the full length on a single passage that took three and a half hours, I have separated the creek into 3 sections that are based on differences in adversity. This separation – and the separate descriptions – will enable readers to decide how much of the stream they wish to run, and in what type of boat (covered or uncovered) they want to run it.

Afterward I have appended a section in which I present my analysis of this challenging stream, and offer some suggestions with respect to paddling techniques and boat types. Only you can judge your degree of competence to handle the fast shallow rapids.

Nesquehoning Creek has no streamflow gauge, nor is there one on any other stream that can be used for comparison. Direct observation is your major guide.

Section 1: Tonoli Road to Industrial Road

Distance: 1.8 miles
Travel Time: 1 hour
Adversity level 2: Challenging due to annoying deadfall
Needs very high water (by observation)
Gradient: 45 feet per mile

This section is so curvy that the paddling distance measures twice the driving distance. Thus what appears to be a short run by road is much longer by water. Picture a corkscrew flattened onto a two-dimensional surface, and you'll have a fair idea of how the creek meanders through the woods.

The gradient is steep but constant: almost like a sliding board whose plane is only

Nesquehoning Creek Section 1 and 2

Section 1 is pretty, but claustrophobic.

slightly inclined. The upper stretch has few exposed rocks, and those that are exposed are small and easily avoided. This is not to say that the creek is without obstacles: only that the obstacles are made of wood instead of conglomerate.

Six logjams bar expeditious passage. The banks are so thickly overgrown with rhododendron that I couldn't step ashore. The only way to get past the wooden barriers was to step out of the boat, wade in knee-deep water, and shove the boat over the top of the debris. These maneuvers were not difficult for me because I was paddling an open canoe. But passing each obstacle consumed time and energy.

Worse than the logjams were the curves. Because the creek averages 10 to 15 feet in width, there was not a lot of room to maneuver a 17-foot canoe. The current was so strong that I constantly got shoved against the bank on the outside of the curves. What makes this a problem is the aforementioned rhododendron. In some places the rhododendron grew in such profusion on both banks that the limbs and leaves intertwined to create a roof some 2 feet above the surface. I had to withdraw my paddle from the water and duck flat over the thwarts as the current pushed the boat through tunnels of greenery.

When the rhododendron grew inward on the curves, I got pinned against the branches while the water flowing under the bottom threatened to flip the canoe. Every curve was a struggle, and once the upstream gunwale nearly got pushed under water as I fought to get free of entanglement.

The obstacles presented in this stretch of stream make for slow going. The saving grace is that the water moves quickly, but not so quickly that I didn't have time to perceive and react to upcoming situations. Even if your boat tips over, you will merely find yourself standing in crotch-deep water that isn't moving fast enough to sweep you off your feet. The shallow water is on your side.

Section 2: Industrial Road to Route 93
Distance: 4.0 miles
Travel time: 1 hour

Adversity level 4: Extremely challenging
Needs very high water (by observation)
Gradient: 61 feet per mile

This section is twice as long as the previous section yet takes about the same time to paddle. The reasons are several: only one fallen tree, no encroaching rhododendron, and faster flow due to increased gradient and more water joining the creek from tributaries. "Wild and woolly" best describes this downstream slalom.

The streambed is punctuated with boulders that are grouped like bristles on a brush. Most of the time the stream flows through patches of bristles like water through a colander, leaving the tops high and dry. But when the creek is in flood, the majority of boulders are covered. Those that are not concealed have rounded tops that don't stick up very high. Even if you do strike a boulder, you're more likely to bounce off it than to have your gunwale dip beneath the surface. That's because the water isn't deep enough to sink or swamp a boat.

You can't help but scrape over rocks that lie barely beneath the surface. Simply try to dodge around the most obvious

The first bend of the dogleg at Paradise Road. When the water level is super high, the gravel bar at the inside of the elbow is submerged... but so are the following boulders, so there's no need to stop and scout.

bumps. This sections has no waterfalls, ledges, or drop-offs; it's a continuous high-speed rollercoaster that charges downstream around gradual bends and leaves you breathless but exhilarated. Paddling this stretch is pure unadulterated fun.

This is not to say that there aren't a couple of big rocks in the way. There are, but they're avoidable. The increased width of the streambed – 15 to 20 feet – provides adequate maneuvering room.

Watch out for the low bridge. The tip of my canoe cleared the steel supporting beams by only an inch or two. I pulled in my paddle and lay down flat until I reached open air. The passage is not marred by obstacles in the river.

The only sharp bends occur at a dogleg at the end of Paradise Road. The take-out is nearly in sight when you see a sheer wall of dirt rising 10 feet high in front of you, at which point the stream turns 90 degrees to the left. The dirt wall also extends along the right bank before and after the upcoming turn. You don't have to paddle blind around the bend. You can beach your boat on the gravel bar on the inside of the curve if the streamflow is medium high. From here you can see 100-feet downstream, to the 90-degree turn to the right, so you can examine your maneuvering options.

This short stretch is a little dicey but not impassable. Running it takes careful observation of the restricted width of the stream. Once you have your route planned and indelibly mapped in your head, shove off the gravel bar and prepare for quick action. Don't worry if things don't go exactly as planned. The rocks are sloped and fairly rounded so that even if you hit one, you'll likely slide off.

Head for the sluice that precedes the elbow where the streambed turns sharply to the right, and paddle through it on either side of the center rock that splits the water flow. Then bounce over the boulders and rock ledges, turn right at the bend, paddle under the driveway bridge (which has plenty of headroom), and proceed through the mammoth highway tunnel under Route 93.

The take-out and/or put-in are located immediately after the light zone, when you see open sky overhead.

To take-out, land on the right bank as soon as possible. Portage your boat 150 feet through the brush to the gravel service road that feeds the treatment plant (on your left), alongside the railroad tracks. Turn right and walk a block or so through the tunnel to the gate that bars unauthorized motor vehicles. You can park a couple of vehicles behind the huge boulder on the outside of the gate. Paradise Road lies just around the bend. This can also be used as a put-in for Section 3.

Nesquehoning Creek Sections 2 and 3

There's no need for a flashlight inside the tunnel. Hug the left side at medium high water levels, as the channel is deeper there than it is on the right side. Go anywhere you want at super high streamflows.

Alternatively, you can park on the pull-over on Route 93, on the east or downstream side of the road, on the north side of the tunnels. The way to the left bank is shorter than the way to the right bank, but is made more difficult by the steep, brush-laden slope to the water. Carrying a kayak or dragging and sliding a canoe downhill is not too challenging, but climbing uphill with a boat on your shoulder(s) is onerous.

Note that in the first paragraph I stated that there was only one fallen tree. Actually, when I ran this stream in its entirety (instead of in individual sections, as I did on other occasions), the tree had not yet fallen. I had a clear shot all the way. The tree did not fall until 2014: not due to a windstorm but because its base was badly rotted. The tree looks as if it's going to stay for a while. Not to worry: the banks are broad and gently sloped on either side, making it a simple task to step ashore on either bank and drag the boat over the trunk.

Section 3: Route 93 to the Lehigh River, thence to Jim Thorpe

Distance: 3.1 miles, then 2 miles
Travel time: 1-1/2 hours
Adversity level 4: Extremely challenging
Needs very high water (by observation)
Gradient: 62 feet per mile

See the final two paragraphs of the previous section for put-in alternatives.

This section has broader banks than the previous section, averaging 20 to 25 feet across at first, then expanding and contracting farther downstream. Although the gradient is only 1 foot-per-mile steeper than Section 2, the incline is not nearly as consistent: some areas are relatively level, while others drop precipitously over series of ledges with no still water at the bottom for recovery. This section is more like an undulating boulder field than a smooth gravel bed.

Before I paddled this stream for the first time, I scouted the entire stretch from Industrial Road to the confluence. I did this by bushwhacking along the right bank, adjacent to the railroad track. I couldn't see all of Section 3 because part of the right bank was bordered by a sheer wall and topped with trees that prevented me from looking down at the water. So I bushwhacked along the left bank from Route 93 to the confluence. I even walked through the tunnel under Route 93. I didn't want to have any last minute surprises.

It was good that I did this. Two-thirds of the way downstream I discovered a hairy cascade that drops 15 vertical feet over the course of 75 linear feet. This series of ledges was an obstacle that I definitely wanted to avoid. I marked a portage point by tying pink ribbons to branches that overhung the left bank. The rest of the creek looked marginally runnable by exercising caution.

Then came the day of reckoning. I passed Paradise Road without stopping, petted the dogleg, passed under the driveway bridge, then paddled through the tunnel under Route 93. This tunnel is massive: 30 feet tall and more than 40 feet wide, with water running all the way from one side to the other.

Large rocks inside the tunnel yielded to larger rocks downstream, and the level streambed angled downward to a sharp incline. The creek was dropping rapidly. Suddenly I found myself scraping over boulders with incredible celerity. There was no time to ponder over the best passage to take. I went where the current carried me, and did my best to fit my canoe between staggered boulders the size of wheelbarrows. There was no let-up.

I don't know how long I paddled in this furious fashion. When I came to a ledge that looked double dicey, I veered toward the left bank and drove the canoe onto shore between a pair of trees. I stepped onshore to examine the lay of submerged land. I determined that it might be possible to paddle over the ledge, but the strange angle of the primary watercourse made the outcome problematical. I wasn't certain that I could turn the canoe sharp enough in midstream to avoid boulders farther down. Rather than take a chance, I hauled the boat out of the water and dragged it to a point below the ledge.

Several hundred yards later I came to, not one ledge, but a series of short ledges with a cumulative drop of 8 feet. I made an instantaneous decision, and did something which in all my years and thousands of miles of paddling I had never done before: I leaped out of the canoe! I *most* definitely did not want to paddle over this ledge.

I landed in a pool of deep water in which I sank up to my neck. For a moment my feet did not touch the bottom. The canoe was getting swept away from me. In my effort to swim, and to clutch and hang onto the boat, I accidently lost my grip on the paddle. The current swept it under the hull. I made a grab for it but missed. I had more important concerns. I kicked with both feet and swam with one arm toward shore as the current swept me and the boat downstream. The pool ended, I found firm footing, and managed to haul the canoe into the near-shore shallows.

Holding onto the gunwale, I climbed over submerged rocks and led the boat downstream. The paddle floated into an eddy some 20 feet away. I caught up with it and tossed it into the canoe. By this time I was partway down the series of ledges. Now I had time to contemplate my initial expedient. My reasoned consideration corroborated my instinctive reaction: I *definitely* did not want to paddle over this series of ledges – not so much because of the consecutive drops, but because the rock angles were all wrong.

The flash of insight that normally guided me through rapids had warned me to avoid this obstacle at all cost. I was glad that I had heeded my subconscious alarm. The question that was now uppermost in my mind was why I hadn't perceived this potential risk on my scouting trips. How could I have overlooked this hazard?

I soon deduced that the reason was the difference in

Typical Section 3 ledge.

water level and flow rate. Both had been only moderately high when I had scouted the creek. Now, four days after the passage of Superstorm Sandy, the stream was a raging torrent: not just high water but abnormally high water. I thought back to the tributaries that I had passed along the way. All of them had been gushing with water that was still cascading down the mountainside. The effect of all this additional water was cumulative, flooding the lower stream beyond anything I had previously seen or anticipated.

In other words, when I originally scouted the stream, it looked as if I could have sneaked the ledge on the left. Now, the left ledge had a torrent of water crashing over it – and the right ledge was positively frightening.

My situation was not untenable. This was not a wilderness creek with no way out but downstream. Civilization lay nearby. I could leave the canoe in the woods and return to run the rest of the creek when the water level was lower. I could walk to a road in less than an hour. I could call for help on the cell phone that I carried in a watertight case; Cheryl, who was waiting for me at the train station, could pick me up at a newly designated location.

On the other hand, a wilderness paddler knows that there is no such thing as an impassable barrier. If a stretch of water isn't runnable, go around it: by walking the canoe through the shoreline shallows (as I had just done), by lining the boat through the rapids, by carrying over a ledge, or by portaging. In this instance I decided to walk the canoe through the shallows, sometime by holding onto the gunwale, other times by holding onto the painters and controlling the canoe's drift and orientation; this latter technique is known as lining.

I started paddling again a hundred feet downstream of the ledges. Now I was extremely cautious. I hugged the left bank because I knew that my planned portage route lay somewhere ahead. Occasionally I gained the middle of the stream and tumbled over the rocks. The high flow rate was an advantage: whenever the canoe grounded on a partially submerged boulder, the water shoved it off and propelled me downstream. All I had to do was maintain balance and point the bow in the best direction.

Finally my pink ribbons came into view. I beached the boat and hiked through the woods to an observation point, where a narrow bridge supported an aged iron pipe across the creek. I had hiked and biked across this bridge on numerous occasions. From the middle of the bridge I could see the entire length of the cascading ledges. I was almost tempted to run it because the water was so high that it reduced the initial 4-foot drop to only a foot; and the following ledges looked more like a waterslide than a series of drop-offs.

I chose not to run it because of the angled half-right turn at the bottom. This narrow passage measured only ten feet across. I judged that the final drop into the turn did not offer sufficient maneuvering room for a 17-foot canoe – although I thought that a kayak could make it with ease. I commenced to portage my boat a hundred yards or so through a rhododendron thicket.

I couldn't perform a true portage with the canoe on my shoulders because the twisted rhododendron trunks and limbs didn't allow me to stand upright. I had to hunch most of the way through the thicket, so I dragged the boat. The bushes grew so close together that in several places the broad beam jammed between trunks. I had to lift the canoe onto its side, then pull, yank, and wiggle it through intertwined branches for the length of a football field.

I put-in below the final drop-off. There were more big boulders ahead of me, but

I knew that the pipe-cross lay only a quarter mile away from the confluence. After a short chancy stretch the gradient moderated and the streambed widened, At this point I was essentially home free.

The only thing to look out for was the cable-cross: two cables that stretch across the stream to enable archaeologists to access the dig on the left bank at the confluence. Depending on the water level, you may have to duck under the lower cable. Then the Lehigh River loomed into view.

Thirty miles upriver, the Francis E. Walter dam was releasing less than 1,000 cubic feet of water per second. Yet the volume of water that flowed through the gorge was extraordinary, flooded by all the tributaries that fed the mighty river. The resulting high level washed out the lower stretch between Nesquehoning Creek and the train station in Jim Thorpe; I didn't see a single exposed rock: only large confused waves and the rapids at the approach to the take-out. Despite spritzing snow, the last two miles was an effortless jaunt.

Analysis

The Nesquehoning Creek is an incomparable paddling experience, but one that must be taken with caution. I have gone to great lengths to describe my full-length trip so that my readers will not be caught unawares by extreme water conditions that might be beyond their ability or experience, or so that they don't have erroneous expectations.

I recommend Section 1 for canoeists who don't mind the challenges that a curvy stream and logjams present. I do not recommend this section for kayakers: not because they can't run it safely, but because most kayakers prefer the challenges of whitewater rapids and rocky obstacle courses. Having to pop the spray skirt and exit the boat in order to carry over half a dozen logjams may not satisfy their motivation for kayaking. And take heed . . .

When I paddle solo I normally wield a double-bladed paddle. I had Iliad manufacture a special 10-foot double-bladed paddle whose shaft separates in the middle for ease in transportation. I could not use this paddle on Section 1 because whenever I dipped one blade, the other blade caught in low-hanging trees or rhododendron thickets. Although a kayak paddle is shorter, it would suffer from a similar fate but not nearly as often.

Section 2 can be paddled by both open and closed boats (kayaks and covered canoes). I wouldn't recommend it for inflatable kayaks because of the absolutely unavoidable action of scraping over exposed and barely submerged rocks, which might tear the fabric. The rapids are straightforward and possess no obstacles that necessitate exiting the boat (except for the newly fallen tree).

Kayakers are warned, however, that this is a shallow-water stream that offers no opportunity for rolling a flipped boat upright. If your kayak turns over, you will be dragged over coarse rocks. All you can do then is pop out – and you'll still get dragged over coarse rocks. Recovery will be difficult. A neoprene wetsuit will protect the skin from nasty abrasions. No naked legs; wear a full-length wetsuit.

I've paddled Section 2 more than once, without paddling the adjacent sections. Doing this stretch alone conveys all the thrills of whitewater paddling without the drudgery of the previous section and without the risk of the following section.

Section 3 is a kayaker's delight and a canoeist's nightmare. I haven't kayaked for

Nesquehoning Creek

I was standing on the pipe cross when I took this picture of the upstream cascade during medium high water.

many years, and when I did my skill level was never more than intermediate. When I read water, I read it from the standpoint of a canoeist. Yet I can't help but think that a skilled kayaker can paddle this lower section without undue risk. Having said that, however, I strongly urge kayakers to scout the pipe cross cascade in order to determine if they feel comfortable with running this potentially treacherous series of ledges.

To reach the pipe cross, drive to the end of Paradise Road (off Route 93, a couple of blocks north of the T intersection with Route 209). Turn left (south, toward the railroad track) and park next to the Nesquehoning dogleg or behind the huge boulder (but don't block the gate to the water treatment plant). Walk east past the gate and along the service road for a mile and a quarter. You'll probably miss the trailhead; I generally do. You'll know you've gone too far when see the retaining ponds of a water filtration system. Turn back and look more closely toward the creek.

You might see a short section of pipe protruding through the stone next to the track. The short trail leads down a hundred yards through a rhododendron thicket that is reminiscent of the Haunted Forest of Wizard of Oz fame. Walk to the middle of the bridge and look downstream.

If you want a closer view of the lower ledges, cross the bridge and follow the trail for 50 feet or so, to where the thicket ends and the forest begins. Turn right (east). There is somewhat of a trail through the rhododendron that leads downstream to the final ledge in the series.

One last thought: the time I paddled all three sections together was in early November. The temperature was in the low 40's. As I prepared for the assault, I thought about whether I should wear a wetsuit or a drysuit. I have several drysuits because my primary outdoor activity is scuba diving. I opted to go dry, with long-johns under my drysuit. This turned out to be a good choice – not because it spritzed snow throughout the day, but because I had to get into the water so many times: at the Section 1 logjams, and in Section 3 where I had to walk or line the canoe.

Keep in mind the possibility of swamping, dumping, or popping out; and take the weather and water temperature into consideration. As I noted above, a layer of neoprene can go a long way toward preventing skin abrasions. There's nothing quite like rubber padding for protection from rocks and boulders.

MAUCH CHUNK CREEK

The water that feeds this stream originates southwest of Summit Hill, in the valley between Pisgah Mountain and Mauch Chunk Ridge. An elevation in this valley is the height of land that separates Owl Creek from White Bear Creek. Owl Creek flows westward to the Little Schuylkill River, thence to the Schuylkill River, which eventually merges with the Delaware River in Philadelphia.

White Bear Creek flows eastward for three miles as little more than a trickle that dampens the forest. When it emerges from the hinterland at Route 902, its width has increased but only temporarily. When you look upstream and downstream from the bridge, you see what appears to be a marsh that is a tangle of deadfall. Some 50 feet downstream stands another bridge: the only visible remains of the old road that predates the present highway.

Half a mile farther downstream, where the water flows through a power line easement, the stream is so narrow that you can step over it without breaking your stride. Immediately east of the easement two things happen: the name of the stream changes to Mauch Chunk Creek, and the width increases due to impoundment. This is the upper end of the reservoir known as Mauch Chunk Lake.

Flooding has been a major problem throughout the history of the borough of Mauch Chunk (now Jim Thorpe). Over the years, hundreds of people have been killed and millions of dollars of property damage has been incurred. At times – particularly during the passage of major hurricanes – the downtown section of Broadway has been temporarily converted from a street to a raging river with a depth of several feet. Torrents of water have swept everything out of its path, sometimes including the macadam and the foundations of adjacent buildings.

In the 1970's, a flood control project was initiated to contain Mauch Chunk Creek and to prevent further catastrophe. Within a month of completion, in 1972, Hurricane Agnes dropped more than seven inches of rain that would have consumed the downtown area had it not been for the dam. Jim Thorpe has been safe from flooding ever since. Two years later, the reservoir was designated as a recreational area named Mauch Chunk Lake Park.

Nowadays, the county park is a mecca to which tens of thousands of visitors throng every year. Activities include camping, hiking, biking, fishing, swimming, boating, and picnicking. Part of the famous Switchback Trail

This historical picture of downtown Mauch Chunk was taken during the flood of 1933.

passes through the park. There are two boat launches. You can bring your own boat or rent one from the park. The park rents canoes, kayaks, rowboats, and paddleboats.

The reservoir measures more than five miles in length. Because the water has no

Mauch Chunk Creek Only Section

Ice fishing is a popular activity on the reservoir.

perceptible current, it is the perfect place to sharpen your canoeing technique, break in a new partner, and practice Eskimo rolls in a kayak.

The original streambed appears at the bottom of the dam. For the next two and a half miles, Mauch Chunk Creek is a babbling brook that averages five to ten feet in width, not a single foot of which is runnable. Okay, there may be stretches between logs and fallen trees where you can paddle a full boat length or two, but these spots are few and far between. I wouldn't even call this stretch an obstacle course, because it is nothing more than one long obstacle that contains enough deadfall to fuel the average household fireplace for the lifetime of the home.

I hardly exaggerate. You can see for yourself by hiking or biking the Switchback Trail from the dam to the outskirts of Jim Thorpe; or hike on the streambed where the water is seldom greater than ankle deep. Downstream of Flagstaff Road, after the stream flows under the highway and passes the sewage treatment plant, large rocks are more prevalent than logs. Now the stream is basically a wet boulder field where even toy boats would have trouble squeezing between rocks. And it's hardly wider than a canoe, to boot.

But then, the stream flows right through the middle of town: not between the buildings, but under them.

Only section: Broadway to the Lehigh River
Distance: 1.5 miles
Travel time: less than 1 hour

Adversity level 2: Challenging
Needs visible water flow
Gradient: 125 feet per mile

The first issue that I need to address to the uninformed is that water that flows through underground aqueducts is not sewage. Nor are the covered passageways called sewers. They are called storm drains. A storm drain is a conduit (if the diameter is small) or tunnel (if the diameter is large) that provides a channel for unwanted surface water to follow so that the water does not flood city streets or rural roadways.

As a teenager growing up in northeast Philly, one of my two primary outdoor activities was exploring storm drains. (My other one was climbing trees.) For a young city slicker with an exploratory bent, and without the means to travel, storm drains had to satisfy my appetite until I was old enough to drive to the country where wild caves abounded: upstate Pennsylvania, Maryland, Virginia, and West Virginia. But that's another story . . .

When it comes to underground exploration, I cut my teeth in storm drains, and had a number of adventures that prepared me for exploring real caves (both dry and submerged) later in life. In this regard I count myself an expert. It was nothing for me to spend hours in storm drains, and emerge miles away from my starting point after passing beneath shopping malls and large housing developments.

This is one of the least congested stretches of the stream between the dam and the storm drain. Worse logjams exist, and downstream of the water treatment plant the incline increases dramatically.

Therefore, while conducting surveys for this book, it was natural for me to follow Mauch Chunk Creek underground when it reached the outskirts of town. The most important feature to understand about this particular tunnel is that the watercourse is not artificial. The original streambed was not moved or altered in any way; it was simply walled-in and roofed-over. In that respect it hardly qualifies as a storm drain: that is, one that was purposely designed and laid out under a paved urban area, in order to create an avenue for rainwater runoff.

The stretch of Mauch Chunk Creek that is not exposed to the sky is not so much underground as it is under blacktop. In that sense it is more of a concealed passageway than a storm drain.

The most astonishing feature about the Mauch Chunk Subway, if I may refer to the subterranean portion of the creek in such a manner, is that the streambed is runnable . . . although admittedly I haven't run it. But I did walk it.

In addition to reminding me of exhilarating childhood adventures, with a strong sense of déjà vu, the Mauch Chunk Subway presented surprises that I didn't expect and that I had never experienced. Whereas most of the storm drains that I explored in Philly were fairly new – they were constructed in the 1950's and '60's as urban development spread into the woods and one-time farmland – most of the Mauch Chunk Subway appears to have been built in the 1800's or early 1900's.

Furthermore, the Subway appears to have been constructed piecemeal. Most segments were assembled from stone, some of brick, a few of concrete, and one short segment was fabricated from corrugated metal, like a Quonset hut (near the downstream end, perhaps under Route 209). All these segments were fairly short, generally not more than a few hundred feet in length, before abutting a segment that was made of entirely different material (and I presume at a different time). In some places stone and brick segments alternate. In other places, stone segments alternate with segments that utilized a different kind or size of stone. Stone blocks were the most common material.

Roman arches predominate when stone or brick was the construction material. Concrete segments were rectangular, likely poured on wooden forms that were removed after the concrete solidified and cured.

The width of the tunnel is consistently eight feet across. The height varies from as high as eight feet to as low as five feet. The streambed appears to be bedrock which for the most part has been swept clean of dirt, loose rock, and miscellaneous debris. There were a few loose rocks scattered here and there, but they were not slippery with moss or algae as you find in an open stream because they can't grow in the total absence of sunlight.

The cliché "clean as a whistle" best describes what in essence is a raceway with a ceiling. The only difference between the Subway and a stream that passes under a bridge is the length: a mile and a half instead of twenty to thirty feet.

The mileage is an approximation because my GPS could not receive a signal. I calculated the distance by rolling a map walker over Broadway on a topographic map, then adding 25% to account for squiggles. It has been my experience that actual stream measurements are usually about 25% longer than a map measurement.

The difference in elevation between the beginning and end of the tunnel is 187 feet. Divided by a mile and a half, this means that the overall gradient is a whopping 125 feet per mile. This would normally scare the spray skirt off me, but in this instance – hard as it is to believe – walking through the Subway was no different from walking down Broadway.

Ancient architectures of various styles will be more noticeable to and appreciated by pedestrians than by swiftly passing paddlers.

The streambed is sloped with nearly perfect uniformity: almost like a flat inclined plane, or a joist with one end propped up by a couple of bricks. There are no ledges, no drop-offs, almost no irregularities. And the minor irregularities that do exist affect only spelunkers, not boaters. Only twice did I step into knee-deep holes; otherwise the water was ankle- to shin-deep all the way.

Although the flow-rate was low when I conducted my survey, the stream was almost runnable, and perhaps not "almost." For one thing, in most places the water did not spread across the full width of the tunnel, but was funneled into a channel that measured half the width, effectively increasing the depth. For another, the angle of descent was so steep that, although a boat would scrape across rocky protrusions on the uneven surface, the combined propelling forces of gravity and current would be greater than the resistance due to friction.

You might think that another six inches in depth of water would make the trip more effortless. While that is undoubtedly true, you might then find that the absence of all friction enables a boat move with a speed that is frightening. I'd rather be in a boat that hung up occasionally than in one that was an unstoppable runaway. I can even envision that a boat dragging a drogue or grapple would be better equipped than one with a paddle.

You really don't need a paddle: there is no need to propel a boat forward because the current and gravity will do that, and there is no need to steer because the walls and the channel will keep the boat on course. In reality, you need an anchor more than a paddle, so you can reduce the speed of the boat if the sensation of terminal velocity gets too scary: the same sensation that motorists feel after comfortably breezing along a wide open highway at 70 miles per hour, then immediately step on the brake inside a tunnel when they realize how fast the walls appear to be moving a couple of feet from the vehicle's window.

I suggest a helmet no matter what kind of boat you choose. There are two overhead obstructions. Each is an 18-inch iron pipe that cuts across the tunnel, leaving a clearance of three feet. You must remember to duck.

Running the Mauch Chunk Subway should be like paddling a downstream slalom: a breathtaking event that is over before you know it. Watch out for the drop at the end. Hug the right wall where a build-up of concrete creates a rise that can be used to snag the hull.

There are four other features that I would like to mention: curiosities, not obstacles.

1) In the first half mile there are several places where the Subway has no ceiling. These roofless stretches range in length from five feet to more than a hundred. In these places the storm drain is confined by walls but is open to the air like the river channels in Los Angeles. By looking up, you can see not only the sky, but yards and the outer walls of houses. The last one is the longest; it lies opposite the Immaculate Conception Church. This is a good place to check the water flow. Don't be put off by the extra steep slope within this final open-air stretch: it's the steepest spot in the Subway, and there are no others that approach this angle of descent.

2) In two places there are floodlights hanging from cut-outs in the ceiling – and they were illuminated when I passed under them! Why they are there, and in what buildings they are located, I have no idea.

3) Twice I heard music toward the end of the tunnel. I couldn't hear it well enough to determine what was playing. I must have been underneath a bar or restaurant.

4) Close to the end, hundreds of delicate speleothems are growing from the concrete ceiling and walls. In caves, these mineral deposits are called stalactites. The slender dripstone formations like the ones growing here are called soda straws. The white purity of this flowstone gallery is spectacular to behold.

All in all, the Mauch Chunk Subway was an interesting experience: one that brought me full circle to the explorations of my youth.

Mahoning Creek Only Section

MAHONING CREEK

Stretched between heights-of-land to the north and south, Mahoning Creek drains water from vast farm fields to the west. Several unnamed branches flow together to form a recognizable streambed in a small patch of forest about three-quarters of a mile west of Normal Square.

Only section: Mill Road to the Lehigh River
Adversity level 1: Not challenging except for annoying deadfall
Distance: 7.8 miles
Needs 800 % on the Aquashicola streamflow gauge
Travel time: 2 to 3 hours
Gradient: 14 feet per mile

If it weren't for deadfall, the Mahoning Creek would be the best all-around family paddling trip in the area. The incline is so gentle that you might think that the streambed was graded as an amusement park ride. The watercourse flows between inconsistent banks that range in width from 10 feet to 30 feet, expanding and restricting without warning. Trees line both banks for most of the way, yielding a supreme sense a wilderness that is deceiving because beyond the thin wooden veneer lie farm fields, businesses, and residential communities: to which the paddler is largely oblivious because these signs of human encroachment are mostly out of sight from the stream.

Although downed trees present obstacles that must be overcome by stepping into knee-deep water, perhaps the greatest hazard occurs when the stream flows through the Mahoning Valley Country Club golf course, where paddlers might get clunked by an out-of-bounds golf ball: an unlikely scenario that worries me not. The greatest intrusion comes from circling around the Mahoning Valley Speedway on a day when races are in progress, when noise pollution interferes with the somber solitude.

When I first paddled this lovely stream, I had to disembark only three times to lift the boat over fallen trees that spanned the banks. After Superstorm Sandy, I had to carry over six of them, and I had to duck and paddle through downward-pointing branches of four others. Despite these annoyances, I highly recommend this stream for a wistful summer cruise, when the water is warm and when most of the way is shaded by a canopy of overlapping leaves.

Even in extremely high water, there were very few places where my blade did not strike bottom when I dipped my paddle. I wore a life vest out of habit, but there was hardly any place where I could not stand in water that swirled around my legs.

The put-in is located near an intersection called Normal Square, where Route 443 crosses Mill Road, several miles west of downtown Lehighton. Turn north onto Mill Road. The bridge crosses the stream a block away. To unload your boat, pull into the dirt road on the north side of the bridge, west side of the road. Slide your boat over the rocks on the left bank, launch, and proceed under the bridge.

In addition to deadfall, you'll have to carry around a low walking bridge in the golf course. This is where I met the astonished octogenarian I described in the Introduction: the one who said, "I've been golfing here for 60 years. Never seen a canoe before."

Aside from golfers, the only other people you're likely to meet on your way downstream are anglers. They fish from the bridges (either under them or from on top), and along the banks near access points. A few backyards touch the water along the upper stretch. Otherwise, you're on your own.

I spotted Canada geese (and their yellow goslings, which looked like the candy chicks you find in Easter baskets), mallards, mergansers, great blue herons, a huge flock of cawing crows, and a pair of very large owls in flight.

You'll know that you're nearing the end of the trip when you pass under the heavily-trafficked Route 443 bridge. As you look ahead to where the stream turns left, you'll see an incredibly steep, tree-covered slope that rises 400 feet above the water. It almost looks as if the mountain might topple over and bury you. Then comes a sweeping right turn, a sharp left turn, and the Lehigh Drive bridge (which looks like a viaduct). You can see the Lehigh River by looking through the four stone arches, A broad stony beach stretches across the left bank, upstream of the bridge. You can drive a vehicle down a short dirt road to the edge of the beach, making for a very convenient take-out.

Don't run the Mahoning Creek unless the streamflow gauge on the Aquashicola Creek registers at least 800% above normal (median). (There is no streamflow gauge on the Mahoning Creek.) The drainage areas for the two streams are 20 miles apart, so be aware that disparities could occur if more rain fell to the east of the Lehigh River than fell to the west of it. But it's a pretty good guide.

At 800 %, I was barely able to scrape over the gravel bars. Higher water is preferable. The only problem with running the stream when the water is extremely high, is that the current will be moving so fast that you'll have more trouble getting yourself and your boat over and through the downed trees.

POHOPOCO CREEK

Pohopoco is pronounced po-ho-po'-co, with long o's and the accent on the second "po." The stream drains water from farmland north of Effort. At least two named tributaries boost its volume.

Section 1: Route 115 to Mill Pond Road

Distance: 4.0 miles
Travel Time: 1 to 2 hours
Adversity level 3: Very challenging because of horrendous deadfall
Needs very high water (by observation at put-in)
Gradient: 35 feet per mile

Ordinarily this stream is little more than an anemic trickle at the Route 115 put-in: more like a wet pebble garden than a runnable waterway. This appearance can change dramatically after a super-heavy rainfall. I ran this section after a freak 3-inch downpour turned the rivulet into gushing whitewater that was seemingly without bottom. According to the USGS streamflow gauge at Kresgeville, the water was flowing 1,100% above normal!

The streambed was 8 to 10 feet wide, but encroaching tree limbs made it tighter at eye level. My canoe rushed along the raceway like a formula car at the Indy 500. Don't let the steep gradient fool you. The gradient is so consistently uniform that the slope is hardly noticeable: like that of a long plank with one end resting on a stub of molding. There are no sudden drops of any kind, and no obstructions for the first couple of miles: just fast flowing water that requires constant but comfortable maneuvering.

Although the stream nears Route 115 as it passes under the Evergreen Hollow Road bridge, you won't see anything but forest to either side. Trees crowd the bank for nearly the stream's entire length, obscuring most signs of human habitation. The stream is like a covered path, employing vegetation as blinders to keep paddlers from knowledge of civilization's proximity.

The creek passes under Route 115, then under Treible Drive a mile and a half from the put-in. After 2 miles (at Altemose Drive) the southward trend curves gradually to the west. By the time the stream reaches Route 209 at Gilbert, the banks have broadened and the water flow has slackened its breakneck pace to one in which the boat becomes more controllable.

Whereas upstream the itinerant floodwaters have swept the way clean, once the water has spread and its speed has been reduced, there enters the problem of deadfall. The creek was 30 feet across when we (Cheryl and I) encountered the first obstruction: a fallen tree whose trunk stretched from one bank to the other. We broadsided the tree, climbed onto its trunk, then hauled the canoe over its branches.

This was only the first obstruction of several: perhaps half a dozen. We were able to paddle around some of the downed trees. For others we repeated the process of clambering over top of them to the downstream side. Each "carry" required a fair degree of exertion that should not be understated.

The stream forked abruptly, with about half the water going down either tine. The left fork was blocked by a huge tree: water flowed under the massive bole but there was not enough clearance for the boat. We took the right fork. Right after that we passed under Gilbert Road (at about the 3-mile point). Then came a broad expanse of still water that, after a passage of 500 feet, funneled down to a breadth of 20 feet, at which point the stream passed under the bridge at Mill Pond Road.

The bridge is too low to allow a boat to pass. We carried it across the road and put the boat in the water on the downstream side, under the curious scrutiny of a small herd of cattle. If I had known what was coming I would have ended the trip there.

Section 2: Mill Pond Road to Route 209 in Kresgeville

Distance: 6.0 miles
Travel time: 3 hours

Adversity level 4: Extremely challenging
Needs 1,000 % at Pohopoco (Kresgeville) station
Gradient: 5 feet per mile

AVOID THIS SECTION AT ALL COST

I suggested taking-out at Mill Pond Road primarily because you have to take out there anyway in order to carry around the bridge. If you end the trip at that point you will have had a pleasant is somewhat rigorous experience without any of the horrors to come.

Section 1 was fast and furious if a little bit difficult due to deadfall. The first two miles of Section 2 are slower and more challenging due to the sluggish flow and the increase of downed trees and the occasional logjam. If you don't mind expending the extra energy, you could lengthen your trip by adding the stretch between Mill Pond Road and Greenhill Road, for a total distance of 6 miles.

The gradient is so slight that there doesn't appear to be any. Consequently the flow is slow and, when the stream spreads through alders, comes practically to a stop. You have to look hard to determine the downstream direction.

There's hardly a stretch of water between those two roads that is straight enough to let you see more than a hundred feet ahead. Not that this presents an obstacle; it just makes maneuvering a chronic headache. Plus there are numerous obstructions to climb over. If I already mentioned that, let me mention it again so as not to catch you off guard. You can't do this stretch without standing in water and climbing over downed trees.

The real horror exists between Greenhill Road and Kunkletown Road. The width of the stream enlarges until the banks disappear through dense thickets and underbrush. In actuality, there probably are no true banks as people normally perceive them to be: vertical barriers that confine the flow of water. This stretch is a swamp with a gradual flood plain that expands and recedes in accordance with differing quantities of water. The banks are not invisible; they are nonexistent.

At first the watercourse flows between stands of jewel weed and alder. In fact, they create a barrier that stands more than 6 feet in height, with tall oaks and maples growing beyond. The stream twists and turns like a maniacal sine wave. Flow decreases as the water spreads through the understory. Even at flood stage, the water in this stretch came nearly to a standstill. I had to look hard in order to see where the water flowed.

Then the impossible happened: the stream came to an end. At least, that's the way it appeared at first sight. Upon closer examination, I could see that the water trickled through a solid phalanx of jewel weed. We were in an enclosure that surrounded us on three sides. There was no way through the weed.

By paddling around the sides of what appeared to be a corral, or a Sargasso Sea of lost ships, we found a horizontal log that stood about three feet above the surface. The log was so completely overgrown with vine that it was discernible only upon close scrutiny. By standing in the canoe and peering over the log, I could see that water

Pohopoco Creek Section 2

flowed feebly on its other side. The water was deeper than I could sink my paddle. We had to brush aside some vine, sit astride the log, balance precariously, and lift the boat over the log between us, then climb aboard.

Then the going got worse. For a short while the stream – such as it was – measured some 15 feet across. Gradually it began to spread outwards on both sides. Just as gradually the definable stream vanished, this time among a thickening barricade of alders. We wormed the canoe through the thicket as the alders grew closer and closer together. A barely perceptible flow spread in three directions before us, providing no clue as to which was the main watercourse – if, in fact, there *was* a main watercourse.

The canoe slowed to a halt as its beam was pinched between impenetrable limbs of alders. Nowhere in any direction could I detect any sign of an opening. Paddles were useless. We pulled the boat forward by grabbing onto alders stems and shoving them aside. It was hard work, and we moved ahead only inches at a time. Finally all forward motion ceased. The alder cordon was so dense that we couldn't see more than a few feet around the canoe.

I stepped out of the canoe into waist-deep water. I worked my way around the alders to the bow of the boat. I towed the boat forward while Cheryl pulled on stems. Mostly I had to step on alder limbs in front of the canoe, and hold them under water while I tugged and Cheryl shoved over the springy obstruction. Then we ran into sticker bushes.

We both wore long pants and long-sleeved shirts so our legs and arms were protected. We were careful to shield our faces. But our exposed hands were stabbed and sliced by daggerlike thorns. We were able to move the canoe only a few inches at a time. Then, I would forge ahead, step down on alders that were in our way, and repeat the process of towing and pulling. The amount of effort that these actions entailed was immense.

I couldn't help but think of Humphrey Bogart and Katherine Hepburn struggling through a jungle marsh in *The African Queen*. The only saving grace was that there were no leeches.

We proceeded in this stop-and-start fashion for perhaps a hundred yards before we detected a slender patch of daylight to the left. Turning the canoe was nearly impossible, as the length of the hull was trapped between alders. Somehow we managed to change our course. Eventually we emerged from the alder forest onto the edge of a flooded soybean field. We were both breathing hard. More accurately, we were gasping.

The water along the edge of the field was shin deep. We left the canoe and walked around one side of the perimeter in search of the main watercourse. By pushing through another thicket we encountered another soybean field. Beyond that we located the creek. Then we returned to the canoe, and dragged it through the water, through the tall thicket, and along the watery edge of the second field to a place where we could launch the boat into flowing water.

Just in case I understated the degree of adversity, be advised that it took an hour and a half to travel the two-mile circuitous stretch between Greenhill Road and Kunkletown Road. Then I had to ride 6 miles by bike to the put-in.

The last mile and a half was pure pleasure by comparison. The main watercourse curved just as badly as in the previous stretch, but the way was blocked only by a couple of downed trees which were simple to negotiate. The flowrate increased. A big wave appeared at the final bend when Route 209 loomed into view. Take the outside of the curve and stay close to the right bank as you pass under the bridge. Most of the water veers toward the left bank, leaving slow water under the bridge and an eddy immediately after it. Plow the nose onto the grassy bank by the USGS stream gauging station.

Notwithstanding the location of the take-out, in Section 3 you'll notice that I suggest putting-in on the left bank upstream of the bridge. On the trip described above I didn't take-out there because the current was too fast to nose the boat against the bank, due to a natural fence of tree limbs upstream of that spot. Check the flow rate before you start this section in order to determine the best take-out. If the current is slow enough, you can take-out at the put-in for Section 3.

Alternative to Sections 1, 2, and 3

Because I didn't know what I was getting into, I paddled Sections 1 and 2 as one continuous stretch that took 4-1/2 hours to complete (not counting the bike ride to the put-in). For my readers and fellow paddlers, I broke this trip into two sections in which the upper stretch presented no obstacles, while the lower stretch presented numerous downed trees plus a horrendous swamp.

Obviously you don't have to run the stream the way I did. You can put-in or take-out at any of the bridges along the way. Here is my suggestion: put-in where I did at Route 115 upstream of Effort, and take out at Greenhill Road. This will give you a taste of fast water and deadfall which will not be overwhelming.

Skip altogether the swamp between Greenhill Road and Kunkletown Road. Put-in at Kunkletown road and pass under Route 209 without stopping, then take-out before the bridge at Trachsville Hill Road, as described in Section 3.

Unless, of course, you are a masochist or enjoy a challenge. In that case run the swamp by itself. For what it's worth, when I ran into the alders that led me to the soybean field, I was heading west. I think if you head north through the alders you'll push through them into the main watercourse that I encountered farther downstream. I am not going back to confirm this speculation. You're on your own.

Section 3: Route 209 in Kresgeville to Trachsville Hill Road

Distance: 3.0 miles
Travel time: 1 to 2 hours depending on flow
Adversity level 1: Not challenging
Needs 800 % at Pohopoco (Kresgeville) station
Gradient: 14 feet per mile

This section is as cute as Section 1 but with broader banks, averaging 15 to 20 feet across at first, then growing to 20 to 25 feet farther downstream. The creek has a rocky bottom with occasional boulders, a few rock dams, and some bedrock scrapes, but no big drops. The slope is so low as to appear almost flat.

Pohopoco Creek Sections 3 and 4

Park at the intersection of Route 209 and Spruce Road, in the clearing alongside the left bank upstream of the bridge. Put in under the bridge right in front of you.

The creek winds through forest that keeps you mostly isolated from signs of civilization. At first it parallels Whitey B Drive and Berger Road, so you might hear some traffic through the trees. A few adjacent homeowners on either side have cleared their properties to the water's edge, but for the most part the yards and houses are out of sight.

About halfway you'll pass under the Berger Street bridge, and about three-quarters of the way you'll pass under the Koch Road bridge. The only hang-up might occur when the creek splits around a small tree-covered island. We took the right fork

Had we known, we could have avoided this ledge by taking the left channel, which is visible through the trees to the right.

and it was a mistake. The canoe grounded on bedrock with a drop of about a foot. It is better to take the left fork. The two forks meet about 50 feet downstream.

You are nearing the end of this section when the water becomes muddy and the flow practically ceases. After a sharp turn to the left you'll see the Trachsville Road bridge. Land on the left bank at the end of a path on the upstream side of the bridge. This path leads uphill to a parking lot where you can stash a bike or leave a shuttle vehicle.

This is the last take-out before entering the reservoir that is part of Beltzville State Park. According to Pennsylvania State Park regulations, boats must be registered for a fee. Unregistered boats are subject to fine.

Alternatively, you can add a couple of miles of pleasant paddling by putting-in at Greenhill Road instead of Route 209. The reason I separate the two is not just because I paddled downstream from Route 209 as a separate trip, but because the upstream stretch has some downed trees across it. Some paddlers might not want to deal with such obstructions.

Section 4 (Trachsville Road to the dam)
Distance: 7.2 miles to the dam, less to the launching ramps
Travel time: Depends on route and destination
Adversity level 0: None
Streamflow is perennial
Gradient: 0 feet per mile

If you're looking for a relaxing cruise to absorb colorful autumn foliage, the Beltzville Reservoir is the place to paddle. As noted at the end of Section 3, boats must be registered for a fee. Unregistered boats are subject to fine. Visit the park office on the north shore to obtain boat registration forms, rules and regulations, and a Park brochure with a map that shows the locations of hiking trails and both launching ramps. The Park rents boats to people who don't have their own.

You're in for a long haul if you decide to circumnavigate the reservoir and explore the northern arms (the Wild Creek arm, the Pine Run arm, and several shorter arms) – I would estimate around 20 miles.

Don't worry about going over the dam if you get too close. There is no spillway, and water does not flow over the top. Water is released through a pipe at the bottom of the dam. The depth is too great to create any suction at the surface.

The reservoir freezes in the winter. The gyrating, freshly-caught pickerel frightened the little girl.

Wear a life vest in case your boat overturns. Unlike Sections 1 and 2, you can't stand up in shin-deep water. The only natural hazard is wind. A northeast wind has a 3-mile fetch. Crosswinds and gusts can cause grief for canoes and kayaks that don't have a keel. If you find yourself boatless in the middle of the reservoir, you've got a quarter-mile swim to the closest shore on either side.

Section 5: Beltzville Dam to the Lehigh River   Adversity level 1: Not challenging
Distance: 5.3 miles   Needs 400 % on the Pohopoco (Beltzville Dam) gauge
Travel time: 1 to 2 hours depending on flowrate   Gradient: 17 feet per mile

Although the streamflow is monitored at the dam, you can check the water level at the North Harrity Road bridge, next to Interchange Road and the turnpike ramps. There are rock bars upstream and downstream of the bridge. If you see protruding rocks, come back another day. If the rocks are barely awash, the creek is runnable but might entail a bit of work when the boat runs aground and you have to walk it over the shallows (of which this is the shoalist). If the water is smooth or ripply, set up your shuttle and prepare for a fun ride with very little exertion.

The creek ends at the confluence with the Lehigh River. To paddle all the way to the end of the creek, you can stash a bike or park a vehicle in the gravel lot on the right bank at the confluence with the Lehigh River. Or you can do the same at the playground in Parryville, at the intersection of Water Street and Centre Street, at the site of the lower dam. Or you can proceed down the Lehigh River; the nearest take-out is about a mile and a half downriver, on either bank above the Route 895 bridge.

The mild gradient keeps the water flowing quickly. You're never far from civilization but for the most part the border of trees will make the banks appear like wilderness. The streambed measures some 30 feet across. About a third of the way downstream you'll pass under the turnpike, then reach the North Harrity Road bridge and an island underneath it, encompassing the center pier. You can pass on either side of the island. After the next curve you'll pass under the turnpike again.

For the next third of the trip the creek will again be bordered by trees. You should be able to pass over the low rock dams without hanging up. A few trees lean into the

Pohopoco Creek Section 5

water from the banks, but the streambed is always wide enough to allow you to paddle around them. The creek then becomes somewhat winding. The cleared areas along the left bank are yards. The streambed is now more than 40 feet wide.

The streambed broadens as it passes under the turnpike a third time. The spreading of the banks and the backwash of the dam reduce the flowrate so that the current will seem negligible. Now you have to paddle in order to make headway. Houses on the outskirts of Parryville line the left bank. Stay close to the left bank as you approach the dam. You'll be out of the current in an eddy. Land on the beach.

The dam is 10 feet tall with a 45-degree slope. Rafts can probably go over the dam without tipping, but I suspect that they might get into trouble when they hit the turbulence at the bottom. I think a skilled kayaker might be able to go over the dam successfully; if he flips over at the bottom he should be able to roll upright in the deep water. But be warned: at high water levels a dangerous hydraulic persists at the bottom.

I don't recommend going over the dam in any boat, especially an aluminum canoe or one with a keel. An ABS or Kevlar canoe with a flat V hull can make it over the dam and slide down the other side. The problem arises when the bow strikes the water and slides under the surface. Some water will pour over the gunwales, but worse than that is the shift in balance when only the tapered stern is resting on the concrete facing. The canoe will tip sharply to one side or the other, and that's all she wrote.

You can carry or portage your boat over the grass to the rocks below the dam. Or you can take-out and carry your boat through the playground to the parking area. The creek ends less than a quarter mile downstream, so you won't miss much if you take-out here.

I lined the boat down the edge of the dam by holding onto the painters and walking down the graduated steps, although it meant getting my shoes wet. I was astonished to see fish leaping several feet out of the waves below the dam, landing on the concrete facing, and wriggling for all they

I took this picture during turnpike bridge construction in 2012.

Po Creek dam.

Three-way confluence: Lehigh River Section 10 on the left, Lehigh Canal Section 1 in the middle, Po Creek on the right.

were worth in their attempt to swim against the flow. None of them made it more than a few feet. They reminded me of spawning salmon that I once observed on the Moisie River in Quebec. In this case I suspect that the fish were trout, although I won't swear to it. It was sure fun to watch.

Below the dam lies a short stretch of standing waves and whitewater that require caution or expertise to navigate. Instead of knifing *through* the waves, backpaddle to reduce your speed and ride *over* the waves.

Pass under the Centre Street bridge. The creek then turns sharply to the right. Pass through some whitewater under the Route 248 bridge. Immediately afterward stands a railroad bridge which has a pier in the middle. If you plan to continue down the Lehigh River to a landing downstream, you can pass to the left of the pier.

If you plan to take-out at the confluence you need to pass to the right of the pier, because you might not be able to ferry to the right bank in the short distance between the bridge and the take-out, especially at high flowrates. Pull into the calm water beneath the canal lock. If you miss it, land on the beach at the confluence a few feet farther downstream. Carry your boat up the grassy slope to the gravel. You can move your vehicle from the parking lot down to the gravel extension.

After writing the words in the paragraph above, I revisited the confluence to take some pictures during a flood. I was shocked to see that since I last ran the creek, a pair of 40-foot-long trees had lodged themselves all the way across the passageway under the right span. Not only did this make it impossible to take-out at the confluence, and reach the still water at the end of the lock, but it created a hazardous situation for anyone who tried to do so. A boat could not go over the log; it would be stopped dead, pushed sideways, and capsized by water rushing under the hull. The occupants would then be pinned underwater against the log. Until these logs rot away or are dislodged, taking-out at the confluence is a treacherous proposition that should be avoided at all costs.

Despite the previous sentence, in 2014 I revisited the take-out and discovered that the logs were gone! Problem solved. This only goes to show how often obstacles come and go in small streams like this.

The 5-mile dam-to-dam passage – from Beltzville to Parryville – is a satisfying alternative for paddlers who intend to run the Lehigh Gorge, and upon arrival find the flowrate too high for their comfort or level of experience. High water on the Lehigh River implies high water on the Po Creek. However, I present a caveat to this option.

I once ran the Po Creek when the dam was releasing water at the phenomenal rate of 1,220 cfs: 1,863% above normal! I figured this would make for a fast ride. I was not disappointed: I made the trip from dam to dam in 51 minutes without even trying. *But* – and there are two cheeks to this *but* – I encountered some whitewater with standing waves which I plowed through or avoided, and found that the water was so high that I couldn't fit under the bridge at North Harrity Road.

Imagine my consternation as I approached the bridge on super-fast water, with extremely little time to calculate if there was sufficient height to paddle underneath it. A warning sign on the left bank – which read "No Boating – Low Bridge" – didn't help; the sign should have been placed a couple hundred yards upstream, before boats got caught in the current, instead of 50 from the bridge.

The midstream island was submerged, but I brought the boat to a halt on the tall thick grass that floated above it. I stepped into thigh-deep water. I walked the canoe to the edge of the bridge; the bow passed under the concrete structure with only one inch to spare. If I had lain flat and tried to float under the bridge, my backbone would have struck its bottom.

If you encounter this situation, beach your boat on the right bank, drag it onto the parking lot, then carry it across the road.

Low bridge at Harrity Road. And this is low water!

SAWMILL RUN

This short stream is almost never runnable because its watershed is so small. The water that feeds it flows down a narrow ravine on the south side of Bear Mountain, then through a constricted pass between Indian Hills to the west and an unnamed rise of equivalent height to the east. As Sawmill Run enters the pass it is joined by Berry Run, which flows down a similar but shorter ravine to the west.

The newly joined stream flows freely for a bit, then is confined by a concrete aqueduct adjacent to a huge and complex structure that looks like a connected series of revetments or settling ponds. The floors and walls of these rectangular holding cells are made of concrete. The walls stand about 5 feet high. Gateways lead from one cell to the next one downstream. The wooden gates are long gone so you can duck under the lintels to pass from one cell to another.

I have no idea of the purpose of this vast edifice. It looks as if water could have been siphoned off the stream through the cells, then redirected back to the main flow farther downstream. The cells are now dry and appear to have been so for a long time. Vegetation has taken root in the dirt that has accumulated on the floors: not just grass, weeds, and shrubs but medium-sized trees.

The aqueduct sports several rough and rocky sheer drop-offs that make paddling problematical. At the end of the aqueduct a pile of breakdown and natural rock create a vertical drop of 4 to 5 feet. After that the streambed regains its natural boundaries with a steep slope rising high above the right bank and a slender flood plain on the left bank. One quarter mile past the vertical drop, the stream flows under Jefferson Street.

The length of Sawmill Run from its origin on the mountaintop to Jefferson Street is less than 3 miles. The length of Berry Run from its origin to the confluence is about a mile and a half.

Only Section: Jefferson Street to Pohopoco Creek
Distance: 1.7 miles
Travel time: 1 hour
Adversity level 2: Challenging
Needs high water by observation
Gradient: 62 feet per mile

Sawmill Run is not a stream for everyone. Paddling it is certainly not a family outing. Yet it possesses a certain attraction for paddlers who are looking to do something different and who don't mind overcoming some obstacles in order to experience that difference. To determine if the stream is runnable after a significant rainfall, look downstream from the Jefferson Street bridge. If most of the rocks are submerged and those that are exposed can be avoided, go for it.

Do not be dissuaded by the steep gradient in the statistical sidebar. Although the gradient is three times that of the Lehigh River gorge, the slope is nearly as consistent as a tilted board. There are ledges to be sure, but only one 3-footer presents a challenge, while the shorter ones can be run almost without thinking.

The streambed averages 10 feet in width. There is hardly anywhere that the water exceeds 2 feet in depth, and for the most part the depth measures less than a foot. If you fall out of your boat, simply stand up and walk or work your way to shore.

At Jefferson Street, lift your boat over the guardrail on the right bank on the downstream side of the bridge. Let it slide 8 feet to the bottom, then climb down and nudge it to the water's edge. This will place you downstream of the 2-foot funnel dam under

Without a flashlight you can see the light at the end of the tunnel, but not the bedrock obstructions in the middle.

the bridge. This spot is perfect for launching.

For the next three-quarters of a mile there is only a single drop-off that may present a problem for canoeists (but not for kayakers). This collection of small boulders can be sneaked on the right; or, if you prefer, you can step out of the boat and drag it around the obstruction. All the other ledges are runnable.

Now comes a feature that I found positively exhilarating: a tunnel under the Pennsylvania Turnpike that is more than a city block in length! The tunnel is straight so you can see light at the other end: much like the dim circle seen by looking through the wrong end of a telescope, or the white light that is seen in a near-death experience. I don't mean the previous line to be a death sentence; or even a near-death sentence. The curved arch stands some 20 feet in height, and the side-to-side span is about 25 feet. This is the longest water-filled tunnel in the Lehigh River watershed.

You can pass through the tunnel without a flashlight but I don't recommend it. Just out of the light zone there's a broad chunk of bedrock that rises high and dry at normal streamflows, but may be submerged during times of flood. This chunk is only half a dozen feet shy of stretching across the entire width of the tunnel. Then another chunk follows it closely. Then yet a third obstacle exists in the form of vertical slabs that stand 3 to 4 feet high: not a drop-off but an uprising solid wall. Not to fear. Should you ram the first chunk of bedrock your boat will simply ride up onto it, for its jagged surface is somewhat slanted. However, although the upstream side of the second chunk is also sloped, the downstream side features a rocky drop that might prove your undoing. And the third obstacle is definitely a boat stopper.

If you don't have a flashlight, enter the tunnel from the middle of the stream, then pick a side and hug the wall so you can slip past these bedrock obstructions. I think the left side is better than the right.

After you clear the obstacles, the rest of the way is mostly open, with only a few

Sawmill Run Only Section

rocks exposed when the streamflow is high enough to be runnable. If you don't avoid these exposed rocks, you'll bounce off them like an errant billiard ball.

Before you reach the light zone at the other end, you'll see a similar-sized tunnel only two hundred feet away. This one – a hundred feet long – allows the stream to flow under Pohopoco Drive. This tunnel sports a smooth concrete floor until the downstream end, so it's clear sailing all the way.

So far the run has been easy-going. Now the waterway gets tough. Two blocks past the second tunnel there's a triple logjam: three large downed trees that are spaced 50 feet apart. You'll have to carry around all three.

One block later, where the stream forks, keep to the right where the water flows quickly. Ahead there's a crumbling rock dam that stands 8 feet high. You can take out on the right bank to carry your boat around it, or you can beach your boat on the island in the middle and lower it down the vertical wall to the rock ledge below.

A block later there's another logjam, this one caused by an extremely fat log that has captured great amounts of debris. Carry right.

Two blocks later there's another dam. This one is built of firm concrete and stands 10 feet tall. The dam does not extend all the way to the left bank, but ends some 20 feet shy of the vertical dirt wall. I suspect that after the dam was abandoned, the streamflow gradually dug through the dirt until erosion enlarged the gap to its present size. Most of the water flows through a tunnel in the dam, but some flows past the left-side abutment: enough at high streamflow rates to paddle around the end of the dam.

The take-out lies only a block away, at Old Mill Road. Shuttle vehicles can be parked in the lot at the Sawmill Run trailhead, 100 feet westward. Or, if the Beltzville Dam is releasing enough water, you can enter the Pohopoco Creek and paddle two miles downstream to Harrity Road, or beyond.

The upper dam can be portaged on the trail on either side of the stream, or a boat can be lowered down the middle of the dam.

LIZARD CREEK

Lizard Creek commences as a host of streamlets that flow together until a recognizable stream is formed and is given a name, in a patch of forest several miles west of Route 309. Much of this water irrigates farmland farther west. Most of Lizard Creek's water is washed down the north side of Blue Mountain, and more is added from farmland to the north.

Section 1: Route 309 to Blue Mountain Road Adversity level 1: Not challenging
Distance: 12.0 miles Needs 800 % on the Aquashicola streamflow gauge
Travel time: 3 to 4 hours Gradient: 9 feet per mile

Although I ran the 16-mile length of Lizard Creek on one continuous trip, I am breaking my description into two sections because of the distinct difference in adversity between the upper and lower sections. Obviously, one can slice this creek into any number of shorter segments by putting-in or taking-out at any of the intersecting roads. But it makes sense to enjoy as much of the stream as possible, so I recommend starting at Route 309 (south of Snyders) and paddling 12 miles to Blue Mountain Road (south of Ashfield).

The total distance along Route 895 (alias Lizard Creek Road) from Route 309 to the Lehigh River is 11-1/2 miles. The shoulder along this road is barely wider than a handlebar. Traffic travels fast. For safety reasons I suggest a vehicular shuttle instead of one by bike.

Lizard Creek is one of those streams that consists mostly of shallow gravel bars unless the water is flowing high. The first time I ran it was after a 5-inch rainstorm. The USGS has no stream flow gauge on the Lizard, but I used the one on the Aquashicola as a guide. This was appropriate because both streams empty into the Lehigh River only a couple of miles away from each other, albeit from opposite sides. Thus the water level of the Aquashicola can be an approximate indication of the level of the Lizard. The Aquashicola was running 1,500% above normal!

As I had already scouted the bridge crossings, I went directly to the take-out to leave a vehicle. Riverview Road parallels the Lehigh River downstream of Route 895. I had intended to take-out at a sandbar on the right bank immediately downstream of the bridge. I was shocked when I saw that the sandbar was submerged and that a raging torrent gushed over it and flooded back into the trees that lined the bank.

The view upstream was frightening: a virtual deluge that looked more like the Johnstown Flood than the docile Lizard Creek. It took only two seconds for me to decide that canoeing a stream that I knew nothing about was tempting the fingers of fate. I canceled the trip without further consideration. I'd rather get hung up on gravel bars than get swept at high speed into logjams. Cheryl and I ran the Aquashicola instead.

By the next day the Aquashicola was running 900% above normal. The outflow of the Lizard Creek was considerably slower, and didn't look nearly as frightening as it had the day before. The take-out sandbar was still under water. In any case, taking-out there meant dragging the boat through the forest, up a steep embankment, and over a guardrail. It was much easier to take-out half a mile down the Lehigh River where there was a parking lot and a concrete boat ramp.

At the put-in, we parked on the wide shoulder of the northbound lane of Route

Lizard Creek Section 1

309. I dropped the canoe in the water on the right bank downstream of the bridge. Thus began an easy-going trip through picturesque farmland and pristine forest, with occasional forays past Route 895 when the stream veered close to the road. By paddling steadily but not hard, we reached the Lehigh River take-out in three hours and fifteen minutes.

As in most small streams, there were a few downed trees that spanned from bank to bank, but only two that necessitated a carry. In neither case was the current strong enough to cause any trouble. Otherwise we were able to push through branches or duck under trunks; one floating log we rammed hard enough to slide over top.

The first firm obstacle was situated just upstream of the first bridge (Ridge Road). Because the stream curved left on the other side of the newly fallen tree, we docked against the 4-foot-high earthen wall of the left bank. When I climbed out of the boat, I was astonished to see that weeds atop the bank were pressed down flat. This meant that water had flowed over the bank the day before. Later we saw high-water marks that were 5 feet above the present level.

We dragged the canoe 40 feet across flat ground, then slid it into the water to continue our exploration of the unknown ahead of us. The next 5 bridges came and went without our encountering any difficulties.

Most of the mud had settled out of the water overnight. The average depth was 3 feet, but when we passed over gravel bars I could clearly see the pebbly bottom that my blade touched on occasional.

I spotted a few trees that were leaning precariously over the stream: deadfall in the making, when some future flood undercuts the bank. A mature eagle flew over our heads. We passed a wild grape vine that was teeming with ripe purple grapes, but the current sped us past it before I could grab a bunch. Pine trees vied for space among hardwoods. There seemed to be an inordinate number of weeping willows dipping their lower branches into the water.

Lizard Creek is muddy only when the water is gushing fast enough to be runnable.

The creek gradually spread in width from 10 feet at the put-in to 20 feet or more about halfway downstream. The waterway curves as you would expect, yet the curves are soft and there are only a few large boulders in the way. There is no call for radical maneuvers.

The second and final firm obstacle is avoidable because it is located between the Ashfield Playground (on the right) and Blue Mountain Road (a block away). This was an old log that had been lodged in place

A school of native trout lingering in the shallows of Lizard Creek.

for a long while. The paved road stood only 5 feet away, but the 6-foot-high bank was covered with tall reeds. We clambered onto the log, dragged the boat over top, then reboarded and continued our journey. With a bit of a struggle, we could have climbed onto the road and hauled the boat out of the water, then carried it to the bridge.

I suggest taking-out at the playground. There is plenty of space for parking, and the lawn is like a beachhead without any slope. Taking-out there will avoid any contretemps with the logjam.

If you decide to continue onto Section 2 instead of taking-out, there is an easy way to avoid the logjam. From the playground take-out you can see that an island is located 50 feet downstream of the beach. The logjam is in the right channel. If you take the left channel, you will merge with the right channel downstream of the logjam, some 20 feet upstream of the bridge on Blue Mountain Road.

Section 2: Blue Mountain Road to the Lehigh River

Distance: 4.0 miles
Travel time: 1 hour (for survivors)
Adversity level 4: Extremely challenging
Needs 800 % on the Aquashicola streamflow gauge
Gradient: 24 feet per mile

Section 2 is everything that Section 1 is not. Whereas Section 1 constitutes a placid family cruise, Section 2 is only for extreme whitewater paddlers – and I stress the word "extreme." I don't want to leave any doubt in your mind that you must be prepared for the horrendous cascades that drop precipitously and unceasingly for the best part of a mile, or for other albeit shorter raging boulder fields both before and after the denouement.

Put-in either at the beach alongside the Ashfield Playground, or a block downstream on Blue Mountain Road immediately upstream of the bridge. A pull-over on the south side of the road is big enough for two vehicles. A cleared swath leads a few feet from the road to the right bank, at the bottom of the island and some 20 feet upstream of the bridge.

Once you leave Blue Mountain Road behind, there is no escape other than by bushwhacking through untrammeled forest. You are committed. Although you will pass

Lizard Creek Section 2

under two bridges, neither one provides a take-out. The first is an ancient stone railroad bridge from which the tracks have long since been removed. The other is the Northeast Extension of the Pennsylvania Turnpike.

The fast-flowing creek appears innocuous for the first couple of miles. Individual rocks are scattered across a streambed that now measures a comfortable 30 feet across. A few minor riffles mar the smooth surface of the water. The railroad bridge looks out of place because it is covered with fully-grown trees. You can make an echo by shouting as you pass through one of the archways. There is no presentiment of the potential doom that lies ahead.

Half a mile past the railroad bridge the creek gets interesting. The gradient increases. Large rocks loom out of the water – only a few isolated boulders at first, but more and more come into view and the stream flows faster around them. Before you know it, you're in the middle of a rampaging slalom with no way to escape: a continuous cascade of wild water – not whitewater as you generally think of it, and certainly no hydraulics, but a true garden of rocks with water screaming over and around these geological obstructions, and with no clear path between them.

This is a kayaker's paradise and a canoeist's nightmare.

It's not like the Rock Garden on the Lehigh River, where you can slither between boulders and always find a discernible path ahead of you. Here there is no path. Here there is no way to avoid scraping over rock. Here maneuvering is difficult because you can't get a full blade in the water without slamming against the bottom. Here you twist and turn, rock and roll, weave left and right, bounce, grate, grind, and groan – all without a moment to catch your breath.

For me this was exciting. For my paddling partner it was terrifying. Cheryl had never paddled whitewater before. Although we had canoed many miles together, she had only paddled flat water, or dead water: in swamps, lakes, and ponds. She had paddled some fast water with me: the Wekiva, Little Wekiva, and Myakka in Florida; the Rio Grande in Texas, with a short sprint through Santa Elena Canyon; and recently the Mahoning, Pohopoco, and Aquashicola. In those cases the water ran fast but without rocks and standing waves. None of those trips prepared her for what we were soon to encounter. This stretch of the Lizard was most definitely out of her league, yet she handled herself admirably under difficult circumstances.

The roar of the rapids was deafening. From the stern I shouted directions: "Left! Right! Now left again! Farther left! Right!" We wound a tortuous course through the rapids and unavoidably left a lot of green bottom paint on rocky surfaces. The rapids were never-ending.

Then disaster struck. Cheryl's blade jammed between two rocks. In striving to maintain her grip and pull the paddle loose, she was yanked partway out of the boat. Her upper body went overboard, parallel to the water with her stomach resting on the gunwale. The canoe listed sharply to the right, with the gunwale dangerously close to the surface.

You may have read about the mountaineering technique of rescuing a climber who has fallen off a snow-covered crest with a sheer drop below. To save the situation, the other climber on the rope must leap off the opposite side of the crest so that both of them are left dangling, but neither one dropping farther off the precipice. I performed a similar feat. I threw my upper body over the left gunwale so that my overboard weight equaled Cheryl's, and rebalanced the boat. This momentary leveling gave Cheryl the opportunity to regain her equilibrium, although the paddle was torn from her grasp as the canoe continued to thunder downstream.

As soon as the boat returned to an even keel, I straightened on my seat, then leaned right and stretched my arm toward the now-floating paddle. I was barely able to catch the T-handle. Cheryl reached back for the paddle, but I didn't have time to hand it to her because we were drifting broadside onto an exposed rock. I dropped her paddle into the boat, then executed a strong pry in order to push the stern away from the rapidly approaching obstacle. The canoe straightened partially. The flow swept the bow past the rock, and the stern rubbed alongside then ricocheted free. I had a split second to hand the paddle to Cheryl before executing another emergency avoidance maneuver.

What took three paragraphs to describe took seconds to occur.

More rocks loomed ahead so there was no time to reflect on our miraculous escape. "Right! Left! Left hard! Go right then left!"

I honestly don't know how long it took us to run the rest of the rapids. Even then, we had only a short respite before encountering another short set. Then another. And another. Suddenly there was only one large boulder in the middle of the stream in front of us. We swept passed it on the right, rounded a slight curve, and saw the bridge for Riverside Road. Through the arches we spotted the Lehigh River. The take-out was only minutes away.

Then we had time to talk about our exhilarating experience. For Cheryl, it was a shocking introduction to whitewater paddling.

In etymology, "dinosaur" means "terrible lizard," a combination of words that originated from the ancient Greek language. I favor naming this rocky stretch of the Lizard Creek the Dinosaur Rapids.

Try it if you dare.

Aquashicola

AQUASHICOLA CREEK

Aquashicola is pronounced ah-quah-shick'-o-lah, with the accent on the middle syllable (shick). It originates in a small wooded area south of Saylorsville, about half a mile south of the beginning of the Buckwha. A narrow ribbon of water then trickles across flatland for more than 12 miles (as the crow flies) before it becomes runnable. In actuality, it doesn't become runnable until after its meager streamflow is augmented by the Buckwha Creek.

You can observe the stream from several places on Lower Smith Gap Road, and also where it passes under Blue Mountain Drive. You might see some patches of clear open water, but what you see is deceptive. For the most part the streambed is little more than runway of wet rocks – or rocks that are not so wet.

Don't try to put-in at Blue Mountain Drive. At that point the stream is wide and deep. Many streams are wide and deep at bridge sites. This is often because the stream was widened and deepened during construction of the bridge. I can't tell you how many times I started under similar circumstances, only to learn that the stream pinched out around the very first curve.

Even when the Aquashicola is flooded, much of the upstream stretch is choked with so much brush growing inward from the sides that a boat can't possibly be pushed through it.

Only section: Lower Smith Gap Road to the Lehigh River
Adversity level 1: Not challenging
Distance: 8.0 miles
Needs 800 % on the Aquashicola (Palmerton) gauge
Travel time: 2 to 3 hours
Gradient: 8 feet per mile

The best place to put-in for this trip is not on the Aquashicola but on the lower Buckwha. Either way, the distance to the confluence of the two streams is the same. I put-in on the Buckwha because the watercourse was wide, deep, and rockless. In fact, more water flows down the Buckwha than down the Aquashicola, lending strength to the argument that the name Buckwha could have been maintained all the way, with Aquashicola being named an accessary after the fact.

As noted above, you can access the Aquashicola from Blue Mountain Drive. However, the stream is so narrow and encroaching vegetation is so thick that I don't think that anything larger than a boogie board can navigate the waterway.

Put-in at Lower Smith Gap Road – not at the bridge over the Buckwha, but one block east where a clearing provides plenty of room for parking at the water's edge. The fast flow will soon carry you under the bridge. Immediately afterward lies a clump of debris that we were able to push through. More debris lies downstream, and at one point a downed tree forced us to step out of the canoe onto the right bank and drag the boat over shallow water through weeds for 30 feet or so. After this you are home free. Well, almost . . .

Half a mile from the put-in you might notice a small stream entering from the left on a nearly parallel but converging course. You'll have to look over your shoulder to spot it. This is the Aquashicola. Even at flood stage it doesn't add much water to the flow.

At this point, the combined streambed is 30 feet wide. It maintains this width for the rest of the trip. Undercut trees are not likely to fall into the creek because the banks consist mostly of gravel instead of dirt, and the banks recede gently. Additionally, the land has been cleared of dense forest on both sides, although individual hardwoods line the banks.

I hate to call the scenery ugly but I have little choice, other than to employ another word that means the same thing. The Aquashicola is a fast and easy float over colorful gravel, yet the terrain on either side is anything but sightly once you leave the near-shore trees behind. Sure you can see the Blue Mountain ridge to the left, where the Appalachian Trail calls to a large number of hikers. But you have to look over slag heaps in the foreground: the leftovers of zinc mining and smelting that have been in continuous operation for a century. The land is badly scarred to the right, where various industries have now taken root.

This is not to say that I didn't enjoy the trip. I like fast-flowing water. I can also add that whereas other Lehigh River tributaries are somewhat claustrophobic because they flow through untrammeled forest with a thick canopy, the Aquashicola presents a breadth of openness that some might find exhilarating. Also, because the streambed doesn't curve as much as much smaller creeks, you always know what lies ahead because you can see downstream for a considerable distance.

The only obstacle is a bridge that is located at about the halfway point. The roadway stands some 6 feet above high water. The bridge is not a span that reaches from one bank to the other. Rather it is solid with a series of culverts resting on the streambed. These culverts measure about 4 feet in diameter. The culverts look large enough to accommodate a canoe, but a plume of whitewater at the downstream end of the center culvert – where most of the water was flowing – made me think that a boulder might be lodged at the outtake. I opted not to try to run through the metal cylinder.

The canoe docked easily against the bridge's bulkhead, between the three central culverts and the one on the left. The bulkhead was conveniently fitted with metal ledges that provided footholds, while four cables that served as a railing provided handholds. Cheryl climbed onto the bridge. I stayed in the canoe and pushed it toward the left bank – in essence a wall of rock – but water flowing through the left culvert nearly capsized the boat.

Too late I saw that we should have landed on the right bank, where a cleared path led up to the road. A boat can easily be dragged up the slope, across the gravel roadway, and into the water downstream.

I was stuck against the bulkhead. I couldn't paddle away from the concentrated current to go back upstream and around the central culverts, so I had to improvise. I handed the painter to Cheryl. I climbed onto the bridge. I lifted the canoe by means of the painter until it was high enough for me to grab the bow deck. Then I hauled the boat up and onto the bridge between the cables. We put the canoe in the water over rocks and weeds on the left bank, then continued on our way.

The rest of the trip was a languorous float. We paddled lightly and steered along the main watercourse. The subsequent bridges had more than adequate clearance.

The shoalest part of the creek occurs just downstream of the bridge that provides access to the zinc plant from the company parking lot. In fact, if you want to gauge whether the water is high enough to paddle, park at the west end of this lot and study the flow. If you see a multitude of rocks exposed, come back another day. If only a few rocks are exposed, accept the fact that you might have to walk the boat in this and a

Aquashicola Creek and Buckwha Creek

few other spots. If you see no rocks exposed, the water is deep enough to provide clear passage for the entire length of the creek.

The U.S. Geological Service has a stream flow gauge on the Aquashicola. The trip that I described above was run when the water was flowing some 1,500 % above normal. Don't run it much less than 1,000 % unless you don't mind walking in a few places. Higher water means a faster trip. You'll notice in the statistical sidebar that we ran 8 miles in two hours, and that was without trying to beat any records.

You can take-out on the right bank at the confluence with the Lehigh River but it's more trouble than it's worth. You have to carry your boat about 500 feet and cross the railroad track to where you can park a vehicle on a siding. It's easier to paddle less than a mile through the Lehigh Gap and take out at the concrete boat ramp on the right bank immediately downstream of the Route 893 bridge. A parking lot lies next to the river.

If you're not rushed for time, I suggest starting this trip by putting-in at the covered bridge in Little Gap. (See the Buckwha chapter for more information.) This will add 3/4 of a mile to the total distance, but the extra short stretch will take only 5 to 10 minutes to paddle. The water flows fast over a streambed that is unobstructed.

BUCKWHA CREEK

The Buckwha Creek first takes form in a forest south of Saylorsburg, about half a mile north of the origin of the Aquashicola Creek. From there it flows for 8 miles (in a straight line) through woodlands. From the few roads that it passes under, it appears to be little more than a tantalizing "crick" that small boys might find fun to explore and look for salamanders under rocks. There is no public access to potentially runnable water until it reaches Kunkletown.

Buckwha Creek passing under the covered bridge in Little Gap. Note the boulders upstream of the bridge.

Buckwha Creek Only Section

Only section: Chestnut Ridge Road in Kunkletown to Lower Smith Gap Road
Adversity level 1: Not challenging except for annoying deadfall
Distance: 5.4 miles
Needs 800 % on the Aquashicola (Palmerton) gauge
Travel time: 1-1/2 to 2 hours
Gradient: 14 feet per mile

This trip is for adventurous paddlers only. A handful of downed trees mar what would otherwise be an effortless float over clear water through a primitive pristine forest. The first mile is the most challenging stretch because the streambed is narrow, and because the paddling surface is made more restrictive by bulging alders and rhododendron.

The widest part of the first mile measures 10 feet across. In many places the width shrinks to 5 feet between ingrown shrubbery. I was barely a hundred yards into the trip when I encountered a log that dammed additional debris precisely at a sharp bend that was only slightly wider than my canoe. I had a difficult time clambering over the log and pulling the boat over behind me. Fortunately, this was the most demanding carry of the trip; the others were challenging but were located in broad areas where maneuvering room was adequate. In one spot on this first mile, I had to put down my paddle and pull my way through alders that completely choked the passageway.

After this choke point the stream widens to 15 to 20 feet. There are no exposed rocks and no drop-offs to make for unsafe passage: only a few riffles that are fun to ride. The downed trees that span the banks are negotiable, although one large tree required not a little climbing and ducking while threading my canoe through its branches. Otherwise, the trip is a gentle float that requires no great effort. Think of it as moving water with a few stopping points.

I ran this stretch when the streamflow gauge on the Aquashicola read 876 %. This flow rate may seem high, but in fact it's the minimum amount necessary to make the water deep enough to cover the rocks; nor was the current too fast. Keep in mind that when the flowrate on the Aquashicola is normal – that is, 100% – the water is less than ankle deep, and the Buckwha is little more than a trickle.

The distance to the covered bridge in Little Gap is 4-3/4 miles. The only obstacle other than deadfall is located 20 feet upstream of the bridge: a collection of boulders that span the stream and create a 2-foot drop. Land on the right bank and drag your boat its length past the drop-off.

You can take-out on the grassy left bank immediately below the bridge, but the next 3/4 of a mile to Lower Smith Gap Road is worth paddling. It has no slow-downs except for a bush-covered island with several cuts that you can easily slide through. Otherwise, this final stretch is fast and fun.

Keep your eyes open for the take-out on the left bank. Tall weeds hide the narrow opening until you're right next to it and passing it fast. If you miss it, you'll have to take-out at the bridge a couple of hundred yards downstream; this is not undoable but it's a lot of work getting a boat through the weeds and up and over the guardrail. The take-out is a pull-over that's big enough to park several vehicles. This is also the put-in for the Aquashicola.

Cheryl snapped this picture of me on Trout Creek.

TROUT CREEK

Why divide a 4-mile stream into three sections, you might wonder? The reason is simple: the upper section has two or three downed trees that some paddlers might find annoying, the middle section is fraught with deadfall that most paddlers would prefer to avoid, while the lower section is obstacle free.

This short stream is a rarity that can almost never be paddled, but when the streamflow is high enough it cannot be beat for mild challenge (Section 1), decided challenge (Section 2), and whitewater (Section 3). Don't attempt to paddle the upper two sections unless the streamflow gauge on the Aquashicola Creek reads at least 800%, or you'll run aground in the shallows. The bottom section can be run at a lower level as long as you don't see too many rocks at either the put-in or the take-out.

You can see most of the runnable portion of stream from the paved bike/hike trail that stretches for 4 miles from the D&L Trail in Slatington, adjacent to the confluence with the Lehigh River, to the athletic field off Factory Avenue in Slatedale. There are parking lots at both places: in Slatington, in the municipal lot on Main Street immediately west of the bridge over the river; in Slatedale, at the athletic field.

The parts of the stream that you can't see lie downstream of the athletic field in Slatedale (which doubles as the end of the hike/bike trail), the stretch in Section 2 where logjams occur, and places in Section 3 where the trail veers away from the stream (or vice versa). The water that feeds this stream flows down from the south side of Blue Mountain, through forest and past farm fields that lie northwest of Slatedale.

Section 1: Factory Avenue to Main Street   Adversity level 2: Challenging
Distance: 1.3 miles   Needs 800 % on the Aquashicola (Palmerton) gauge
Travel time: 15 minutes   Gradient: 33 feet per mile

I include this section only because I surveyed it. I don't think it's possible to start farther upstream because the streambed is so narrow at the next upstream access (the bridge at County Bridge Road), that the possibility of ever having enough water to run that stretch is extremely rare. Plus, the put-in at the bridge is difficult due to the high, tree-covered embankment.

Park in the southwest corner of the parking lot of the athletic field, closest to the water. From there you have to carry your boat about 100 feet to the left bank. Launching is easy because the bank is nearly level with the water. Despite the fairly high gradient, the incline is consistent and the streambed has no ledges or drop-offs. The average width is 20 feet.

There are two main challenges and one minor one. The first one is a pair of fallen trees that will require getting out of your boat to either drag over or around. The second one is a fallen tree which you can circumvent to the left if the water level is high enough; otherwise drag over the rocks. The minor one looks imposing at first sight: a huge logjam that appears to stretch across a broad watershed; in fact, however, you can continue paddling by hugging the left bank and following the S-shaped curve.

You can take out upstream of the Main Street bridge by climbing up the gentle slope on the right bank, to the plateau that divides Trout Creek from the stream to the east, which lies 50 feet away. (This converging stream is unnamed on the USGS topo map.)

Section 2: Main Street to the Covered Bridge at 7th Street

Distance: 1.5 miles
Travel time: 30 minutes

Adversity level 3: Very challenging
Needs 800 % on the Aquashicola (Palmerton) gauge
Gradient: 25 feet per mile

There are two places to put-in: one is the take-out that's described in Section 1, the other is on the right bank upstream of the bridge over the unnamed tributary that lies 50 feet to the east of Trout Creek. You can park in the adjacent clearing at the intersection of Main Street and Old Mill Road.

Once I tried the alternative put-in on the tributary. I got hung-up on exposed boulders at first, both under and shortly after the bridge, and had to hump or pole my way off. The tributary joins Trout Creek 100 yards or so downstream.

Trout Creek is twice as wide as the tributary; the water is deeper and the current is faster. Once you get going you could race all the way to the finish line if it weren't for the deadfall. Four downed trees block the way, and for every one you must climb out of the boat in order to lift it over the obstructing log. The water is only knee-deep.

Four bridges cross this stretch: a trail bridge, the Center Street bridge, a turnpike bridge, and another trail bridge. The deadfall lies between the first trail bridge and the Center Street bridge. The rest of the way is smooth paddling with fast current but no whitewater.

You might wonder why I didn't break this section at the Center Street Bridge, instead of the way I did. The reason is that the banks are high, steep, and covered with thick vegetation, making put-in and take-out extremely difficult if not impossible at that location.

Take-out after passing under the covered bridge. This is a trail access area with a large parking lot. Pass under the bridge along the right bank, then steer left and land upstream of the car-sized boulder in the middle of the stream. A short path leads to the parking lot. This is also the put-in for Section 3.

Section 3: Covered Bridge at 7th Street to the Lehigh River

Distance: 1.5 miles
Travel time: 15 minutes

Adversity level 3: Very challenging
Needs 800 % on the Aquashicola (Palmerton) gauge
Gradient: 39 feet per mile

This section consists almost entirely of fast-moving whitewater with short standing waves. It is incredibly exciting. I based the adversity level not on wave heights (which measure a foot or two), but on the sharp curves that necessitate quick and skillful turning so as to avoid being shoved against the outside banks. Anticipate your turns by angling the boat before you enter the curve, then paddle hard as soon as the bow clears the inside bank. Despite the high gradient, the saving grace is that there are no ledges or sudden drops: just a continuous slide down a steeply inclined plane.

Put-in downstream of the covered bridge. Pass left of the car-sized boulder. Then give up all thoughts of relaxing. The stream is a constant flow with no let-ups. I ran it so fast that I beat Cheryl to the take-out: the only time that I paddled a stream faster than she drove on the streets. Mostly all I did was steer and maneuver.

Take out on the left bank under the third of three bridges before the Lehigh River, and walk up the path to the parking lot. You'll recognize the bridge because you'll see the Lehigh River a hundred yards in front of you. For a longer ride, drift into the river and coast downstream to the next public access.

HOKENDAUQUA CREEK

The rain and spring water that eventually becomes Hokendauqua Creek seeps down the south slope of Blue Mountain, west of Smith Gap: an area that is designated as State Game Lands #168. It then seeps through farmland for a mile or two before the trickles merge to become recognizable as a creek. Farmland continues to the very outskirts of Northampton. The stream is mostly bordered by trees that keep it isolated from view of civilization.

In the statistical sidebar I give 750 % on the Aquashicola Creek gauge and/or 450 % on the Monocacy Creek gauge as suitable streamflows. These amounts are no guarantee that Hokendauqua Creek is runnable. Hokendauqua Creek's watershed lies between that of Aquashicola Creek and that of Monocacy Creek. I give these streamflows as references because they were the streamflows that were registered when I ran Hokendauqua Creek, and I did not get hung up on gravel bars, although I scraped over a couple of them.

Hokendauqua Creek has a large population of trout.

One could opine that the gauge on the Aquashicola Creek is more accurate because the watersheds are closer, albeit on opposite sides of Blue Mountain. On the other hand, if the streamflows were reversed, with the Monocacy higher than the Aquashicola, Hokendauqua Creek might still be runnable. This situation indicates that hard rain fell in one watershed but not in the other. In either case, it is questionable whether Hokendauqua Creek receives enough rainfall to cover the gravel bars. You'll just have to go and see for yourself.

Note that my designation of sections is somewhat arbitrary. Look on any road map, and you'll see that there are any number of bridges that can be used as alternate put-ins and take-outs. However, in Section 1 the streambed is narrow and dotted with logjams. Section 2 is wide but also has some deadfall, plus a dam. Section 3 has a dam but no deadfall, and the water flows swiftly to create standing waves that require caution.

Section 1: Glase Road to Route 248
Distance: 4.2 miles
Travel time: 2 hours

Adversity level 3: Very challenging
Needs 750 % on the Aquashicola or Monocacy gauge
Gradient: 7 feet per mile

This stretch is for paddlers who either seek challenges or who are not bothered by them. The challenges are not paddling challenges (note the gentle gradient) but deadfall challenges. Some of the massive fallen trees have created massive challenges. This is not to say that they are insurmountable, only that much strength and effort is required to overcome them.

The saving grace is that the giant trunks that span the waterway are not bunched together but are spread far apart, so there is time to rest between carries and lift-overs. I am overstating the case somewhat so that my readers won't be taken by surprise. In actuality, there's not as much deadfall as you might expect for a narrow streambed – 10 to 20 feet in width – but a couple of the most challenging ones make up for the rest.

The worst logjam completely clogs the stream by creating three distinct channels, each of which was blocked by logs and was overgrown with thick vegetation. The resulting channels are less than 5 feet across, and flow for more than a hundred yards through lesser deadfall before they merge to let the water regroup. Furthermore, I had to wade in thick mud that had not been washed away because of the damming effect of the natural obstructions. Wherever the stream flowed freely, the bottom consists of boulder fields and gravel bars.

On the good side, the banks are devoid of encroaching vegetation, undoubtedly due largely to the rocky nature of the terrain. I had to duck under a few low-hanging branches now and again; and some hung so low that they swiped across the gunwales. But foliage like this was a minor annoyance.

I was able to duck under a few of the downed trees: sometimes barely scraping through, and twice getting stuck when there wasn't enough space for my back to clear the low height. Others I rammed and forced my way over top.

The water flows nicely between obstacles. The banks are spread far enough apart so that there is plenty of room to maneuver around exposed boulders and shallows. Except for bridges and occasional buildings, the stream is bordered by dark primeval forest and tall rock cliffs, some rising sheer more than 50 feet in height. Wherever a cliff adorns one side of the stream, a floodplain graces the opposite side. This stretch rates high on my scale of rugged beauty.

Sufficient depth of water is a prime directive for easy-going paddling. When I paddled this section of the Hokendauqua Creek, Jim Thorpe received an inch and a quarter of rain overnight. The streamflow on the Aquashicola gauge registered only 130 % at sunrise, while the Monocacy gauge registered 974 %. A couple of hours later, as I prepared to leave the house, the Monocacy streamflow had dropped to 740 %. By the time I reached Hokendauqua Creek, it was only marginally runnable.

I ran it anyway. Matted grass on floodplains that stood a foot and a half high attested to recent flooding. The water was falling so fast that halfway downstream I started scraping rocks. By the end of the trip I was leaving bottom paint everywhere.

As Cheryl and I sat on the bank next to Route 248, we could actually *see* the water falling. In a matter of ten minutes, more and more rocks were exposed until shallow and barely runnable riffles became scratchy, then turned into walkways. I theorized that most of the previous night's rain had been absorbed by surrounding farmland; only the rain that fell on the stream's bordering forest poured into the waterway. I canceled my plan to paddle the rest of the way to the Lehigh River.

Use rain accumulation and streamflow gauges on adjacent watersheds as guides. Do not rely on visible water depth at Glase Road or intermediate bridges, because streambeds are excavated at bridge sites prior to construction. Instead, check the water depth at Route 248. If the downstream stretch looks runnable, then the upstream stretch should be runnable. But don't lollygag. Start as soon as possible after a downpour.

Section 2: Route 248 to Indian Trail Road Adversity level 2: Challenging
Distance: 5.4 miles Needs 750 % on the Aquashicola or Monocacy gauge
Travel time: 2 hours Gradient: 23 feet per mile

As noted above, adjacent streamflow gauges should be used only as guides. If both

Hokendauqua Creek Sections 2 and 3

the Monocacy gauge and the Aquashicola gauge are high, it's a pretty good bet that heavy rainfall inundated that land in between. Ultimately, though, the only true guide is visual observation at the Route 248 bridge. Look downstream about a hundred yards. If you don't see exposed rocks and the water is flowing unobstructed through the riffles, then go for it.

There is deadfall on this stretch, but not much and nothing that requires much effort to circumvent. It's more of an annoyance than a hardship. One time I had to drag my canoe some 20 feet or so along a soggy bank. Other times I merely had to step over logs. The scenery more than offsets these minor inconveniences. A thick veneer of trees lines the banks so that you'll almost never know that you're passing farm field after farm field that are literally only a stone's throw away – if you could cast a stone through the foliage. The feeling of remoteness is broken on occasion by bridges and powerline easements.

This section is the prettiest stretch of the Hokendauqua Creek, and well worth scampering over and around a few downed trees in order to enjoy the pleasant beauty. You'll even get to paddle under an old-time covered bridge.

A runnable dam that was created by a log.

A dam is located a quarter mile past the covered bridge. It stands vertically and drops three feet or more, adjacent to a large house (or small mansion). Not to worry. The streambed splits when the dam comes into view. Take the left channel to avoid the dam, then duck under the tree that has fallen across the water. You can look upstream and see the dam after the channels rejoin.

Standing waves are a joy to pass over. The water gets rough at the approach of Indian Creek. Plow through it, then veer left. The take-out is located only a block after the confluence. Hug the bank. There are no eddies, but the water moves slower than it does in the middle. Grab a handful of vegetation to bring your boat to a stop. Climb out of the boat onto the steep embankment. Kick or crawl 8 feet to the top, with your boat or painter held tightly in hand. Then drag the boat onto the level ground above.

There's not much more that I can say about this stretch, but I do want to reiterate my sentiments and reinforce my viewpoint that, despite a few obstacles, this is the most scenic part of this incredibly curvaceous creek. Don't miss it.

Section 3: Indian Trail Road to the Lehigh River   Adversity level 2: Challenging
Distance: 4.7 miles   Needs 750 % on the Aquashicola or Monocacy gauge
Travel time: 2 hours   Gradient: 18 feet per mile

Despite a lower gradient, this section has more standing waves than the previous section. The primary reason is that the streambed lacks a consistent slope. Instead, it has a saw-toothed configuration in which relatively level stretches are punctuated by ledges or drops. Only one of these rocky drops stands high enough to present a problem: the one under the Horwith Road bridge. I sneaked it on the right. Otherwise, the waves were fun to ride in roller-coaster fashion without rising high enough to splash over the gunwales.

Another reason for the increase in wave heights is the additional water that is supplied by Indian Creek, which nearly doubles the streamflow.

This stretch passes farmland and quarries that you'll never see because of

A ledge rather than a dam, at low water the lintel stands less than one foot high, and impounds water for only a couple of hundred feet.

the fringe of trees. Except for occasional bridges, more than half the trip is reminiscent of a wilderness experience.

The only obstacle is the Lappawinzo Dam. This is the strangest dam I've ever seen. The stone and concrete breastwork has a full-width lintel that you can walk across. Under the lintel there is a channel in the middle that allows water to flow unimpeded over a low shelf that creates the impoundment. Walls extend perpendicularly from each side of the stream to the central channel, which measures some 15 feet across. Thus the water is both funneled and accelerated through the channel.

There is enough height between the water and the lintel for a boat to pass as long as the paddler ducks. I didn't try it and I don't advise others to make the attempt. The actual drop is only a couple of feet, but the venturi effect helps to create a serious hydraulic that might capsize a kayak or tip a canoe, and that might capture the paddler.

The lift-over is short. I broadsided my boat against the vertical breastwork on the left, stepped onto the lintel, dragged the boat over the top, then lowered it down the convenient steps into the water on the other side. The whole operation took only a couple of minutes, then I was on my way.

The feeling of remoteness is dispelled upon approach to Northampton's environs. Industrial centers and trucking traffic are exasperatingly noisy; the sight of commercial buildings ruins the sense of back-woods paddling . . . but the water is fast and furious and fun to paddle.

Then a fringe of trees blocks the view of other buildings and the upcoming housing developments. Except for the bridges, the natural barrier recalls the previous sense of isolation all the way to the finish line.

Prepare to take-out when you see the Lehigh River. I took-out on the right bank between the Canal Street bridge and the D&L Trail bridge. The steep slope has poor footing. I slipped and fell, and planted my hand on the nettles that cover the 8-foot-high embankment. I have always been particularly susceptible to the poison. The nickname "seven minute itch" is a misnomer in my case. My hand and fingers were still stinging several hours later.

The parking lot lies at the top of the slope.

An easier but longer take-out is located on the left between the D&L Trail bridge and the river. A convenient concrete apron extends into the water so that you can paddle your boat right onto it. However, you then have to portage your boat 50 feet up the trail and then across the walking bridge to the parking lot. Choose your poison!

INDIAN CREEK

The water that ultimately becomes Indian Creek trickles down the south slope of Blue Mountain, east of Little Gap: an area that is designated as State Game Lands #168. It then flows through a mix of farmland and housing developments, most of which is unseen from the stream due to thick surrounding forest. The streambed is little more than a ditch that passes under roadways by means of culverts. It skirts a golf course but you'll never see it; there is no need to worry about getting clunked by an errant golf ball: it will never make it through the trees.

The streambed starts to grow in width about half a mile north of Sycamore Drive, but the best place to start a trip is half a mile farther downstream at Indian Trail Park: west of the stream, on the right bank. There's plenty of parking right next to the put-in, and a gentle slope leads to the water's edge.

Only Section: Route 248 to Hokendauqua Creek, thence to Indian Trail Road

Adversity level 2: Challenging
Distance: 2.7 miles plus .1 mile
Needs 750 % on the Aquashicola gauge
Travel time: 1.5 hours
Gradient: 30 feet per mile

This creek looks inviting at the put-in, but the invitation is deceiving. A stream that could be a scenic and relaxing family cruise is made challenging by deadfall. I was able to duck under three downed trees, but I had to disembark and carry around six others. Five of the carries were not exceptionally challenging; they were just onerous. But the fifth and last one required quite a bit of finesse because the huge tree that spans the banks blocks sight of a pair of ledges, the first of which cannot be run because it lies so close to the tree.

I made the mistake of veering toward the left bank because the top branches of the tree lay across the right bank. I figured that stepping over the base of the trunk would be easier than working my way through the upper limbs. I was wrong. Instead of a level landing, the bank consisted of a short vertical rock face. When I laid the boat alongside the trunk, I had to hold onto it tightly because the friction against the bottom hull threatened to flip over the boat by dipping the upstream gunwale under water.

At the same time I had to sit on the trunk, swing my legs over it, stand in the water, and haul the boat over the trunk and into the water downstream of the tree but practically within reach of a 3- to 4-foot ledge. The flat rock under my feet was slippery: a precarious perch at best. I then lined the canoe over the drop-off and moored it on a semi-dry ledge while I took photographs.

The next ledge lay some 50 feet downstream. I walked in water as I lined the canoe close enough to the drop-off that I could see what it looked like. It appeared to be runnable. I jumped into the boat and was still situating myself on the kneeling pads as the current swept me almost against the base of a tree that protruded from the bank. I barely had time to pick up my paddle and get the boat past the trunk and over the drop-off.

In retrospect, it would have been better to beach the boat on the right bank upstream of the first tree, where a flood plain extends all the way past the second ledge, then portage or drag the canoe around the treetop and over unobstructed and level ground. Readers, heed my caution.

Runnable log on Indian Creek.

By the way, had it not been for the upstream tree, the upper ledge would be runnable near the right bank, where part of the ledge slopes down so that the drop-off measures less than a foot.

There is some low whitewater at the confluence with the Hokendauqua Creek, but nothing that a properly paddled canoe cannot handle. The trickiest part is making the right turn into standing waves that are perpendicular to the streamflow of Indian Creek.

After that, it's only a block to the take-out upstream of the bridge on Indian Trail Road. Keep left and grab hold of vegetation on the short but steep bank to stop forward momentum as you climb out of the boat and get a foothold on the sloping dirt. Drag your boat up the 8-foot-high embankment.

The shuttle distance on Indian Trail Road is 2.2 miles.

In the statistical sidebar I give 750 % on the Aquashicola Creek gauge as a suitable streamflow. This amount is no guarantee that Indian Creek is runnable. Indian Creek's watershed lies between that of Aquashicola Creek and that of Monocacy Creek (skipping over that of Hokendauqua Creek, which doesn't have a gauge). When I ran Indian Creek, the gauge on the Monocacy Creek registered 456 % above normal. I figured that if the streamflows were high on both straddling watersheds, Indian Creek (and Hokendauqua Creek) should be runnable.

If either of the adjacent watersheds is low while the other one is high, this indicates that hard rain fell in one watershed but not in the other, in which case it is questionable whether Indian Creek (and Hokendauqua Creek) – between the two – received enough rainfall to cover the gravel bars. In that case you'll just have to go and see for yourself.

One of many downed trees on Coplay Creek.

COPLAY CREEK

It was only out of curiosity that I surveyed this stream by biking the Ironton Rail Trail in Coplay. The trail closely parallels part of the stream. I didn't expect to find more than a narrow ribbon of water, so I was surprised to find a stream that measured 8 feet in width, and which appeared to be unobstructed by deadfall. So I decided to give it a run for the money. Big mistake!

The stream originates in a shallow depression between two rises that barely rise. It appears as a drainage ditch that meanders southward through farmland for 8 to 9 miles until it skirts the western edge of the Iron Lakes Country Club and golf course. It then makes a sweeping curve northward, first through more farmland, then between quarries that are either active or flooded, until it reaches the terminus of the spur of the rail trail.

Only section: Quarry Road to Lehigh River
Distance: 5.8 miles
Travel time: 3 hours
Adversity level 4: Extremely challenging
Needs high water (by observation)
Gradient: 20 feet per mile

Although the most common width of the streambed is 8 feet, in places it stretches as wide as 10 feet. In either case, encroaching vegetation often reduces the navigable width. In some spots, sagging branches from adjacent trees touch the water all the way across the streambed. The only thing you can do in these cases is to pull in your paddle, duck your head, and let your hat take the brunt of the damage.

My canoe rapidly filled with green leaves and rotted branches that broke off limbs at the slightest contact. I didn't have a rake with me, so twice I beached the boat and flipped it over to dump the accumulated debris. Despite these dumps, for a couple of miles I was accompanied by a hyperactive "old ugly" that dashed fore and aft as I shooed it away from my knees.

An "old ugly" is Cheryl's name for a large hairy spider whose appearance is scary (to her). For the most part the "old ugly" stayed in the bow. On one occasion, as I crashed through low-lying limbs and leaves, a spider, or a mite, or something with long legs, wrapped its appendages around my nose. I didn't take time to examine it. I plucked it off my nose and tossed it overboard without seeing exactly what it was. It might have been a granddaddy longlegs.

But none of the above was the worst part of this trip. Although I saw no deadfall from the Ironton Rail Trail, it grew to mountainous proportions where I couldn't see the stream from the trail. At first there were just a few isolated logs. The water was shallow – seldom more than knee deep – so lifting the canoe over wooden barriers was little more than annoying. But isolated logs soon became more frequent. Then logs morphed into fully-grown trees. Then fully-grown downed trees came in clusters.

Finally, I found myself fighting for survival in a naturally made obstacle course. In some places I had to abandon the stream altogether, in order to drag, lift, and shove my boat through thickets and thorn bushes, to say nothing of downed trees that occupied the forest floor. For a couple of miles I carried the canoe more often than I paddled it. The trip was exhausting to say the least.

This is not to say that there weren't some fun stretches to paddle, especially near the end, but all in all the experience was one that I would not like to repeat. The most interesting part of the trip was paddling through the tunnel to the Lehigh River.

Plus there were two bridge crossings that I had to make over dry land. The first one was a trail bridge that was too low to pass underneath. The second one was an old concrete bridge that had collapsed into the streambed. Dragging the boat around them was a minor annoyance.

Just before the confluence, the stream passes under an old railroad bed, then under Water Street. The tunnel measures some 50 feet in length, and is split into two parts. The left part consists of an arched passageway that stands 12 feet high and measures 8 feet in width. Halfway through the passageway the ceiling drops flat to a height of 6 feet or so. This tunnel was dry when I scouted it on the day of my bike ride.

The right part is actually a pair of small parallel tunnels. The right tunnel of the pair is either sealed off or blocked by breakdown. The left tunnel stands 6 feet high and measures 27 inches in width at the narrowest point of the jagged rock construction. I measured it with a rule to determine if I could fit through in my boat. I couldn't.

As luck would have it, a rainstorm flooded the area two nights after my bike ride, so the following day found me on the water – which was already receding and barely deep enough to float my canoe in some places. When I reached the tunnels, both small ones were completely blocked by tree limbs and brush all the way to the top. But the large tunnel had enough water flowing through it to float my boat: a cheap thrill that I thoroughly enjoyed as it was like paddling through a cave. The tunnel even had short off-white stalactites growing from the ceiling.

After exiting the tunnel I crossed the outflow of the right tunnels – both of which were letting water strain through the debris buildup – and landed on a stony beach. From there it was only 30 feet to the road, and another 50 feet to a pullover where Cheryl had parked the Jeep.

The first thing I said to her was, "I'd like to see the Great Leslie try that one." It's a quote from Professor Fate in the movie *The Great Race*.

I really pushed the envelope when I decided to paddle such a narrow stream. But you never know what you can do until you try it. But you won't find me trying it again unless the deadfall is removed. Then this stream would be a little charmer.

Anglers should note that I spotted schools of fingerlings in the stream when the water was clear before the storm. I see no reason why native trout shouldn't live there, too. I've seen them in much smaller streams.

As a guide for water level, I used the Jordan Creek streamflow gauges because the watersheds of the Coplay Creek and the Jordan Creek lie next to each other. Even so, although the rain fell overnight, and I paddled the following morning, the water had already receded a foot by the time I started my trip. I saw long grass on the flood plains that was still wet and lying flat against the damp ground. For what it's worth . . .

LITTLE LEHIGH CREEK

The meager beginning of this stream lies at the base of Topton Mountain, which is located a couple of miles south of Topton. After leaving the forest, the water irrigates 6 miles of farmland before it reaches a depth that becomes potentially navigable after a large rainfall. Upstream of the confluence with Spring Creek, the designated streambed is little more than a thin strip of sunken land that can transport water when there is enough to create flow.

After leaving farm country and entering suburbia, the stream carves a circuitous course past a number of recreational grounds on the way to and through Allentown: Ancient Oak West Recreation Area, Little Lehigh Creek Flood Plain – Miscellaneous Open, Winding Brook Manor Recreation Area, Danfield Run Passive Recreation Area, Harris-York Public Open Space, Millbrook Farms Recreation Area, Wildlands Conservancy, Lehigh Country Club, Devonshire Park, Little Lehigh Park, and Fountain Park (eleven in all).

Thus the Little Lehigh Creek has more recreational access than any other tributary to the Lehigh River.

The reason I designated Section 1 from the Millbrook Farms Recreation Area is because there is considerable deadfall above this location. The upstream waterway can become navigable after a massive rain event, but there could be more portaging than paddling. I might attempt some upstream stretches someday, but I had not done so when this book went to press. Technically then, my Section 1 could be considered Section 2.

Note that the stream cannot be run unless the Little Lehigh gauge in Allentown registers at least 200 %. Of all the Lehigh River tributaries, this is the lowest streamflow above normal that results in runnable water. As a caveat, however, this amount of streamflow is the absolute minimum necessary to make the stream *barely* navigable. A streamflow of 300 % is more desirable if you want to avoid scraping over gravel bars and grinding to a halt on manmade rock dams.

The stream is fairly consistent all the way. You'll hardly notice a difference in gradients until the confluence with the Jordan Creek, after which the streambed slopes downward noticeably along a flat incline to the river.

Also consistent are wildlife and vegetation. I spotted numerous mallards, mergansers, Canada geese, great blue herons, and a lone, pure white, great egret, which was either lost or out of place. I also saw turtles that were sunning themselves on logs. The trees are typical pines, oaks, sycamores, and so on; but what struck me the most was the number of weeping willows that line the banks.

The sole reason for breaking the stream into three sections is because of dams and deadfall, which add a challenge to Sections 1 and 3, and which are totally absent from Section 2. As information, I paddled all three sections together in three and a half hours, and that was without exerting myself.

Section 1: Mill Race Road to Fish Hatchery Road   Adversity level 2: Challenging
Distance: 4.8 miles   Needs 200 % on the Little Lehigh (Allentown) gauge
Travel time: 2 hours   Gradient: 10 feet per mile

There are six rock dams along this stretch, but none present a problem to paddlers, although at the bare minimum runnable level you might scratch some paint off the bot-

Despite the dam, this scene typifies the natural beauty of the Little Lehigh Creek.

tom of your boat. The real challenges are deadfall and dams.

First the deadfall. As far as deadfall goes, these are fairly amenable to passing. I was able to duck under a cluster of four downed trees, but at higher water levels my boat or my back would have struck or scraped bark. I had to clamber over two logs by stepping on the hard gravel bottom and sliding the boat over top of them. Neither of these maneuvers was challenging, but the average paddler doesn't want to get his feet wet or have to expend the energy to drag a boat over a log.

The big turn-offs on this section are two vertical rock dams with concrete lintels. Each measures three feet or so in height. I paddled over the first one but not intentionally. I wanted to beach the boat on the lintel, step on it, and lower the boat over the lip. The mild current and the depth of water on the lintel conspired to thwart this maneuver: my canoe was shoved over the lip before I could get my feet out from under the seat. Fortunately I was scraping along the bushes that lined the left bank. I grabbed them for stability, and managed to maintain an even keel as the stern dropped over the lip.

I took greater care with the second dam. I kept to the right bank because I saw some large tree trunks that were stranded on the lintel, away from where the bulk of the water was pouring. This time the canoe ground to a halt. It took but a moment to lower it over a lip.

Other than these obstacles the trip was a pleasant experience which, because of my inclination toward challenges, was to my liking. Definitely do this section if you don't mind a few obstacles in the way.

There's a parking lot and boat access on the right bank upstream of Fish Hatchery Road.

Section 2: Fish Hatchery Road to S. 10th Street   Adversity level 1: Not challenging
Distance: 4.5 miles   Needs 200 % on the Little Lehigh (Allentown) gauge
Travel time: 1.5 to 2 hours   Gradient: 10 feet per mile

This is the stretch for you if you want a pleasant cruise with no obstacles to bar clear passage. The water flows slowly but steadily, without riffles or speed-ups due to rock dams. For the most part, a buffer of trees on both banks offers a sense of seclusion. The covered bridge is a treat. Take time to land on the right bank and explore this maintained relic.

Little Lehigh Creek Sections 2 and 3

Paths border this stretch of the stream for much of its length. Bikers, hikers, joggers, and dog-walkers are common sights that don't detract from the "family" experience. Some of these pedestrians were moving faster than I was drifting.

The streamflow stalls near the end of this section due to the backwash of a dam. As you approach the take-out bridge you'll see an abandoned multi-story building on the right. I don't know the history behind this huge industrial facility, but it parallels the bank for a block and a half: a truly amazing sight.

Take-out on the left bank upstream of the bridge at South 10th Street. Street parking is available next to the ballfield. You're safe unless someone hits a really long fly ball.

Section 3: South 10th Street to the Lehigh River and Canal Park

Adversity level 2: Challenging
Distance: 2.0 miles
Needs 200 % on the Little Lehigh (Allentown) gauge
Travel time: 1 hour
Gradient: 10 feet per mile

This "down and dirty" stretch is fairly noisy due to nearby traffic until it reaches the Jordan Creek about a mile downstream. Worse than the noise are the obstacles: a 6-foot-high dam and a serious logjam.

First the dam. This dam is scheduled for removal because it no longer serves a purpose. In fact, it is counterproductive as it prevents migratory fish such as shad from reaching their spawning grounds upstream. It is also an impediment to boaters.

The best way around it is down the bypass channel on the right. Hug the right bank as you approach the dam. The concrete abutment extends 10 feet from land. This will prevent you from being swept over the lintel. You'll see a narrow stream of water being diverted past the abutment. Climb onto the abutment or step into the water and let the current take your boat into the channel. It won't go far because of deadfall and boulders, so don't worry that your boat will get away from you. Either line it or drag it down the channel to the shallows at the bottom. Then shove off from shore and swing around the downstream sandbar.

Now for the deadfall. The problem with any deadfall is that it does not allow floating objects to pass. This means boats as well as debris. Debris such as tree limbs and plastic bottles accumulate – and keep accumulating. On this stretch I passed a midstream trash dump that started when overhanging branches contacted the water and

The Section 3 dam.

snagged drifting objects which then became trapped. This developed into an island that measured some 6 to 8 feet across, filled with rubbish.

Afterward, I met a thick downed tree that had collected others of its kind. High banks prevented me from carrying the boat around the trunks, so I had to step onto one, then onto another, and balance myself as I hefted the boat onto and over the collection of loose boles and junk. This passage was precarious but not hazardous. Worst case scenario was a dunking into water that was so deep that I could not touch bottom.

Rubbish raft.

A high streamflow would have increased the challenge. A super high streamflow might have submerged the trunks. Speaking of which . . .

I once endeavored to paddle this stream after a severe rain event when the streamflow gauge rose to 4,000 % above normal. The water was so high that it nearly touched the bottom of the bridge on Riverbend Road; this would have necessitated climbing up the left bank and carrying the canoe across the road. Worse than that was the pedestrian bridge for the Little Lehigh Parkway Path: water flowed *over* the bridge, and the bridge was stacked high with tree limbs and other debris. The park itself was flooded because the river overflowed the banks. Both these bridges normally have 5 feet of clearance.

Anyway, it's clearing sailing after the logjam. The junction with the Jordan Creek is attended by a pair of abandoned railroad bridges, followed shortly by the Basin Street bridge and an active railroad bridge (where I took-out on one of my Jordan Creek trips). Bridge, anyone?

The influx of water adds speed to the streamflow. The steeper gradient is visible but flat and without drop-offs. The veneer of trees is so thick on either side that you'll feel as if you're in the wilderness. Then comes the confluence with the Lehigh River. Ferry across the river to the Canal Park boat launch.

The creek overflowed its banks and this pedestrian bridge after a severe rain event, littering the walkway with debris and detritus. When I paddled this stretch at a lower level, I passed under the bridge without even having to duck my head.

JORDAN CREEK

This stream is a cruiser's delight. Except for Section 1, the low gradient is consistent from beginning to end, with no drop-offs or hydraulics lying in wait around blind bends, and with only one fallen tree which can easily be negotiated. The only obstacles are two dams in Section 4. You can carry around these dams, or you can avoid them altogether by running selected stretches that lie elsewhere.

The latter scenario is likely the preferable one because most paddlers will not want to pass through areas that are less than scenic, particularly the final stretch between Jordan Park in downtown Allentown and the confluence with the Little Lehigh River. I will describe the entire stream, then suggest ways to break trips into comfortably short stretches that avoid the less appealing areas.

Numerous mallards and Canada geese quacked and honked all along the stream. I saw several great blue herons. I spotted one pure white bird that was either a great egret or a great white heron; I am not knowledgeable enough to distinguish between those species at a glance. I also saw a groundhog and a muskrat. Don't get tangled in fishing lines that dangle from overhanging tree limbs; anglers cast flies, lures, and baited hooks into these waters because the stream is stocked with trout.

High water is necessary to keep from constantly running aground. I don't recommend paddling any stretch of this stream unless the streamflow gauge at Schnecksville reads at least 1,000%. Ten times the normal flow might sound excessively high, but keep in mind that under normal circumstances the stream is little more than a wet rock garden that is shoe-sole deep: ladies wearing platform shoes won't even get their toes wet.

For example, if the normal depth is one inch (100%), then ten times that amount (1,000%) is only ten inches: sufficient water to float a boat but without strong enough current to knock you down if you stood in it. Most of the time I could see the rocky bottom; it was only as deep as my blade was long. Deeper areas exist upstream of the dams where the flow rate is reduced due to water impoundment. In short, the stream consists of mildly flowing water with occasional rocks and ripples. The only true whitewater occurred in Section 1, and the only riffles downstream of Jordan Park.

Higher streamflows will shorten your passage time without significantly increasing water depth.

Kayakers should definitely wear helmets. Canoeists should stand up if the boat tips over or they fall overboard; nowhere did I encounter waves that could swamp an open boat that was properly handled. Rafters and tubers: enjoy!

The Jordan Creek flows down the south side of Blue Mountain west of Bake Oven Road. After trickling out of the forest it flows through farmland for 5 miles, passing through Germantown along the way. It might be possible to put-in at Germantown, but I think it would take an extreme weather event to provide enough water to float a boat. I started a couple of miles south of Germantown.

Section 1: Route 309 to Route 100   Adversity level 2: Challenging
Distance: 2.2 miles   Needs 1,000 % on the Jordan (Schnecksville) gauge
Travel time: 30 minutes   Gradient: 28 feet per mile

The first time I saw this section, the streamflow gauge was registering 2,200 %.

The water was flowing so fast that it was scary, because I didn't have any idea about what obstacles I might encounter. I could see much of the stream from five bridges, and more of it alongside Route 100. It was the stretches that I couldn't see that worried me. The water was moving so fast that, if I had to abandon ship in order to drag the boat over a logjam, I wouldn't be able to stand in it without getting bowled over. Plus the depth was unknown.

Too bad I didn't know then what I learned the next day, when I ran it after the streamflow had dropped to 1,200 %. This short section is a dream delight for whitewater paddlers.

I parked on the shoulder on Route 309, carried the canoe on the outside of the guardrail to the left bank upstream of the bridge, hugged the abutment, and then launched from the rocks under the roadway.

Not to worry. There's enough space to pass under the tree between the branches.

Shortly after embarking, I encountered the only tree that lay all the way across the streambed. It was located before the beautiful stone bridge that carries Werleys Corner Road over the creek. I had to stand in the water in order to lift the boat over the barrier. Had I run this section the day before, I could have passed over the log – perhaps without ever seeing it.

The rest of the trip was pure fun. There was plenty of height under the Route 100 bridge. After that, the surface of the fast-flowing water changed from smooth to uneven, with plenty of standing waves to add excitement. A huge tree straddled the stream alongside Route 100; you can see it from the road if you want to scout it. This proved to be no impediment because its massive trunk lay more than 4 feet above the water surface. I passed under it without even ducking, drifting straight and fast between fat down-thrust limbs that were spread far enough apart that I could pass between them.

Perhaps the creek's only hydraulic lay immediately downstream of the tree. I ran over the middle of it to prove that it wasn't a safety hazard, and kept on trucking. The course winds a bit after veering from the highway. A number of fallen trees reach into the stream from the banks, but none stretch all the way across, so it was easy to ply a circuitous path around them.

I barely saw the Hollenbach Road bridge in passing. Then came more curves and more deadfall. I felt as if I were running an obstacle course: one that always had an open passage. I stopped at Route 100 by pulling into the eddy on the right bank upstream of the bridge. This is an excellent place for taking-out and putting-in. The low embankment rises gently upward to Narris Road.

My advice to paddlers who enjoy thrilling but non-hazardous whitewater is to establish a shuttle on this short section, and run it over and over again until you have had your fill. Unlike the Lehigh River, you're commitment is always short. You can quit any time you want, and take-out at three places along the way.

Jordan Creek Sections 2 and 3

Section 2: Route 100 to Kistler Road Adversity level 1: Not challenging
Distance: 5.1 miles Needs 1,000 % on the Jordon (Schnecksville) gauge
Travel time: 1 hour or more Gradient: 14 feet per mile

Put-in on the right bank upstream of the southern Route 100 bridge, at the intersection of Narris Road. The embankment slopes gently down to an eddy. Float under the bridge and the one a block away that passes under Bittners Corner Road. Then say goodbye to civilization for the next five miles, and prepare yourself for a wonderful wilderness experience.

The streambed on this section carves four long sweeping curves that turn from north to south through a forested landscape that separates the creek from cultivated farm fields that lie out of sight. Nearly vertical escarpments rise a hundred feet on either side, always facing a flood plane on the opposite bank. If you look up high you might catch a glimpse of several homes on the bluff above, but after the first mile even those signs of human habitation are no longer visible.

This section is not bothered by obstacles or standing waves. I floated easily over one sloped rock ledge that dropped nearly a foot. Otherwise, there was nothing but fast rolling water – and the feeling that I was passing through the middle of nowhere. The only intrusion was the remnant of an old ford which, with a streamflow of 1,200 %, was unfordable.

For the most part I could touch the bottom with my blade, but my hull never scraped rock – even when I went over the ledge, because the depth of water was sufficient to cushion my passing. I paddled steadily but mechanically, without ever exerting myself. My one-hour passage was due to an able assist from the current.

Take-out at Kistler Street, on the left bank downstream of the bridge.

I heartily recommend this stretch for people who appreciate paddling in solitude.

Section 3: Kistler Road to Kernsville Road Adversity level 1: Not challenging
Distance: 8.3 miles Needs 1,000 % on the Jordon (Schnecksville) gauge
Travel time: 2-1/2 hours Gradient: 9 feet per mile

I ran this section when the Schnecksville streamflow gauge read 2,000 %. Even at that high flow rate, I scraped bottom half a dozen times; on only a couple occasions did I encounter waves more than six inches in height. I would describe the current as "lazy." When I passed around the Trexler Nature Preserve, unattended children were playing knee-deep in the water. One father was walking in the middle of the stream with his 3-year-old daughter; the water was up to her waist but only up to his shins. I chatted with the father for a bit as I drifted slowly past them. At a streamflow less than 1,000%, I might have run aground often enough to make the trip agonizing.

I put-in on the left bank on the downstream side of the Kistler Road bridge. Bear Road intersects Kistler Road a hundred feet from the bridge; Cheryl parked the car on the grass next to Bear Road while I unloaded the boat. After I slid the canoe into the water, there was nothing to bar the way for the next 8 miles: an easy cruise that required little effort. The width of the stream averaged 25 feet.

Almost the entire passage was forested on both sides of the stream. A few back yards intruded on the wilderness experience, as well as an occasional cornfield that was visible through the barrier of trees that lined the banks. In many places the banks consisted of steeply sloped bedrock, sometimes as much as 80 degrees; nonetheless, trees managed to maintain a grip on the slanted surface. I passed under seven bridges, three of which were covered.

The stream curves around three sides of the Trexler Nature Preserve. This was where I met bathers and picnickers. At one spot I passed under a covered bridge and a pedestrian bridge, then floated over a dam that was less than a foot in height. About a mile later, as I approached another pedestrian bridge, I was astonished to see a pick-up truck splash across the creek in front of me. I soon learned that it had crossed a concrete ford. The downstream drop-off was only a few inches in height. In all my canoeing experience, this was the first time that I had to be on the lookout for vehicular traffic. I looked both ways before paddling over the ford.

A car braving the ford where I was nearly run over by a pick-up truck. The road leads to an outdoor zoo that sports roaming elk and bison.

I took-out at the grist mill dam at Kernsville Road. This dam stands six feet high. I paddled through the dead water along the left bank to the diversion channel for the grist mill. Logs blocked the opening, so I stepped ashore in the weeds and dragged the canoe 20 feet to the clearing next to the wall of the building, which was past the dam. Parking is available on the other side of Grist Mill Road.

This segment of the Jordan Creek has much to recommend it: pretty scenery, the feeling of remoteness, and easy-going paddling with no obstacles.

If you want to get the flavor of the stream without the need for a shuttle, you can do a 3-mile stretch around the Trexler Nature Preserve. Start at the Mill Creek Road bridge on the west side of the Preserve, paddle downstream around the northern tip of the preserve, then head south past the ford to the Old Packhouse Road bridge, and walk half a mile across the base of the peninsula to your starting point.

By the by, at five covered bridges, Jordan Creek has more than any other stream in the watershed.

The dam and abandoned grist mill at Kernsville Road.

Jordan Creek Section 4

Section 4: Kernsville Road to Basin Road (after the Little Lehigh River)

Distance: 13.7 miles
Travel time: 3-1/2 to 4-1/2 hours

Adversity level 1: Not challenging
Needs 1,000 % on the Jordon (Schnecksville) gauge
Gradient: 9 feet per mile

I did this stretch in one fell swoop without resting longer than it took to snatch a drink of water as I drifted with the current. Add an hour to my time if you want a more leisurely trip.

You can also shorten the length (and duration of passage) by running only the stretch between Wehr Mill Road and MacArthur Road: 8 miles of pleasant paddling along tree-lined banks with no dams or obstacles to bar the way. To do this, put in downstream of the covered bridge and take out upstream of the bridge at MacArthur Road. Both ends have plenty of available parking. I recommend this stretch for paddlers who don't want to deal with obstructions.

Kernsville Road passes over the stream at the site of an old gristmill, which is located – appropriately – on Grist Mill Road. Park opposite the gristmill. Launch your boat on the upstream side of the gristmill, which is conveniently located downstream of the dam. Slide the boat to the edge of the concrete pad, slip it into the water, and push off into the current. Pass under the bridge. From here the distance to the dam and covered bridge at Wehr Mill Road is nearly 3 miles, through pristine forest all the way.

The width of the stream averages 40 feet.

I was not surprised to see a great blue heron dart away from the treetops at my approach. But I marveled when a bald eagle followed its flight path.

A mile and a half downstream I encountered a fallen tree that stretched all the way across the stream. I drifted toward the left bank, passed over one partially submerged limb, pulled myself under an overhead limb, and continued on my way without a hitch. I passed under the bridges at Route 309 and the Northeast Extension of the Pennsylvania Turnpike.

The Wehr Dam in Covered Bridge Park.

The major obstacle on this stretch is the dam at Wehr Road. A picnic area graces both banks. I drifted along the shrubbery to the upper edge of the dam (where the water flowed slowly), stepped onto a concrete pad on the right bank, then dragged the boat across the grass to a concrete staircase that led down to the water. The current is quite fast immediately downstream of the dam, but I had no trouble in sliding my canoe into the water and pushing off. This might pose a problem for kayakers who have a greater need to steady their craft while getting seated.

If you don't like the looks of this fast-water entry, carry your boat across the road and put-in at another set of concrete steps that ends in an eddy. I met a pair of local kayakers who were putting-in there. This is the place I recommend as a put-in for paddlers who prefer a shorter trip without having to contend with portaging a dam.

A mile downstream there is another covered bridge, this one somewhat dilapidated. A mile afterward there is a solid railroad bridge whose dual waterways pass through elbow-shaped arches that seem like tunnels because of their 100-yard length. I've never seen anything like it.

The next 3-mile-stretch consists of a winding watercourse through woodlands that give the appearance of wilderness, yet working farms exist on either side, out of sight beyond a thick veil of trees. Then comes Mauch Chunk Road and a possible take-out, although the banks are covered with shrubbery.

Four more bridges followed before I reached the monstrously overflowing dam that preceded the crossing of MacArthur Road (Route 145). I took-out on the left bank where a hundred-foot-wide swath of lawn separates the river from the White Castle restaurant. There is plenty of parking here because this is a municipal park with its own designated parking spots.

To continue downstream, I dragged my boat over boulders between the trees – a distance of 30 to 40 feet – then paddled under the bridge. Paddlers should note that this dam has since been removed. But this still makes a convenient take-out and put-in.

Jordan Park is half a mile farther downstream. I ran my boat onto the concrete apron on the upstream side of the dam. I chose the right bank but the left bank was identical and equally as serviceable; more so if playground crowds had presented a problem. I dragged my canoe a boat-length past the low dam and got right back on the water. Again, paddlers should note that this dam has since been removed.

Now you get to paddle through the middle of downtown proper. The flow is the same and trees hide most of the urban squalor, but the smell is noticeably different. I paddled over two miniature dams that stood less than a foot in height.

Now the bridges come one after another as noisy vehicles ply the cross streets overhead: seven bridges if I counted correctly, and all with embankments that are too high and too vertical to afford a practical take-out. Not to worry: the important landmark is the confluence with the Little Lehigh River, which merges from the right immediately upstream of a tall-sided iron railroad trestle, which is quickly followed by another, smaller trestle, neither of which has seen recent use.

A block or two afterward comes the Basin Street bridge. Hug the left bank and steer into the still water left of the pier. Here you can step onto a muddy bank and haul or portage your boat up a narrow path on the downstream side to the parking area above.

The confluence: Little Lehigh Creek on the left, Jordan Creek on the right. The abandoned railroad trestle is overhead.

Or you can continue down the Little Lehigh Creek and take-out at Canal Park. It's only another mile, and the take-out is more user friendly.

In closing I repeat: if you are not a completer and are simply looking for a pleasant and fast-moving trip, do the 8-mile stretch between Wehr Road and MacArthur Road. For shorter trips, scout the intervening bridges for suitable put-ins and take-outs.

MONOCACY CREEK

Monocacy Creek commences in farmland north of Chapman. Water trickles along tiny rivulets for several miles before they merge to form a recognizable stream – and then it is recognizable only after a heavy rainfall. South of Chapman a definite streambed exists: one that works its way south through Bath, after which the rocks that line the bottom might be wet fulltime. Not until a mile or so south of Bath does the stream become runnable, and then only on rare occasions, such as when a flood of Noachian proportions strikes the area.

When I examined stretches upstream of Jacksonville Road, I found a narrow ribbon of streambed that was largely choked with deadfall and accumulated brush and debris. Downstream looked clear and potentially runnable despite encroaching vegetation. So I bided my time and waited for forty days and forty nights of rain: enough to drown all but Mount Ararat and to fill the streambed to a depth that would float my boat.

A regular morning check of the Lehigh River watershed streamflow gauges revealed that the one on the Monocacy in Bethlehem was flowing at only 125 % normal (median). I shrugged and went to work on my computer. Three hours later, Cheryl told me that the weather station reported that three to five inches of rain fell overnight in Bethlehem. When I rechecked the website, I was astonished to discover that the streamflow had increased to 957 %!

I called downstairs to Cheryl and told her that we were paddling today. (In this case "we" meant that I was paddling and that she was running the shuttle.) We arrived at the put-in a couple of hours later. The creek was indeed flowing high and fast. I soon learned that the water had already dropped a foot and a half. By the next morning the streamflow dropped to 288 %! It was a good thing that I had not hesitated, and started when I did. Or perhaps it was a bad thing.

What followed was my most arduous canoe trip on Lehigh River tributaries. Reflecting on it at the take-out, the trip reminded me of the joke about banging your head against the wall; the only redeeming value was that it felt so good to stop . . . after six hours of grueling effort, with emphasis on "grueling."

This was only one of several dozen logjams, some of which were worse.

I don't mean to downplay the creek. On second thought, I do. In the few places at which I was able to take proper notice, I saw a kind of pristine beauty that partially redeemed the exertion that was required to appreciate it. Great blue herons were prominent, mallards and Canada Geese concentrated in flocks, deer and speckled fawns observed my passing. Otherwise, maneuvering my canoe downstream was cumbersome, strenuous, or painful drudgery – or all of the above: more like all twelve labors of Hercules one after the other. I don't exaggerate.

The only kind statement I can make about the stream is that it wasn't hazardous.

I lost count of the number of downed trees and logjams that I had to carry over or around. I estimate that there were between 30 and 40. And this doesn't count other carries or portages past numerous railroad trestles, two abandoned concrete bridges, manmade dams, and a cattle crossing. One logjam consisted of nearly a dozen trees that extended for 50 feet. Many times I had to drag my canoe through nearly impenetrable thickets that were spiced with thorn bushes.

Originally I intended to have only one section for this creek. After running it, I decided to break it into three sections with decreasing levels of adversity.

By the way, the name of the stream is pronounced mo-knock'-ah-see, with the accent on the second syllable.

Section 1: Jacksonville Road to Brodhead Road   Adversity level 4: Most challenging
Distance: 5.7 miles   Needs 600 % on the Monocacy (Bethlehem) gauge
Travel time: 3 hours plus   Gradient: 12 feet per mile

This section is for completers and masochists only. Even at the high flow rate on the day I canoed, the water was usually only a foot or so deep. My double-bladed paddle did not touch bottom because of the angle of the sweep, but when I had to use my single-bladed paddle – due to ingrowing shrubbery that snagged the uplifted blade of my double-bladed paddle – the blade barely scraped the gravel streambed for the first several miles. Depth proved not to be a problem.

Initially the banks stood less than 10 feet apart. But leafy branches reduced the navigable width to 5 feet or less. Many times I had to duck my head and let my hat take a beating because the branches extended inward from both sides all the way across the stream. At least the branches were thin and bendable.

I did not go far before I encountered the first fallen tree or logjam – there were so many that I can't remember which. Then came another . . . and another . . . and another . . . and another . . . well, you get the point. Most of the time I could stand on the streambed while I hefted the canoe over the logs. Sometimes the water was bunched up by the jam, perhaps waist deep or deeper. Then I had to drag the canoe through the brush on the banks, again and again and again and . . .

The railroad approximates the course of the stream. Whereas the track was laid straight or in sweeping curves, the streambed meanders like a one-legged alcoholic after a weekend binge. These winding peregrinations take the stream under trestles, many of which are so low that they block the way for boats, so that I had to drag my canoe across the tracks. Stop, look,

I encountered more than one massive logjam like this, requiring portage through the woods.

Monocacy Creek Section 1

One of three low railroad trestles that forced me to carry my canoe across the tracks.

and listen were the orders of the day.

The railroad track was often visible, but the buffer of trees mostly blocked my view of the land adjacent to the stream. Surrounding farmland was usually out of sight except for brief glimpses through thin groves. For the most part, I felt as if I were paddling through a remote wilderness area.

Road bridges for vehicular traffic never presented a problem. They all stood high enough for me to duck under.

About two miles downstream from the put-in I encountered a cattle crossing at the site of the bridge on Township Line Road. A pair of guard straps was stretched across the creek. Although the bottom strap stood close to the water, I was able to lift it with the outstretched blade of my paddle, and lift it over the bow. The straps were not intended to prevent boats from passing – if anyone else was ever stupid enough to paddle this stretch – but to act as a visual reference for cattle fording the stream. Another pair of straps was stretched on the downstream side of the double ford on the other side of the bridge. Thus the cattle could roam in four different fields: on either side of the road and on either side of the stream. I was fortunate in that no mooing bovines blocked the way as I drifted past the fords. I wondered, "Where's the beef?"

For a while I had a grand view of the ranch and grazing land until I entered another veneer of dense foliage.

Just before Steuben Road I was blocked by the worst logjam of all. Nearly a dozen trees were laid across the stream like giant Pickup-Sticks. Adjoining brush was thick. I fought my way for fifty feet through brambles and sticker bushes, either pushing or dragging the canoe: whatever worked.

Then came more isolation . . . and exasperating logjams. I apologize for repeating myself. I am merely attempting to provide my readers with a realistic description of the rigors of the stream, so they won't have to learn it firsthand. Sometimes passage was blocked by a single massive trunk. Other times a slender trunk acted like a huge wooden colander that captured logs and loose brush.

There are multiple access points along the way – Route 512 (Bath Pike), Township Line Road, Steuben Road, Georgetown Road, and Hanover Road – but what's the point of knowing about them. Unless you are into self-inflicted torture, or want to play a sick joke on a paddling partner, avoid this stretch of water at all costs.

I estimate that I made more than two dozen carries on this stretch alone. That's about one every quarter mile. It took me 3 hours to complete this section. I was already exhausted, yet I had another eight and a half miles to go.

Monocacy Creek Section 2

Section 2: Brodhead Road to Illic's Mill Park Adversity level 3: Very challenging
Distance: 5.5 miles Needs 600 % on the Monocacy (Bethlehem) gauge
Travel time: 2 hours plus Gradient: 8.5 feet per mile

This stretch consists largely of more of the same but with downed trees and logjams somewhat fewer and farther apart. The streambed now measures 20 to 30 feet across. Yet a number of hefty trees managed to fall and span the banks to create low bridges or solid barricades.

No way through.

A newly fallen tree blocks passage only a hundred feet downstream of the Brodhead Road. The carry was easy due to a low grassy bank that was mowed like a lawn. This deadfall was a harbinger of more come. A quarter mile later the stream passes beneath Route 22 (which is not an access). Shortly afterward is a railroad trestle that must be carried (on the right). Traffic noise from the highway is annoyingly loud.

The noise mitigates as the stream turns away from the highway and enters the Archibald Johnson Conservation Area (although there's nothing on the stream to designate this). There may not be as many downed trees and logjams as there were in the previous section, but those that exist are generally larger, and the way around them is longer.

After passing under Township Line Road (again), from which the banks are accessible, the stream passes beneath a walking bridge and over a couple of low rock dams – nothing to worry about. You can duck under the upcoming railroad trestle but not the one a block afterward. Immediately comes a low concrete bridge with a logjam underneath it. This single-lane bridge has long been abandoned and is overgrown with grass; there is no sign of a road leading away from either end. The same goes for the next abandoned concrete bridge (minus the grass), which has partly collapsed into the stream.

After these highlights, which overlook a couple of downed trees, the creek looks as if it's going to run into Route 22 – but it turns left in the nick of time and enters the Gertrude B. Fox County Park. Being a county park does not absolve the stream from logjams; this stretch certainly has its share. Also, there's a railroad trestle that requires a carry on the right.

Bath Pike comes as a breath of open air, although traffic guarantees that the air won't be fresh. Large flocks of ducks and Canada geese gather here. You can take-out or put-in from the adjacent parking lot. This point is 3.5 miles from Brodhead Road, but as long as you've made it this far you might as well paddle 2 more miles with some challenges ahead.

At this point the unobstructed width made me think that my troubles were over. Not by a long shot! Downed trees and logjams were significantly reduced, but two

Monocacy Creek Sections 2 and 3

Collapsed bridge.

dams and two railroad trestles had yet to be carried or portaged (some in the following section).

The first dam lay only a quarter mile away. The 5-foot height looked imposing but it turned out to be easy to dock against the left-bank retaining wall and lower the canoe over the drop into still water below. You can avoid this dam by putting in a block downstream on single-lane Bella Vista Drive.

At this point there are housing communities on both sides of the stream, but you won't see most of the dwellings through the bordering vegetation, except perhaps in winter. The following West Macada Road is a difficult access that lacks water-level entry.

A low dam spans the creek a block past Bridle Path Road. I ran it without difficulty. Three-quarters of a mile later, I was barely able to duck under a railroad trestle. Then comes Illick's Mill Park, on Monocacy Creek Road, with a public parking lot that serves as an excellent take-out because it avoids the tall dam a block downstream.

Section 3: Illick's Mill Park to the Lehigh River   Adversity level 2: Challenging
Distance: 3.1 miles   Needs 600 % on the Monocacy (Bethlehem) gauge
Travel time: 1 hour plus   Gradient: 17 feet per mile

Illick's Mill Park is the historic site of a famous grist mill. The park is worth visiting just to see the wonderful stonework of which the two pavilions are constructed. The dam stands 10 feet high. A pavilion is perched on either side of the dam. A high walking bridge a hundred feet downstream enables visitors to cross the stream.

If you plan to put-in here, put-in below the dam. Either portage your boat from the parking lot upstream, or drop it off below the dam before proceeding to the parking lot. I passed through the park without using it as an access, so I grounded my canoe on the narrow gravel beach immediately upstream of the dam, on the left bank. I portaged the boat through the pavilion without bopping anyone on the head.

You might think that by avoiding the dam you won't have any carries on this final stretch of waterway that is comparatively wide. Think again. Just because you're paddling through a municipal area doesn't mean that the municipality has cleared the stream of debris and other obstacles. In fact, for the next mile and a half you won't even be aware of the municipality, because of the dense forests on either side of the creek.

The railroad trestle that crosses the water three-quarters of a mile downstream of the dam is not only impassible; it's hazardous. Swift current wants to carry you to the middle of the trestle where the clearance is measured in inches. This isn't an active railroad track but a disused siding. Hug the right bank, nose into the small eddy ahead of the bridge, paddle hard, spin around to face upstream, grab a boulder, and scramble onto the sloped embankment of loose stone. Drag your boat uphill and over the abandoned railroad bed.

Around the bend, some 200 feet downstream of the trestle, is a cascade that's filled with raging whitewater and tall standing waves that can upset a boat that isn't handled properly. I ran the 4-foot drop, but you might want to carry around it through the woods on the left. Be careful of the concrete rubble downstream of the cascade.

Hazardous trestle.

Now the area becomes citified. The bridge at Schoenersville Road is high enough for easy passage, but the trestle a block and a half downstream requires bending down low.

Then comes a bridge that is high and mighty – for West Union Boulevard – followed by yet another low but passable railroad trestle, followed by a tall walking bridge, followed by another high and mighty bridge (this one for West Broad Street), which is followed by a dam that was buried. The water was so high that I passed right over it without seeing it.

You're surrounded by trees again but knot furlong. The bridges come fast and furious: a walking bridge practically underneath a super high bridge, followed by the Main Street Bridge. After the dogleg you'll see three overhead structures all at once, crossing the stream only a few feet from each other: the West Lehigh Street bridge, a railroad trestle, and the aqueduct that carries water for the canal that passes *over* the creek. There's plenty of headroom under all three.

The blind left turn is free of obstacles. Sit back and relax, and let the current carry you downstream for half a mile between the canal and the D&L Trail. The confluence with the Lehigh River is located immediately after the walking bridge that connects the D&L Trail with the Sand Island Trail. Take-out on the peninsula that separates the two bodies of water. From there it's a block to the parking lot.

You'll notice that this section has a higher gradient than the previous two sections. The water runs faster but is nearly free of obstacles, making this an ideal run for people who like to stay dry, and who don't like to carry around too many downed trees and logjams.

Beautifully terraced dam and associated stone structures are architectural delights.

SAUCON CREEK

Saucon Creek results from the drainage of high ground south of the Lehigh River, primarily between Limeport Hill and Chestnut Hill (an actual hill, not the township outside of Philadelphia). It winds northward then eastward then northward again, boxed in by South Mountain to the northwest and a series of hills to the southeast. Minor streams contribute water along the way. Forest yields to farmland which yields to suburbia.

In between farmland and suburbia, the stream makes is most obvious appearance as it flows past one golf course, cuts through the edge of another, and finally bisects the biggest one in the area: the massive spread of the Saucon Valley Country Club, which boasts three complete 18-hole courses plus a host of ball courts and other activities. Sand traps dot the courses, as do water traps, but the longest trap of all is the shallow Saucon Creek.

Section 1: Route 378 to Bingen Road
Distance: 2.9 miles
Travel time: 1 hour

Adversity level 1: Not challenging
Needs 500 % on the Little Lehigh (Allentown) gauge
Gradient: 13 feet per mile

Saucon Creek is not as much of a hazard to golfers as golfers are to paddlers. For one thing, although there is only one small logjam, more than two dozen bridges cross the healthy ribbon of water. I counted 26 bridges, but I might have lost count because I kept count in my head.

For another, there is the potential risk of paddlers getting bonked by errant golf balls whose trajectories either take them out-of-bounds or are too short to reach the green. I don't mean to imply that club members are poor drivers. But it must be stressed that the stream not only passes within a stone's throw (or a golf ball's aerial course) of a score of fairways, it also slices right through the middle of some of them. This latter circumstance puts paddlers directly in the flight path.

Not since my kayaking days have I worn a crash helmet while paddling. For all these reasons, paddlers must decide for themselves whether they want to intrude on this intricate maze of tee-offs, fairways, roughs, and greens.

The logjam consists of a single downed tree that I rammed in order to get the bow on top. I then stepped onto the log and dragged my canoe over it.

Most of the bridges have adequate headroom. About 6 of them require severe ducking. By "severe" I mean that I had to lie flat on the center thwart and lower my head between the gunwales. Two or three times the back of my life vest scraped the bottom of a bridge. Once I got clunked in the head, my life vest jammed temporarily, and the boat was twisted sideways until the force of the current freed me from the obstruction.

Common merganser on the Saucon Creek.

Other than those slight detriments to clear passage, the stream is a pleasant delight of fast water that snakes through club grounds over occasional riffles where the banks stand 20 feet apart.

Saucon Creek Section 2

Section 2: Bingen Road to the Lehigh River
Distance: 6.9 miles
Travel time: 2 hours
Adversity level 1: Not challenging
Needs 500 % on the Little Lehigh (Allentown) gauge
Gradient: 19 feet per mile

Despite one dam and two partial dams, I think of this stretch as a family trip that can be enjoyed by most paddlers whose children are older than tots. The slope is consistent without any surprises than those that are mentioned in the previous sentence. The riffles are bigger than the ones in the golf course but are fun to paddle instead of cause for worry. And when the water is up, the streamflow is fast. Most of the time I could touch bottom with my blade. Plus the width of the streambed averages 30 feet or more.

The biggest challenge is the put-in. The shoulder on Bingen Road is only two feet wide, so you have to block traffic while unloading boats. Equally as frustrating is the lack of a cleared path to the water: the way is choked with tall weeds. But once you're over the put-in hurdle, you can sit back and relax for a speedy float downstream.

Saucon Creek is unobstructed for most of the way in Section 2. Note that Saucon Park can also be used as an access.

The dam is located two miles from the put-in, immediately upstream of the piers that support the bridge on the Saucon Rail Trail. The dam stands only two feet high, but falling water creates a small hydraulic that is followed by rocks and churning waves so that upsetting a canoe could be easily accomplished. You can carry around the dam on either side.

The first partial dam is located a mile later. I call it partial because you can paddle through the breakdown alongside the left bank. Another partial dam is located in Saucon Park; this one is open in the middle so you can shoot straight through the waves that are created by the funnel effect.

The only other obstacle is a downed tree that spans the banks. Yet enough water flows over the slender trunk next to the right bank that I was able to float over it, propelled in part by the strong current.

Because most of the stream is lined with trees on both sides, you won't see much of the urban areas that exist on the other side of the fringe of woods.

If you're looking for a shorter trip you can use Water Street Park in Hellertown as a midway access. Plenty of parking is available. Keep in mind that, because of intermediate trees, the park is difficult to spot from the water if you want to use it as a take-out. Check the right bank after bridges at about the halfway point.

The most convenient take-out is located a quarter mile before the confluence with the Lehigh River. Start watching the geography after passing under the second railroad

Saucon Creek Section 2 225

bridge, where the stream parallels Shimersville Road. After another quarter mile, the stream swings around the sewage treatment plant by turning right, left, and left. Keep to the right side of the stream as you approach the Shimersville Road bridge.

You'll see a tree that has fallen partway across the streambed from the left bank. The take-out is on the right bank upstream of the tree. A short path leads from the gravel landing to Applebutter Road, where a pull-over can accommodate two or three vehicles. Don't block the fireplug.

For completers, skip the take-out and pass to the right of the tree. Proceed under the highway bridge and the railroad bridge beyond it. A perfect take-out is located on the left bank, anywhere between the railroad bridge and the confluence, because a gravel road stands just a few feet away and leads to a river landing. Alternatively, hug the left bank as you enter the Lehigh River, then paddle upstream for twenty feet past the discharge outlet to the paved boat landing.

However, the road that leads to the gravel road and the landing apron is gated with an 8-foot-high chain-link fence. Sometimes the security gate is closed, and sometimes it's open. If it's open, and if you don't mind ignoring the stay-out warning, you can drive a vehicle from the driveway a block or so to the boat landing.

If the gate is closed, paddle into the river but stay close to the right bank. After passing a few trees you'll see a long indentation with a narrow gravel beach that is backed by low vegetation. Take-out before you reach the next grove of trees, under the high-voltage cables. Portage your boat up the narrow path through the shrubbery and over the railroad tracks to a short gravel road (to the left) that leads to Shimersville Road, where there is also room to park on the other side of a gate.

The next public landing on the Lehigh River is 4 miles downstream, past the Route 33 bridge, on the left bank adjacent to the middle of Turkey Island. This landing has a concrete pad for launching boats, and a large parking lot that will hold more than three dozen vehicles with trailers, and more than two dozen vehicles without trailers. Pick your poison.

The Lehigh River is in the foreground, flowing from right to left. The Saucon Creek is flowing toward the camera from under the bridge on the left. To the right the gravel bar below the paved apron is exposed when the water is low.

Watershed Clearwater Revival
(A rock band of different density)

The Shad Sack

Among others, one species of fish that used to inhabit the Lehigh River and its tributaries, is shad. Shad is a migratory fish that is born in freshwater streams in summer, lives in the Atlantic Ocean in winter, then returns to the place of its birth in summer to spawn. Shad used to be an important staple in the diet of Lenni Lenape Indians. Historically, shad used to swim upstream as far as the Great Falls of the Lehigh, at Stoddardsville. Thus they were able to reach every major tributary in the Lehigh River watershed, and a number of minor tributaries.

The completion of the lower canal system in 1829 prevented shad, and other transitory fish that swam up the Delaware River, from entering the Lehigh River watershed. The reduction in local fish inhabitants was then exacerbated by various forms of pollution: coal dust from mining operations, acid drainage from coal mines, industrial waste from zinc refineries and iron mills, and untreated human sewage.

Local resident Kent Roberts told me that when he was a kid in the 1960's, he and most of his friends avoided swimming in the Lehigh River because those who did habitually contracted ear infections. Today this is no longer true: a fact that I know from personal experience. On a few occasions I have been dumped into the river when my canoe upset. I have swum my mountain bike across the river in order to reach a trail on the opposite side. And during a three-day power outage a few summers ago, Cheryl and I took baths in the river (washing with liquid biodegradable backpacking soap).

The Clean Water Act of 1970 has certainly cleaned up the river's act.

I have also eaten fish that I caught in the river, with no ill effects except a hunger for more. The river and the fish in it are clean and uncontaminated.

As for shad, they are slowly making a come-back into their native spawning grounds – but only so far upstream. As noted above, shad have been kept from returning to the Lehigh River watershed by dams. Initially these dams enabled full-time navigation on the river. Despite the destruction of much of the system by the Great Flood of 1861, shad could not jump over the dam at Easton. Thus they were still barred entry to the watershed.

To ameliorate the situation, fish ladders were added to the dams at Easton, Glendon, and Allentown, in 1994. These fishways have proven to be a boon to restoring shad to the lower Lehigh River, yet they have been only partially successful. They have fallen far short of the projected goal of creating a self-sustaining population. It has been estimated that only 10 % of returning shad find and utilize the fishway. The rest keep trying to leap over the dam until they wear themselves out and die. Thus this stopgap solution has achieved only minimal success.

The obvious solution to the shad issue is removal of the dams, especially as these dams are no longer needed for their intended purpose. Furthermore, dams accumulate silt and other debris, which decay over time and create an unhealthy local environment. A river without dams is continually flushed clean by every rainfall. Dams also present a potential drowning hazard for swimmers and boaters. I repeat, the obvious solution to all these problems, as well as to the overall health of the river, is to remove the dams and let nature takes its course.

Watershed Clearwater Revival: Tributary Dam Demolition

The primary objections to removing dams are threefold for the Easton Dam and Chain Dam (at Glendon): the lower water level would expose sanitary sewers and storm drains, requiring them to be either lowered or relocated; without high water the tourist canal at Hugh Moore Park and the Delaware Canal at Easton would go dry, so that pumping stations must be installed in order to keep them flooded; and some bridge piers would have to be reinforced.

A recent feasibility study determined that it would cost some $11 million to remove the dams at Easton and Glendon. This would enable 100 % of migratory fish of all species to reach as far upriver as the Hamilton Street bridge in Allentown. The natural flow of water would increase water quality. It would also eliminate safety concerns for boaters and swimmers, as well as future maintenance costs. However, it does not take into account the construction and maintenance costs of pumps and piping that will be required to feed water to the canals.

Nor does this plan include removal of the dams at Allentown and Northampton, which will ultimately be necessary for a free-flowing river that stretches from the mouth as far as the Francis E. Walter Dam north of White Haven. The only major tributaries that migratory fish could not reach, and in which downstream resident fish could not mingle, would be Tobyhanna Creek, Tunkhannock Creek, and northern Bear Creek: all of which are dammed and as a consequence prevent local fish populations from mingling and from living in a healthy habitat.

A free-flowing Lehigh River is a long row to hoe. Now is the time to start hoeing.

Tributary Dam Demolition

Meanwhile, in addition to three dams near the headwaters of the Lehigh River, nearly all the river's tributaries are also blocked by dams that serve either the public, or private interests, or no one at all.

Moving downriver from north to south, Trout Creek has two large impoundments. The one closest to the river is called Arrowhead Lake, and serves a gated community from which non-property-owners are excluded. Farther upstream is Brady's Lake (which used to be called Trout Lake); this one lies wholly within the boundaries of Pennsylvania State Game Lands #127; it is a popular boating and fishing reservoir.

A hazardous private dam is located on the lower stretch of the Tobyhanna Creek. Instead of a spillway, water is funneled under the lintel via cylindrical pipes. Fish can get sucked downstream through the pipes but cannot swim upstream due to the downstream force of the water. Swimmers and boaters can get trapped by the suction, and drowned. The top of the dam is utilized as a roadway that obviates the need of a bridge.

Farther upstream is the 20-foot-tall dam that has impounded water for a mammoth reservoir called Pocono Lake. Not only is this stretch of water closed to fish from downstream, but it is also closed to non-resident humans as well, despite the fact that the water is held in trust by the Commonwealth for the populace. Sailboating is a popular activity on this exclusive recreational reservoir. Going over this nearly vertical dam would almost certainly result in death.

Yet another dam is located near the headwaters of the creek, at Tobyhanna State Park, where canoeing and kayaking are popular activities for all comers.

The Upper Tunkhannock Creek, which feeds into Tobyhanna Creek where it is now flooded and called Pocono Lake (see above), is dammed to create a number of impoundments: one that is unnamed, then tourist resorts called Lake Naomi, Stillwater Lake, and Lynchwood Lake; plus a slew of others that are on various tributaries: all in all, a vast network of reservoirs that are separated not only by dams but by privatization.

An ancient wooden dam on the Tunkhannock Creek is located at Hemming Road. This dam is particularly dangerous for canoeists and kayakers because when the water is high enough to paddle, the approaches preclude landing due to fast water and high-walled embankments. The dam is too high for fish to jump.

Bear Creek is blocked by a private dam at Route 115. This dam impounds water so that people in the surrounding housing development can boat and float in the large reservoir. Visitors are not welcome. Two other dams lies farther upstream.

A privately owned dam on Mud Run blocks fish from ascending more than a couple of miles from the confluence with the Lehigh River, thus preventing them from reaching the Great Falls of the Mud: the ultimate natural barrier to all fish except perhaps to shad, which can leap incredible heights. Farther upstream there are no less than six more dams whose impoundments serve local residents (and local residents *only*).

Hickory Run is dammed within State park boundaries. One of its tributaries, Sand Spring Run, is dammed in three places.

Quakake Creek is impounded some two and a half miles above its confluence with Black Creek, some 100 yards upstream of Route 93. One of its unnamed tributaries is also dammed. Both impoundments appear to be used as municipal water supplies. A rock dam exists a few feet downstream of Route 93; it gets washed away by every super-heavy rain event, but someone keeps rebuilding it.

Nesquehoning Creek is obstructed by two huge private impoundments from which non-residents are excluded. One of its tributaries, Jeans Run, has an ancient concrete dam that separates native trout into two distinct colonies that cannot meet and mingle.

Mauch Chunk Creek has a dam that was built for flood control. Prior to its construction, the borough of Mauch Chunk (now named Jim Thorpe) was practically washed away a number of times by uncontrolled deluges. The reservoir is a popular public park that caters to boaters, anglers, campers, and hikers.

The Parryville Dam stops fish from swimming upstream barely half a mile from the mouth of the Pohopoco Creek. Without this dam, fish could swim upstream for 5 more miles to the Beltzville Dam (but not into the reservoir because the flow through the outlet pipe is too strong; although fish in the reservoir can swim or get sucked downstream through the pipe). A proposal to remove the Parryville Dam was vetoed by the borough of Parryville, which owns and maintains the dam, because the impounded water is siphoned off to slake the thirst of the borough's residents. As an alternative, the borough approved a plan to install a modular prefabricated fishway at a cost of nearly $200,000, but so far the funding for the project has not been forthcoming.

The Beltzville reservoir is a hugely popular area for motor boating, water skiing, canoeing, kayaking, angling, picnicking, and hiking.

Two dams obstruct fish and boat passage on the Hokendauqua Creek. Neither one serves a purpose or creates much of a backwash. The hydraulic at Lappawinzo Dam must be avoided by lifting boats over the lintel along the sidelines. The next one upstream rises only a couple of feet where the channel is split in two by an island; the left channel is open to both fish and boats.

The truly bad dam on the Hokendauqua Creek, on the outskirts of Northampton, was recently removed by the Wildlands Conservancy.

In 2015, the Wildlands Conservancy provided funding to remove a dam on Coplay Creek. In fact, this removal was only a small part of an overall "regional watershed management plan" that the Wildlands Conservancy has initiated. After the natural streambed and floodplain were re-established, "The next phase involves establishing a riparian buffer to provide pollinator habitat and further enhance the health of the stream."

The sentence that is quoted above means that volunteers will then plant native wildflowers on the newly exposed banks in order to prevent erosion and to provide habitat for animal species such as birds, insects, and small mammals. Free-flowing water will wash away the unhealthy sediment that has been deposited over the years at the base of the dam.

In 2013, The Wildlands Conservancy commenced a huge project to remove nine dams on the Jordon Creek and Little Lehigh Creek. During that summer, four dams were removed from the Jordan Creek, and two from the Little Lehigh Creek. These dams were removed from the bottom up; that is, from the mouths of the creeks upstream. These removals restored some 15 miles of free-flowing water: 9 miles on the Jordan Creek and 6 miles on the Little Lehigh Creek.

The dam debris was hauled away. The newly exposed banks were graded. Hundreds of native trees and shrubs were planted on the reclaimed land, "to help filter pollutants and nurture viable wildlife habitat." The roots of vegetation will also help to prevent erosion.

Pebbles and small stones are now exposed on the streambed after being swept clean by free-flowing current. This is the kind of substrate that trout find attractive because it is home to insects and other organisms that they eat. Unobstructed flow helps to oxygenate the water: another benefit for fish of all species. Also, water that sits behind a dam is warmed by the sun; trout thrive best in cool or cold water. Additionally, the concentration of sediment behind a dam buries bugs on which many fish feed; fish die without nourishment. Dammed streams possess spots of local sterility; they become doubly damned, as it were.

Not only did this reclamation project abet the health of the ecosystem, but it increased public safety. For example, the dam in Jordan Park bordered a playground, where the depth of impounded water has been a constant concern for parents whose children played in the park.

Still water attracts Canada geese, which then wander over adjacent dry land and cover it with goose poop: a health hazard to playing children as well as an ugly nuisance. The release of impounded water forces Canada geese to roost elsewhere.

Not everyone wants the health of the aquatic environment improved. Consider the Wehr Dam on the Jordan Creek. It was constructed to provide power for a grist mill. The grist mill is long gone, so the dam no longer serves the purpose for which it was built. Yet the citizens of South Whitehall Township want to save the dam from wreckers, so as to continue to impede the free-flow of water, simply because in their memory the dam has always been there.

Their main concern was the esthetic value of the structure and the impoundment to the adjacent park. Yet they also cited environmental rationales. An endangered freshwater mussel inhabits the streambed upstream of the dam, and might be washed away by fast-moving water which the dam currently decelerates. The dam also prevents sea lampreys and eels from wandering upstream.

Proponents for the dam's removal, including the Pennsylvania Fish and Boat Commission, noted that the accretion of sediment behind the dam creates an environment that is harmful to fish and other wildlife.

The condition of the Wehr dam is deteriorating. The floodgate is so badly rusted that it can no longer be opened in case of emergency. The retaining structure is cracked, leaking, and in need of repair at a cost of nearly a million dollars, and this estimate does not take continuous maintenance into account: money that has to come out of the township coffer. Should the dam fail, the township would be liable for clean-up costs.

The dam can be removed for less than half the cost of much needed repairs, and the cost of its removal can be paid by grant money. Yet township citizens vetoed its removal. And there the matter rests.

The Little Lehigh Creek has two dams remaining.

Monocacy Creek is in the process of having one of its two dams removed. Yet dam removal represents only part of the process of clearing a stream to permit water to flow freely. In the chapter about this creek, I noted that the stream was clogged by more than *forty* logjams, some of them massive and consisting of a number of fallen trees, in one case nearly a dozen. These logjams trap everything that floats and much material that is submerged. Thus they keep growing larger with the accumulation of tree limbs and similar debris, including unsightly plastic water bottles. Once I spotted the bloated body of a dead dog that was snagged in the branches of a logjam.

The Saucon Creek has a small dam that prevents fish from migrating farther upstream.

All of the above does not account for small dams on tributaries to tributaries.

Acid Mine Drainage

Remediation of acid mine drainage is an ongoing concern in the Lehigh River Watershed. Walking point on this issue is the Wildlands Conservancy.

Coal mining was a major occupation throughout the 1800's. It employed thousands of miners, and furnished clean-burning coal to tens of thousands of homes and businesses in metropolitan areas. Coal-burning stoves were absolutely essential for heating homes and industrial buildings in winter. The legacy of this one-time necessity is drainage from underground mines that were dug below the water table.

Pumps kept the water level down when the mines were in operation. After the mines closed, ground water gradually seeped into the mines and rose to its former natural level.

Most people think of rock as solid and impermeable. In reality, rock is more like a sponge than a block of steel. Water slowly works its way through interstices: tiny, sometimes microscopic cracks or channels in the rock. This water eventually emerges and collects in streams farther down a mountainside. Water from flooded coal mines carries dissolved acid from coal. The result of this process is acidic water that eventually drains into the Lehigh River via its tributaries.

This artificially increased concentration of acid is abnormal, and is therefore harmful to plants and animals that inhabit the watershed downstream of the intrusion. This

Watershed Clearwater Revival: The Zinc Factor

problem has long been recognized. Efforts to reduce pH levels are ongoing, but there is much work that needs to be done in order to restore the natural balance.

The streams that carry acid mine drainage into the Lehigh River are Sandy Run (via Pond Creek), Buck Mountain Creek (at Rockport), Black Creek (via Hazle Creek and Quakake Creek), and Nesquehoning Creek. All these streams are located on the west side of the Lehigh River between White Haven and Jim Thorpe.

If you remember your high school chemistry, pH stands for percentage of hydrogen. Neutral pH, which is neither acidic nor alkaline, is 7 on the numeric scale. Numbers higher than 7 are alkaline (as in bleach); numbers lower than 7 are acidic (as in vinegar). The pH of water from mine drainage generally lies between 3 and 3.5.

The goal of acid mine mitigation is to restore the pH to its previous balance, which is near neutral.

The most vigorous remediation project is currently being conducted near the mouth of the Nesquehoning Creek, which contributes more acid to the watershed than all the other streams combined. The Lausanne Tunnel drains water from the Panther Valley mines into the stream just before its confluence with the Lehigh River. Most of this water has now been diverted through a pair of aerators into a two-stage separation pond. When mineral-laden water is aerated, the iron it contains then combines with oxygen in the air to form ferrous and ferric molecules which are precipitated out of the solution and fall to the bottom of the pool, where the iron rust coats and colors the substrate with a reddish hue. The cleansed water on the surface of the pool then flows over a barrier into the creek.

Other contaminating minerals such as aluminum, manganese, and sulfur are also oxidized and precipitated by the same process.

By itself, anthracite or hard coal does not leech much acid into the underlying terrain. The high levels of acid that are presently being generated are a result of past processing of coal, which was done on site. After the coal was extracted from the ground, it was crushed or broken into manageable chunks. The leftovers of this process are collectively called culm: coal dust and other fine particles that remain after the usable chunks are carted away.

The discharge from Buck Mountain is treated in a different manner but with the same result. A portion of the water has been rerouted so that it passes through a pond that is laden with limestone: a sedimentary rock that abets the precipitation of minerals.

These and other measures will ensure that acid mine drainage is treated so that the inevitable overflow will be less acidic when it reaches the Lehigh River.

The Zinc Factor

Speaking of minerals . . . in the late 1800's, zinc deposits were discovered on the north side of Blue Mountain, east of the Lehigh Gap. A pair of processing plants was established in Palmerton to extract zinc from the ground and to refine it for commercial use. As a byproduct of the refining process, the smelters' tall chimneys emitted smoke that contained a concentration of heavy metals – not the kind of music that we have all grown to love or hate, but zinc, cadmium, sulfur, copper, and lead: elements that are high in atomic weight on the Period Table.

Fumes wafted onto the north-facing slopes on both sides of the gap, which had already been denuded of trees that had been felled to fuel pig iron furnaces. To make a century-long story short, heavy metals that polluted the soil prevented the growth of new vegetation.

Understand that zinc was and continues to be an essential product. Steel pails, guardrails, and chain-link fences are coated with zinc to prevent corrosion: a process that is called galvanization. Zinc is used as a sacrificial anode for cathodic protection of boat propellers, shafts, and rudders. Zinc is a vital ingredient in dry-cell batteries. Among hundreds of other uses, perhaps most important is mixing zinc with copper to make brass: a non-corroding alloy that is especially useful in a saltwater environment: for seacocks, valves, gauges, and other parts of ships that ply the seven seas.

Another important, even crucial, use for brass is for cartridges and canon shells. During two world wars, the Palmerton plant was the prime supplier of zinc that was used in the manufacture of shell casings: millions of them. I won't go as far as to state that zinc won the war, but I will state that at the very least both wars might have lasted longer than they did, with a commensurate increase in the loss of life. It's even conceivable that without zinc for ammunition, America might be led today by a Kaiser or a Fuhrer instead of a President.

The zinc refineries have received all the blame for the barren mountainsides. Yet there were other factors that contributed to the Moonscape appearance. As noted above, by the time the zinc refineries commenced operations, loggers had already clear-cut the forests on Blue Mountain. Subsequent fires destroyed much of the undergrowth. Without roots to bind the ground together, erosion from hard rains washed away much of the topsoil, exposing the rocky substrate; the resulting run-off carried heavy metals into the Aquashicola Creek and the Lehigh River. During dry spells, the thin layer of remaining dirt became desiccated by the heat of the sun. The absence of moisture prevented new growth from taking hold. It was in this unstable environment that high levels of zinc in the soil inhibited seed germination.

Thus it was the combination of all these destructive agents that ultimately created an environment in which vegetation could not gain a foothold, so to speak; or to grow if it did manage to get its roots into the ground.

One should also keep in mind that the New Jersey Zinc Company always operated with contemporary state-of-the-art emissions control. Throughout the years, the company employed thousands of workers, supported their families, and even built houses for them: a progressive attitude that paralleled the Krupp armor and munitions factories in Germany.

Today, zinc remediation is being conducted by the Wildlife Information Center, which is housed at the Lehigh Gap Nature Center. The Center's volunteers and hired commercial service providers have spread limestone, fertilizer, and compost on target growing areas. Zinc bonds with calcium carbonate (of which limestone is comprised) by means of a chemical reaction, so that the concentration of pure zinc in the soil is reduced. The fertilizer and compost promote seed germination and root growth in vegetation. The target areas have been seeded with varieties of vegetative ground cover that can tolerate medium to high levels of zinc toxicity.

These ongoing efforts will eventually revegetate and, in the long run, reforest Blue Mountain to its pre-disturbance condition.

Linear Measurement

The length of a river can be measured in a number of ways.

The most common method is to roll the wheel of an opisometer (a map walker) across a printed map that has a mileage gauge in the legend. This will yield a rough approximation that could be off by 10 % or more (too long or too short), depending upon the size and scale of the map as well as the accuracy of the person wielding the instrument.

A method that is sometimes employed to designate a political boundary is to survey the thalweg. The thalweg is a boundary line that is drawn along the deepest part of a river. This line is not necessarily the midpoint between banks. In essence, the thalweg is the deepest channel in a watercourse (but not always the best navigable channel). The thalweg may be used to assign jurisdiction to States or countries that are separated by a river.

In the field, geologists use survey equipment to draw the twists and turns of river banks. This yields an extremely accurate drawing but not necessarily a measurement of length. Length is generally determined by spacing a line midway between banks, then measuring the length of the line. This isn't as straightforward as it sounds.

I suppose if you could lay a string between the banks, you could straighten the string and measure its length. Obviously this is impractical. The alternative is to calculate the length of the curved line between banks by using calculus or differential equations. This can be done but it's time consuming. (In college, my calculus teacher once had the class spend an entire 45-minute period calculating the volume of a potato chip. This was a laborious exercise because a potato chip is curved in two dimensions. Like Archimedes, I determined that it was simpler and quicker to dunk the potato chip into a glass of water and measure the amount of liquid it displaced.)

The problem with using river banks as limiting factors is that they aren't constant; they're variable. Banks are not like vertical walls in a hallway, with a specified distance between them. They can be sloped, stepped, low, or high.

Take a bank that is sloped and convoluted with curves and indentations. Do you draw your centerline when the water is low, medium, or high? Add the fact that the angle of a slope is also subject to change, and you can see the complications.

How about banks that are stepped? When the water rises higher than the lowest step, it floods the adjacent plain and, in effect, becomes immeasurable. (While I'm on the subject, you should know that often when a stream overflows its banks, the speed of the current is reduced. This is because the volume of water is spread over a larger area.)

The way to account for these vagaries of nature is to specify a water level at which the centerline should be measured. By doing so the length of a stream is standardized and unchangeable. The common denominator is mean low water, or average.

Yet, as far as paddling is concerned, this arbitrary centerline length is not always meaningful – not if you want to know how many miles you have to paddle to get from one point to another.

The method that I have employed in the present volume is to measure what I call the "main flow course." Water in a stream almost never flows precisely along the centerline between banks. Streambeds are uneven both vertically and horizontally. Bottom contours push water aside. Obstructions such as boulders or islands divert the flow along meandering courses and down divergent channels. Most of the water generally flows along the outside of a curve.

All these factors serve to lengthen the paddling distance with respect to river length.

Picture the main flow line as a convoluted or asymmetrical sine wave between opposite sides, or a sidewinder moving forward between parallel lines. This line constitutes the distance that a boater must actually paddle as the boat caroms from side to side like a billiard ball on a pool table. The way I measured this line was with a GPS unit.

The Global Positioning System that my receiver utilizes is the same as that which is used in automobiles, except that instead of showing streets and points of interest like a road map, mine displays a topographic map complete with waterways and contour intervals. This enabled me to obtain "paddling distance" rather than "river length."

There's not much dissimilarity between these two distances on a narrow stream whose width measures, say, a couple of boat-lengths. But on a major river like the Lehigh, the difference can be considerable. In addition to the natural lack of uniformity, there are intentional deviations from the centerline. For example, if the main watercourse is fraught with wild standing waves that threaten to swamp a boat, the paddler may opt to take a circuitous course in order to avoid imminent doom. Because rapids are not always run in an undeviating manner, my track might differ somewhat from the track of another paddler; or from my own track on another day when the water level is dissimilar.

Furthermore, GPS is not without its quirks. For one thing, the line it draws is not curved: it is drawn from a series of short straight lines that are connected end to end. I use a sampling rate of 15 seconds; this means that every quarter of a minute, the unit marks my position and draws a line from the previous position: one that was obtained 15 seconds earlier. The faster I travel, the longer the lines. The slower I travel, the shorter the lines; but this also means that more lines are drawn: more *straight* lines. The cumulative effect is to induce inaccuracy that results from straight lines that are connected instead of a smoothly drawn curve.

Another inaccuracy is induced by positional differences. Although people tend to think of GPS coordinates as a pinpoint, that is almost never the case. There are always variances that result from the number of satellites in view at any moment, and the angle of those satellites above the horizon. Signals from satellites that orbit close to the horizon can triangulate a position more accurately than satellites that orbit directly overhead.

Signals can be blocked or distorted by adjacent mountains, overhead vegetation, cloud cover, precipitation, condensation in the atmosphere, and so on. What all this means I can amply demonstrate.

Suppose that I am standing still. The unit receives a signal that approximates my position. That position might be 50 feet off of my actual position. Fifteen seconds later, the unit receives another signal that is also 50 feet off – but 50 feet in the opposite direction. The distance between these two positions is 100 feet – a distance that is recorded as movement – and I haven't strayed from the spot!

On one trip down the Lehigh River, I stopped at Lunch Rock to eat a sandwich. I walked around the rock, mingled with rafters, snapped a bunch of pictures, and chatted at length with some anglers. By the time I departed, some 45 minutes later, my GPS unit logged my travel distance as half a mile! I subtracted this distance from waypoints that I marked downstream.

Because river conditions change, I don't claim that my streambed mileage is perfectly accurate. Think of it as a "close approximation."

Streamflow

None of the waterways in the Lehigh River basin can be paddled under normal flow conditions, including the river itself. All the tributaries need rainfall. The Lehigh River upstream of the Francis E. Walter Dam also needs rainfall. Downstream of the dam, the runnability (or paddleability, to create another nonce word) of the Lehigh River depends mostly on the amount of water that is released (plus the amount of water that is added by the tributaries). Therefore it is critically important for potential paddlers to understand how much water is needed to float a boat. Otherwise, they might put-in at a landing where the flow rate looks sufficient, only to find that farther downstream or around the first bend the water is too low for the boat's draft, and they wind up walking and towing their boats on a nearly dry streambed.

The U.S. Geological Survey maintains a website called WaterWatch. The Internet address is http://waterwatch.usgs.gov/?m=real&r=pa&w=map. The home screen presents a map of Pennsylvania with colored dots that represent the location of every streamflow gauge station in the State. Not every stream has a gauging station, but most of the major tributaries to the Lehigh River are equipped with one or two. The Lehigh River has six. The gauges at these stations provide real-time streamflow conditions. This handy tool enables paddlers to know before leaving home whether the stream they want to paddle is runnable that day.

Of course, this system works for paddlers only if they have an established baseline of the amount of water that is needed before a particular stream can float a boat, and to what degree. I created such a baseline by annotating the streamflow whenever I paddled a stream.

In the statistical sidebar for each section of a stream I have indicated the minimum streamflow that is needed to make that stretch of water runnable. For the Lehigh River downstream of the dam, I have given the amount of water in cubic feet per second, or cfs. That is the common convention that private boaters and raft outfitters have always used.

For all other streams I use "% normal (median):" (not "% normal (mean))," which is given underneath "% normal (median)" in the gauge station's statistical sidebar. This choice was simply my personal preference when I started to annotate streamflows. (In fact, I don't know how or why the USGS differentiates between "median" and "mean." Both words are defined as "the middle point.")

None of the streams is runnable when the streamflow is given as 100%, or normal. In most cases, this means that you can walk across a streambed without getting your ankles wet. If the percentage is less than 100, you might not even get your shoe soles wet; at the very least your uppers will stay dry. Multiples of 100% are needed before the Lehigh's tributaries become runnable.

For example, I once paddled a stretch of the Jordan Creek when it was flowing at 2,000% above normal (median). As I passed the Trexler Nature Preserve, I drifted past a man and his 3-year-old daughter, both of whom were standing in the middle of the stream. The water was up to his knees and her hips.

To use WaterWatch, hover your cursor over the dot that represents the stream you want to check. There's no room on the map for names, so you'll have to play around with the dots until you learn the streams by their placement. A dialogue box pops up to provide statistical information. The website does not define the words used in the statistics. Here are my interpretations:

Top line: station location (click on the number for more information about the station

Drainage area: how many square miles of land feed into the station

Discharge: the amount of water (in cubic feet per second) that is presently passing the station

Stage: in feet (meaning unknown to me, but from my experience it doesn't mean depth of water)

Date: current year, month, and day, plus time of most recent update

Percentile: meaning unknown to me

Class symbol: a quick-glance color code for dots in which:
  red means very much below normal
  brown means much below normal
  orange means below normal
  green means normal
  light blue means above normal
  dark blue means much above normal
  black means very much above normal

% normal (median): percentage of water above or below normal

% normal (mean): percentage of water above or below normal (difference from median unknown to me).

If you click on the dot instead of just hovering the cursor over it, you may get two additional items of information:

Flood stage: in feet (amount of water that is considered to be flood)

Water temperature: in degrees Celsius, plus current year, month, and day, as well as time of most recent update.

Note that not all the above information is displayed for every dot, and some information that is displayed only by clicking on one dot may be displayed by hovering the cursor over another dot (for another stream, of course). There appears to be no firm rhyme or reason for these disparities. Est quod est, as the Romans used to say. It is what it is.

Despite my lack of understanding of all the statistics, the only item of information that you need to know for the purpose of runnability, is the discharge (for the Lehigh River) or the % normal (median) for the tributaries. Now check my statistical sidebar to determine if there is enough water flowing for a stream to be runnable.

Not every stream possesses a gauging station. For those that don't, check the streamflow of adjacent streams that are fitted with a gauge – but use those streamflows only as a guide. Correlate nearby streamflows with area rain accumulations before leaving the house. Even then you might find an ungauged stream unrunnable, and for a number of reasons. Consider the following . . .

Much of the rain that falls after a period of drought soaks into the ground and does not contribute to run-off. Rain that falls on tilled farmland is largely absorbed by the soil, whereas rain that falls on forests where the terrain is rocky or consists of hard-packed dirt will flow along the surface. A high percentage of rain that falls *after* a previous but recent rainfall that soaked the ground will work its way to streambeds. Keep all these variables in mind when determining whether an ungauged stream might be worth investigating.

When all else fails, the final recourse is to examine the stream at both the take-out and put-in.

Adversity

Adversity levels are subjective. Whitewater that is scary to one paddler may be fun for another. In this sense, a paddler's skill and experience usually define the difference between levels. But factors other than the speed of the current and the height of standing waves contribute to overall adversity: gravel bars, boulder fields, restrictive passages, ledges and drop-offs, fallen trees, dams, and so on.

The adversity levels that I have ascribed refer largely to water conditions. In parentheses I have noted additional characteristics, such as "annoying deadfall." In the body of the text I have expanded sidebar statistics with necessary description. In the latter context, I may provide in-depth detail about how much struggle was required to get around the deadfall.

Keeping the above in mind, I have ascribed five levels of adversity that are based largely on water conditions but not necessarily on obstacles such as rocks and deadfall, unless the latter is particularly obstructive:

Adversity level 0: None (like a canal, pond, or reservoir)
Adversity level 1: Not challenging (water that is flowing but not fast)
Adversity level 2: Challenging (riffles with occasional but avoidable obstacles such as boulders that are either exposed or awash)
Adversity level 3: Very challenging: (fast whitewater with waves standing no higher than 2 feet, many boulders that require technical maneuvering)
Adversity level 4: Extremely challenging (very fast whitewater, waves standing higher than 2 feet, tight boulder fields, ledges, drop-offs, or waterfalls that require portaging)

Books by the Author

The Popular Dive Guide Series
Shipwrecks of Maine and New Hampshire
Shipwrecks of Massachusetts: North
Shipwrecks of Massachusetts: South
Shipwrecks of Rhode Island and Connecticut
Shipwrecks of New York
Shipwrecks of New Jersey (1988)
Shipwrecks of New Jersey: North
Shipwrecks of New Jersey: Central
Shipwrecks of New Jersey: South
Shipwrecks of Delaware and Maryland (1990 Edition)
Shipwrecks of Delaware and Maryland (2002 Edition)
Shipwrecks of the Chesapeake Bay in Maryland Waters
Shipwrecks of the Chesapeake Bay in Virginia Waters
Shipwrecks of Virginia
Shipwrecks of North Carolina: from the Diamond Shoals North
Shipwrecks of North Carolina: from Hatteras Inlet South
Shipwrecks of South Carolina and Georgia

Shipwreck and Nautical History
Andrea Doria: Dive to an Era
Deep, Dark, and Dangerous: Adventures and Reflections on the Andrea Doria
Great Lakes Shipwrecks: a Photographic Odyssey
The Great Navy Wreck Scam
The Fuhrer's U-boats in American Waters
Ironclad Legacy: Battles of the USS Monitor
The Kaiser's U-boats in American Waters
The Lusitania Controversies: Atrocity of War and a Wreck-Diving History (Book One)
The Lusitania Controversies: Dangerous Descents into Shipwrecks and Law (Book Two)
The Nautical Cyclopedia
NOAA's Ark: the Rise of the Fourth Reich
Shadow Divers Exposed: the Real Saga of the U-869
Shipwreck Heresies
The Shipwreck Research Handbook
Shipwreck Sagas
Stolen Heritage: the Grand Theft of the Hamilton and Scourge
Track of the Gray Wolf
Underwater Reflections
USS San Diego: the Last Armored Cruiser
Wreck Diving Adventures

Books by the Author

Dive Training
Primary Wreck Diving Guide
Advanced Wreck Diving Guide
The Advanced Wreck Diving Handbook
Ultimate Wreck Diving Guide
The Technical Diving Handbook

Nonfiction
The Absurdity Principle
Lehigh Gorge Trail Guide
Lehigh River Paddling Guide
Wilderness Canoeing

Science Fiction
A Different Universe
A Different Dimension
A Different Continuum
Entropy (a novel of conceptual breakthrough)
A Journey to the Center of the Earth
The Mold
Return to Mars
Second Coming
Silent Autumn
Subaqueous
Tesla and the Lemurian Gate
The Time Dragons Trilogy
    A Time for Dragons
    Dragons Past
    No Future for Dragons

Sci-Fi Action/Adventure Novels
Memory Lane
Mind Set
The Peking Papers

Supernatural Horror Novel
The Lurking: Curse of the Jersey Devil

Vietnam Novel
Lonely Conflict

Videotape or DVD
The Battle for the USS Monitor

Visit the GGP website for availability of titles:
http://www.ggentile.com

www.ingramcontent.com/pod-product-compliance
Lightning Source LLC
Chambersburg PA
CBHW051046160426
43193CB00010B/1084